THE GEOGRAPHIES OF AFRICAN AMERICAN SHORT FICTION

THE GEOGRAPHIES OF AFRICAN AMERICAN SHORT FICTION

Kenton Rambsy

University Press of Mississippi / Jackson

Margaret Walker Alexander Series in African American Studies

The University Press of Mississippi is the scholarly publishing agency of the Mississippi Institutions of Higher Learning: Alcorn State University, Delta State University, Jackson State University, Mississippi State University, Mississippi University for Women, Mississippi Valley State University, University of Mississippi, and University of Southern Mississippi.

www.upress.state.ms.us

The University Press of Mississippi is a member of the Association of University Presses.

Any discriminatory or derogatory language or hate speech regarding race, ethnicity, religion, sex, gender, class, national origin, age, or disability that has been retained or appear in elided form is in no way an endorsement of the use of such language outside a scholarly context.

Copyright © 2022 by University Press of Mississippi
All rights reserved

First printing 2022
∞

Library of Congress Cataloging-in-Publication Data

Names: Rambsy, Kenton, author.
Title: The geographies of African American short fiction / Kenton Rambsy.
Other titles: Margaret Walker Alexander series in African American studies.
Description: Jackson : University Press of Mississippi, 2022. |
Series: Margaret Walker Alexander series in African American studies |
Includes bibliographical references and index.
Identifiers: LCCN 2021055328 (print) | LCCN 2021055329 (ebook) |
ISBN 9781496838728 (hardback) | ISBN 9781496838735 (trade paperback) |
ISBN 9781496838759 (epub) | ISBN 9781496838742 (epub) | ISBN 9781496838773 (pdf) |
ISBN 9781496838766 (pdf)
Subjects: LCSH: American fiction—African American authors—History and criticism. | African Americans—Fiction. | Geography in literature. | Geographical perception in literature. | Place (Philosophy) in literature. | Space in literature. | Geocriticism. | Setting (Literature) |
BISAC: LITERARY CRITICISM / American / African American & Black | LITERARY CRITICISM / Modern / 20th Century
Classification: LCC PS647 .A35 R36 2022 (print) | LCC PS647 .A35 (ebook) |
DDC 813/.0109896073—dc23/eng/20220202
LC record available at https://lccn.loc.gov/2021055328
LC ebook record available at https://lccn.loc.gov/2021055329

British Library Cataloging-in-Publication Data available

For my parents, Howard & Phillis Tean Rambsy

CONTENTS

Introduction 3

Chapter 1—Locating the Big 7: One Hundred Anthologies
and the Most Frequently Anthologized Black Short Stories 19

Chapter 2—Writing the South: Charles Chesnutt,
Zora Neale Hurston, and Richard Wright 40

Chapter 3—The Paradox of Homegrown Outsiders:
Ralph Ellison, James Baldwin, and Alice Walker 63

Chapter 4—New York Cityscapes: James Baldwin
and Toni Cade Bambara 86

Chapter 5—Up South: Geo-Tagging DC and
Edward P. Jones's Homegrown Characters 106

Conclusion 128

Acknowledgments 137

Notes 139

Selected Bibliography 153

Index 165

THE GEOGRAPHIES OF AFRICAN AMERICAN SHORT FICTION

INTRODUCTION

One of America's most well-known authors achieved her first major literary success as a short story writer. In 1925, Zora Neale Hurston's short story "Spunk" earned second place in the *Opportunity* magazine literary contest. In the same year, editor Alain Locke included "Spunk" in the Harlem Renaissance anthology, *The New Negro*.[1] By 2000, "Spunk" and Hurston's stories "Sweat" and "The Gilded Six-Bits" were fixtures in literature anthologies, having appeared in more than thirty collections. Despite widespread circulation though, Hurston's stories have received relatively little critical notice. Instead, scholarly and popular discourses have primarily devoted attention to her novel *Their Eyes Were Watching God* (1937). In other words, Hurston the novelist has largely overshadowed Hurston the short story writer.

Yet stories by Hurston, which appear in several different anthologies, expand our views of her engagements with Black cultural explorations and the power of storytelling. As an author of short fiction, Hurston produces work that corresponds to stories by Richard Wright, Alice Walker, Toni Cade Bambara, and Edward P. Jones, to name just some examples. Short stories by Black writers constitute a rich body of artistic composition that depict Black characters in an array of settings and circumstances. Some of those stories are well traveled. They have journeyed across dozens of anthologies, having been routinely selected for inclusion by editors.

Anthology editors shaped the landscape of Black literature starting in 1925, by repeatedly publishing stories by a core group of writers: Charles Chesnutt, Hurston, Wright, Ralph Ellison, James Baldwin, Bambara, and Walker. In that way, editors essentially created a "Big 7" of African American short fiction writers. The continual inclusion of these seven writers in anthologies solidified their presence in American and African American canonical histories. The appearances of short stories by those seven writers and nearly three hundred others defined geographic parameters of African American literature. The circulation of short fiction in anthologies gave the South and New York City an outsized presence in literary representations. A history of African American short stories, which necessarily concerns the formation of the Big 7 and the explorations of varied cultural locales, is long overdue.

The Geographies of African American Short Stories explains how the Big 7 and other selected writers such as Edward P. Jones, Rudolph Fisher, Amiri Baraka, and Henry Dumas made character depictions and culturally discrete settings consequential to the production of short fiction. That production was facilitated by anthology editors. Consequently, this book is not a comprehensive study, but instead takes into account how the most frequently republished stories by the Big 7 plotted a diverse range of characters across multiple locations—small towns, a famous metropolis, city sidewalks, a rural wooded area, apartment buildings, a pond, a general store, a prison, and more. In the process, short fiction by the Big 7 has highlighted the extent to which places and spaces shaped or situated racial representations. Black short story writers are cultural cartographers. They crucially orchestrate relatively short narratives about the interplay between characters and settings.

The Big 7 set stories in a variety of geographic settings and, in the process, underscored place-specific dimensions of the locales that they depict. Visions of the South presented in short fiction by Hurston and Walker highlight intraracial tensions in Florida and Georgia, while Wright dramatizes conflicts between Black and white people in Mississippi. Ellison manages to include intraracial as well as interracial conflicts in a single story, "Battle Royal," set in a small Alabama town, where the unnamed male narrator boxes against his Black teenaged peers for the amusement of wealthy, white businessmen. Baldwin and Bambara project a range of different sights and sounds that Black people encounter in New York City, and thus showcase the sensory dynamics of an urban environment. The multiplicity of locations in African American short fiction indicates the ways writers make settings integral to their artistic creations.

This book also pays special attention to Edward P. Jones and offers an analysis of the twenty-eight stories, all set in Washington, DC, that comprise his two collections, *Lost in the City* (1992) and *All Aunt Hagar's Children* (2003). His meticulous city narratives are particularly rewarding when read with attention to spatial and historical references. His virtual map of DC constitutes an outstanding achievement in the production of African American short stories. His stories evidence his penchant for details as he incorporates more than four hundred DC locations into his two collections of short stories. The locations he references are embedded with cultural signifiers to Black people and neighborhoods in DC. More attention to short stories by Jones and the Big 7 reveals how this important mode of writing contributes to the artistry of African American storytelling.

James Nagel defines the short story as "a brief fictional narrative, sharply focused on a central character with a unified plot and progressive intensity of action."[2] He further classifies American short stories by pointing out how "these stories often involve the process of immigration, acculturation, language acquisition, identity formation, and the complexities of formulating a sense of self that incorporates the old world and the new world" (15). Even though elements of the form vary from artist to artist, short stories often include a main character interacting with a small cast of supporting characters in a self-contained incident in a distinct setting. African American short story writers have been especially attentive to Black characters and the places that they occupy.

Scholars have produced a substantial number of analyses of African American literature. The critical discourse has largely concentrated on novels, especially books by prominent authors like Hurston, Wright, Ellison, and Toni Morrison. Prominent literary scholars including Henry Louis Gates Jr., Deborah E. McDowell, Barbara Christian, and Robert Stepto have produced extensive work on novels.[3] Nonetheless, their works usefully provide a context for exploring the historical trajectory of short fiction by writers.

The brevity of short fiction may account for the relatively small amount of notice it attracts from scholars, who have historically concentrated on longer prose narratives. The brief glimpses that individual short stories offer may be found as insufficient for those interested in more extensive treatments. But what is useful about the concision of short fiction? And what can short stories by Black writers tell us about African American literary art that poetry and novels cannot? A search for the answers to these kinds of questions can build our knowledge of short stories and the writers who composed them.

For many Black writers, short stories anticipated longer works. Perhaps short stories serve as a model—or sketch pad—for authors to experiment with structural features of writing and develop distinct stylistic approaches. The displays of Black vernacular expression that permeate Hurston's short fiction from the 1920s anticipate the cultural representation in *Their Eyes Were Watching God* (1937). The experimentation with racial blurring that Toni Morrison enacts in her 1983 story "Recitatif" would later emerge in her novel *Paradise* (1999). Ellison's "Battle Royal" would later become the first chapter of his novel *Invisible Man* (1952). For Hurston, Ellison, Morrison, and other writers, stories were like trial runs for novels. Short story writing, though, is valuable as a practice beyond the connection to later works. Authors have collectively produced a robust and outstanding body of short fiction. An examination of how writers utilize relatively brief narratives to explore and display cultural ideas illuminates the artfulness of their compositions.

Brevity matters. Precision of language and setting as well as glimpses of the lives of characters exemplifies the extent to which writers hone their creative abilities to drive a plot and build suspense. A short story deviates from the novel form by containing relatively little character development, a limited number of settings and scenes, and a contained plot. The intricacy of short stories as a genre rests in the abilities of writers to focus on a single character or small group of characters in condensed settings to achieve overall effects. More attention to short stories reveals how this important mode of writing contributes to the artistry of African American storytelling.

THE IMPORTANCE OF ANTHOLOGIES

In addition to pinpointing the artistic qualities of short fiction, this book highlights the defining role of anthologies in the transmission of compositions. The breadth of short stories by Black writers is vast. However, I was curious about the short story writers that editors chose to republish most frequently. As a result, I created "The Black Short Story Dataset—Vol. 1," a dataset of one hundred anthologies, which contains information about the various collections.[4] Bibliographies often organize entries alphabetically and chronologically, but a dataset opens additional possibilities for arrangement by publication date, author birth year, author gender, publisher, anthology type, and story title. "The Black Short Story Dataset" includes over six hundred short stories by nearly three hundred authors selected by more than seventy editors.

A sample of one hundred anthologies is hardly exhaustive, but a dataset of this size nonetheless offers a rather large body of information on some of our most canonically significant writers and stories. This project privileges inclusion, even though the exclusion of Black writers is a central feature of American literature anthologies and literary histories. That is, while my research concentrated on one hundred collections that reprinted works by Black writers, there are hundreds of anthologies that exclude African American short stories. Thus, we should keep the long history of Black writer exclusion in mind. At the same time, studies of preferred or selected texts reveal the decisions editors have made to keep particular stories by Black writers in privileged positions on literary playlists, so to speak.

The presentation of Black writers in literature anthologies contributes to our understanding of Black writing and the contexts through which stories circulate. Anthologies constitute one of the most important ways to examine the histories of Black short fiction. "African American writers are perfect examples," Joseph Csicsila has noted, "of how the dynamics of academic scholarship and taste can radically reconfigure the contents of literature anthologies—and thus what gets taught in college classrooms—overnight."[5] The field of African American literature is not static and is constantly fluctuating. Shifts in African American literary studies during the 1970s and also the 1990s led anthology editors to include works by writers who were previously excluded or represented only sparingly. Anthologies are especially important for reprinting literary works and thus expanding the circulation of author compositions. An analysis of the publishing histories of the Big 7 reveals how these authors and their stories became recurring choices for editors.

The proliferation of scholarly works and active organizing related to African American literary studies from the mid-1980s through the 1990s highlighted Black writers in unprecedented ways. Scholars were placing renewed attention on prominent African American authors and introducing audiences to a variety of *new* Black writers. Making room for new contributors while preserving space for familiar writers was challenging. As Darryl Dickson-Carr explains, "critics and scholars have collectively struggled to expand different canons while not completely disregarding their mainstays."[6] Either way, attention to and republication of Black writers were expanding.

African American publishing histories are multifaceted, and conventional bibliographies offer only so much information. Gates has noted that most editors of African American literary anthologies "have tried to include as many authors and selections (especially excerpts) as possible, in order to preserve and 'resurrect' the tradition."[7] Thus, we might embrace the use of datasets in order to enhance our understanding of the circulation histories of Black short fiction. A dataset on the thousands of items associated with the transmission of African American short stories moves us closer to uncovering the details behind phrases like "frequently anthologized" and "widely anthologized." The defining roles of editors in the formulation of literary canons reveal how anthologies shaped perceptions of Black writers and Black literary history.

Anthologies are significant gateways into literature. These collections introduce readers to a variety of authors, while also framing literary artists and texts within historical periods under distinct labels. The students at the "more than 1,275 colleges and universities worldwide" that use *The Norton Anthology of African American Literature* are likely to view the Harlem Renaissance as taking place between 1919 and 1940.[8] *Black Voices: An Anthology of African American Literature* presents Baldwin primarily as an autobiographical writer even though other anthologies present him as a novelist. *The Heath Anthology of American Literature* indicates that Richard Wright belongs to the "Modern Period (1910–1945)," while the *Norton Anthology of African American Literature* presents Wright as a part of "Realism, Naturalism, Modernism, 1940–1960." An examination of anthologies clarifies why the transmission of short fiction is crucial to understanding the presentation of African American literature.

For decades now, Chesnutt, Hurston, Wright, and Ellison have been mainstays in anthologies featuring short fiction by American and African American writers. Chesnutt's "The Goophered Grapevine" and "The Wife of His Youth" are among the most widely anthologized nineteenth-century African American short stories. For Wright and Ellison more so than Chesnutt, successful novels generated later interest in their short stories. Anthologists did not have the space to include the entirety of *Native Son* or *Invisible Man*, so they could and did reprint Ellison's "Battle Royal," "Flying Home," or "A Party Down at the Square" and Wright's "Almos' a Man" and "Bright and Morning Star." Of course, writers hardly control the transmission of their short fiction over long periods of time. Underpublished writers would likely have chosen to appear more frequently, and widely published writers would perhaps want a more diverse selection of their works to appear. However, editors, not writers, largely dictated the circulations of hundreds of works. Editors formulated cohorts of writers. Editors established the Big 7.

Although my interests here concern African American short stories, my dataset creates opportunities to address questions about a range of information about Black writers and anthology editors. It's a humbling experience to spend years reading dozens and dozens of short stories by Black writers and then realize how much more there is to read. Robert Elliot Fox notes that "most canonical anthologies seem based on an assumption of the greatness of previous writings to which we are perpetually appending footnotes and an occasional new monument."[9] Hundreds of short stories by Black writers have been published in anthologies since 1925. Still, thousands more short stories were never reprinted. A dataset on stories appearing in anthologies begins allowing us to account for some of what editors have selected and highlighted for readers.

According to Maryemma Graham and Jerry Ward, "In the twenty-first century, literary histories may achieve a limited degree of comprehensiveness in dealing with a vast amount of literary and cultural data."[10] Investigating several anthologies as data points reveals how the repeated inclusion by editors of select short stories reinforces the geographic settings that readers are most likely to encounter. Even though authors set their stories in a variety of locations, the thirty most frequently anthologized stories showcase the South and New York City. Editors are especially drawn to the South.

Stories by writers set in this region account for nineteen of the thirty most anthologized compositions. Surveying the circulation histories of African American short fiction reveals how anthologies contribute to accentuating attention to distinct places and spaces.

CULTURAL GEO-TAGGING

The processes by which writers identify locations are analogous to the practices of utilizing electronic devices and social media to pinpoint the precise whereabouts of a person or group of people. People who use Facebook, Twitter, and Instagram often utilize geo-tagging technology to make "friends" and "followers" aware of where they are. Moreover, travelers make use of GPS to navigate through unknown terrains or frequently visited points of interests that may not be listed in any travel guide. We can use similar methods to track locations presented in short stories. We can chart and quantify the variety of settings, landmarks, streets, buildings, and neighborhoods in order to understand the extent to which writers make geography central to their compositions.

I coined the term "cultural geo-tagging" as a way of describing the processes of identifying, quantifying, and organizing artistic depictions of settings and geographic markers across several stories. By documenting the number and variety of geographical references, including the types of settings, landmarks, street names, neighborhoods, and regional dialects, we begin to understand how Black writers make cultural spaces integral to their artwork. Black writers use geographic markers to inscribe their stories with layered and resonant social histories. References to the physical layout of a setting, descriptions of social attitudes, and allusions to cultural practices contribute to impressions of a given location and reveal the interplay between race and geography.

Cultural geo-tagging illuminates what we are witnessing regarding positioning, location, mapping, and geographic matters in the works of Black writers. Authors compose settings, across different geographic locales, that represent what Caroline Knowles has called "an active archive of the social processes and social relationships composing racial orders."[11] A setting, according to Knowles, is active because "it interacts with people and their activities as an ongoing set of possibilities in which race is fabricated." Short story writers sometimes rely on specific streets, neighborhoods, city landmarks, and regional expressions. By incorporating a range of distinct places and spaces in their works, Black writers reveal that the sites where stories occur are central to the compositions. City life provides Jones, for instance, with an abundance of sights, sounds, and real-world locales. Elements of the urban landscape are not merely add-ons for his stories. Instead, Washington, DC, is integral to Jones's storytelling.

According to Brooke Neely and Michelle Samura, "A race-space framework also illustrates how the processes of difference and inequality converge around the organization of both race and space."[12] Both Hurston and Wright set stories in the South. Hurston's stories focus on folk culture in Florida and the interactions between Black characters exclusively and also represent her fondness of her Florida hometown. Wright's stories, on the other hand, represent racial conflicts and suggest the explosive nature of white violence, all of which would have been familiar to him growing up in Mississippi. Neely and Samura explain how "Linking race and space explicitly helps us understand how the fluid and historical nature of racial formation plays out around on-going negotiations over the meanings and uses of space." They further note that "this conceptual marriage highlights how the definitions and meanings of race and space are enacted and embodied social processes." Taken together, stories by Hurston and Wright reveal that their childhoods in the South had a bearing on their literary creations. An awareness of short fiction by Black writers broadens and diversifies our views of how integral cultural geographies are to artistic composition.

Short stories by Black writers present a plethora of places and settings. Even though authors set their stories in Chicago, Detroit, and Los Angeles, the compositions situated in the South and New York are particularly compelling and pervasive, clarifying the significance of location-related activities and settings in short stories. Works by Hurston, Wright, Bambara, and Baldwin show characters sitting on front porches in a rural Florida town, swimming in a lake in Mississippi, running along Amsterdam Avenue in Manhattan, and riding in a cab in New York City, respectively. Walker presents a family home in rural Georgia. Baldwin depicts a jazz club in Greenwich Village, and Bambara sets a story in the FAO Schwartz Toy Store on Fifth Avenue. African American short story writers have charted fairly succinct tales across numerous settings and geographic regions. Geo-tagging or classifying a rather large body of spatial locations and information in numerous short stories makes it clear how often Black writers are utilizing landmarks and locales in the course of presenting narratives.

In *Southscapes*, Thadious Davis "acknowledges the connection between society and environment as a way of thinking about how raced human beings are impacted by the shape of the land."[13] Descriptions of rural environments and landscapes, as well as practices such as porch gatherings by Black folks and lynching by white mobs, constitute some of the many distinguishing features of stories set in the South. Black short story writers pull from, contribute to, and alter southern representations in diverse ways. Maya Angelou takes up the topic of two racially antagonistic white men threatening a Black man on a commercial bus ride from Memphis, Tennessee, to Cincinnati, Ohio, in her story "Steady Going Up." In her story "Brownies," set in the suburbs of Atlanta, ZZ Packer alters familiar histories of racial prejudice and segregation by presenting a group of Black girls preparing to enact violence on white girls. While most African American fiction deals with characters making permanent migrations from the South to the North, William Melvin Kelley chronicles Dr. Charles Dunsford's traveling from his home in New York to attend his twenty-year college reunion in Nashville, Tennessee— a locale filled with memories from Charles's childhood. The regional and thematic diversity of short fiction by African American writers unsettles the notion of the South as a monolithic location.

Southern settings give Black writers chances to present Black people in a variety of contexts. In "The Passing of Grandison," Chesnutt depicts an enslaved man who successfully manipulates his owner and escapes with his entire family from a Kentucky plantation. In her story "Nineteen Fifty-Five," set primarily in a rural Alabama town, Walker depicts a harmonious relationship between a middle-aged Black woman and a young white male, challenging the notion that interracial relationships were not possible in the Jim Crow South. In "Bright and Morning Star," Wright portrays a Black heroine in rural Mississippi who sacrifices herself to defend her son and a local civil rights group. Ellison spent a brief period as a young man in Alabama. Accordingly, in his story "King of the Bingo Game," though the primary action is set in an unnamed northern city, the unnamed protagonist has flashbacks to his life and upbringing in the Deep South.

Canonical southern short fiction by white and Black writers also depicts various instances of violence in compelling and dreadful ways.[14] Approximately twenty-six short stories by the Big 7 reveal the prevalence of violence in southern stories published before 1950. For several African American short story writers, depictions of violence facilitated the presentation of captivating moments. Ranging from conflicts between Black and white characters to domestic disputes between married couples, writers incorporate violence into short fiction to heighten the intensity of the drama. The sometimes-brutal scenes they created disrupt widely held views about southern hospitality and tranquility.

African American Vernacular English varies across the country and appears in a variety of literary settings; however, short stories that take place in or feature characters from the South are more likely to showcase Black vernacular speech than stories set in other areas. The speakers in Hurston's "Sweat," "Spunk," and "The Gilded Six-Bits" all use Black vernacular English to enhance the character dialogue of the rural Florida setting. Rudolph Fisher's "City of Refuge" (1925) is set in New York City, yet the vernacular speech of the protagonist King Solomon Gillis serves to highlight his North Carolina origins. The southern-born characters in Jones's "All Aunt Hagar's Children" (2003), set in Washington, DC, are identifiable by their vernacular speech patterns as well. Short story writers present vernacular speaking southerners as a way of highlighting the distinctive language use of the region.

While the Great Migration remains a significant subject in African American history and literary studies, the decision among many writers to present stories in southern settings is noteworthy. "No matter where an African American writer is born in the United States," explains Trudier Harris, "he or she feels compelled to confront the American South and all its bloody history in his or her writing."[15] Alice Walker, Charles R. Johnson, James Baldwin, Ernest Gaines, Dorothy West, and Henry Dumas all situated stories in the South. Harris believes the American South is "a rite of passage for African American writers." The composition of stories with southern settings or characters becomes a way for writers to actualize or explore aspects of their cultural identities. And while well-known stories highlight multiple places across the South, the most anthologized northern stories have one central location: New York City.

In *The City in African-American Literature* (1995), Yoshinobu Hakutani and Robert Butler note that urban settings have been "crucial symbols" in Black fiction for "the rich variety of ways it has used urban settings and themes."[16] Toni Cade Bambara portrays a group of kids traveling to Fifth Avenue in "The Lesson." James Baldwin's "Sonny's Blues" depicts a strained relationship between two brothers living in Harlem. These and other New York-based stories reference neighborhoods, landmarks, and specific addresses in addition to showing characters walking down streets, using cabs and subways, and congregating in parks and cabarets. Baldwin and Bambara both utilize New York as a central setting in their short fiction, but each writer uses the place to different degrees and thus portrays multiple settings within a single metropolis.

Amiri Baraka explains that New York and any other urban places for that matter "must escape any blank generalizations simply because it is alive, and changing each second with each breath any of its citizens take."[17] Hakutani and Butler echo these sentiments, asserting that because of the complexity of urban environments, critics should "resist any simple categorizations and neat generalizations" in our exploration of how writers use city settings.[18] Baldwin and Bambara use urban settings, specifically New York City, to highlight various aspects of city living. Bambara's tendency to focus primarily on children characters and Baldwin's interest in portraying two adult brothers influence the types of settings they incorporate into their stories and the ways characters navigate their environments. While characters are free to roam throughout the city in Baldwin's "Sonny's Blues," Bambara's characters do not travel outside of their neighborhood unless accompanied by an adult. Ultimately, several factors such as the historical era, references to landmarks and navigation routes, and even the age of the protagonist influence the story.

Several Black writers present a range of urban spaces in their stories featuring Black characters. Paule Marshall has a college-educated, politically active Black woman as the protagonist in her story "Reena," which is set in Brooklyn, New York. Wright's "The Man Who Lived Underground," also set in New York City, describes how a Black man falsely accused of murder goes underground and lives in the city's sewers to escape captivity by police officers. In "Like a Winding Sheet," Ann Petry characterizes how, even in a northern city, remnants of the Jim Crow South still impede upon Black people's lives as she follows a Black couple and depicts how the prejudices and injustices they face disrupt their marriage. And in Edwidge Danticat's "Seven," a Haitian-born husband and wife reunite after seven years apart and start a new life in New York. New York is a central locale across all of these stories, though the writers find diverse uses for the metropolis.

Some stories by Black writers incorporate music or musical settings. Baldwin, Fisher, Dumas, and Baraka, in particular, depict the convergence of music and location as they present stories in which large numbers of Black people gather to take in the sights and sounds of jazz. In *The Music in African American Fiction: Representing Music in African American Fiction*, Robert H. Cataliotti notes, "The clubs and cabarets that fill the cityscape in *Home to Harlem* provide the meeting ground for professional blues and jazz artists and their audiences."[19] Music—especially jazz—has been influential in terms of style, language, attitude, and consciousness of New York and other metropolises. Writers utilized these types of settings in their stories to demonstrate how jazz music was central to the landscape of New York City and other urban environments. As a result, these locations were vital to illustrating the livelihood and entertainment of urban centers.

Cultural geo-tagging charts the place-making that comprises artistic compositions. In addition, cultural geo-tagging draws attention to the significance of positioning. How a protagonist is placed in proximity to rivals and supporting characters calls attention to a given setting. Surveying several geographic factors accounts for how authors situate characters in cultural contexts and in relation to ideas.

HOMEGROWN, OUTSIDER, AND HOMEGROWN OUTSIDER CHARACTERS

In discussions of the craft of creative writers, Janet Burroway, Orson Card, David Corbett, Donald Maass, and others have noted that the production of notable characters is essential to compelling storytelling.[20] Beyond mentioning various places and settings, writers explore locations through the characters that they present. There are multiple ways to describe the protagonists who appear in fiction, though a focus on geography prompts considerations for what I refer to as homegrown and outsider characters. Homegrown characters are those native to a region who are familiar with the local environment and customs. Outsider characters are strangers or visitors to a region and its social norms. There are even homegrown outsiders—figures who are native to a region but, for some reason or another, are distant from those in their home environment. The presentations of homegrown, outsider, and homegrown outsider characters in short stories constitute an element of cultural geo-tagging that further accentuates settings and ideas.

"Characters infuse a story with conviction," explains Corbett, to reveal how people "get things done, the beliefs that guide them and the errors that betray them, their crucial decisions, their hopeless failings, their critical deeds."[21] Consequently, writers incorporate homegrown characters into their stories as a way of offering insider perspectives on a region. The protagonist of Bambara's "Raymond's Run" pinpoints specific locales and navigates her Harlem neighborhood with ease. Hurston presents several residential figures in "Spunk" that shed light on the inner workings of their Florida community. In "Going to Meet the Man," Baldwin describes a public lynching from the perspective of someone inside the community and is thus able to depict the frenzied and troubling excitement that filled the narrator and other onlookers as they watched a Black man suffer an agonizing death. These and other homegrown characters allow authors to shed light on environments that might otherwise be hidden.

Edward P. Jones makes exquisite use of homegrown characters, imbuing them with deep knowledge about the spaces and places that constitute Washington, DC. In numerous stories, including "Lost in the City," "All Aunt Hagar's Children," "The Girl Who Raised Pigeons," and "Bad Neighbors," Jones presents characters knowingly navigating the city by walking down the street, standing on street corners, taking subways, and riding in cars. Moreover, his homegrown characters grant him the ability to show the abundant and assorted locales of the city. In the process, he displays his expansive knowledge of his hometown. The depiction of dozens of characters with overwhelming familiarity with the environs of Washington, DC, empowers Jones to fully explore an assortment of areas, primarily occupied by Black people, in the District.

Outsider characters, on the other hand, are unfamiliar with those in a particular setting in a story. Novelist Orson Card has noted that a character's role is defined by a "network of relationships with other people and with society at large."[22] Writers present some characters, though, who have strained or distant relationships with other people. Those characters are unaccustomed to the social norms of the communities they visit. They are unaware of the local histories that inform the general populace of a setting in a story.

James Baldwin's unnamed character from "Sonny's Blues" is a relative stranger among a crowd of people in a Greenwich Village jazz club. King Solomon Gillis in Rudolph Fisher's "City of Refuge" is oblivious to the manipulative advances of a streetwise con artist he encounters when arriving in Harlem from North Carolina. A wealthy white couple from the North in Charles Chesnutt's "The Goophered Grapevine" stand out among locals. Three white people from Henry Dumas's "Will the Circle Be Unbroken" are strangers among the patrons in all-Black Harlem jazz club. The outsiders in these and other stories inevitably confirm that there are inner places and insiders and that there are those who must learn and experience settings with only basic knowledge of its parameters and possibilities. Outsider characters raise the likelihood of a conflicting viewpoint with those in a setting since these figures do not hold the values of a set community and can thus cause disruptions.

In several stories, writers present figures who are a combination of homegrown and outsider characters. These characters emerge from a local environment but for some reason become detached. Donald Maass explains that "you can deepen the psychology of place in your story by returning to a previously established setting and showing how your character's perception of it has changed"; he continues, "You can also give your characters an active relationship to place, which, in turn, means marking your characters' growth (or decline) through their relationships to their various surroundings."[23] The presentation of characters that for whatever reason have become alienated from their home environments intensifies the drama of a narrative by raising the possibility of conflict within a common group.

The protagonist of Ellison's "Battle Royal" is a local, yet he becomes unsettled and ruminates about following a path not taken by other Black boys where he lives. In "To Hell with Dying" by Alice Walker, the central character returns to her southern home only to realize how distant she has grown from her childhood environment. In "The Screamers," Amiri Baraka presents a local who has grown frustrated with his life in Newark, New Jersey, and is longing to rebel against the Black middle class for adopting standards that suppress Black art and culture in general. Homegrown outsider characters are bridges. They link the old and the new, the familiar with the unfamiliar, the residents with the guests.

Writers other than the Big 7 also accentuate cultural geographies by presenting characters that offer distinct views of settings or regions. In "City of Refuge," Rudolph Fisher shows the moments of awe a Black southerner experiences when he moves to Harlem. In "The Sky Is Gray," Ernest Gaines challenges stereotypes about the South in a touching interracial scene in which a Black boy and his mother encounter an elderly white woman shop owner who seems to take pity on them as they wander around in the cold in Bayonne, Louisiana. Terry McMillan writes about a seventy-two-year-old woman named Hazel in her story "Ma'Dear," using vernacular to embellish the narrative prose with geographic elements and thus offering a narrative that reflects the perspective of an elderly Black person. The wide variety of characters presented by writers in hundreds of stories indicates the prevalence of geography in relatively short compositions.

OVERVIEW OF THE BOOK

Chapter 1, "Locating the Big 7: One Hundred Anthologies and the Most Frequently Anthologized Black Short Stories," clarifies how generations of editors solidified a Big 7 of major writers by repeatedly republishing their stories. Decisions by editors to publish select works by Chesnutt, Hurston, Wright, Ellison, Baldwin, Bambara, and Walker shaped the canonical history of African American short stories. Drawing from a dataset of one hundred anthologies published between 1925 and 2017, the chapter reveals how a relatively small number of writers and stories became so pervasive. The chapter explains how the imperative of recovering and promoting women writers advanced the circulation of stories by Hurston, Bambara, and Walker. Finally, consideration of a chronological approach, the preferred mode of arrangement by editors, pinpoints the reason the Big 7 emerged as they did.

Chapter 2, "Writing the South: Charles Chesnutt, Zora Neale Hurston, and Richard Wright," explains why depicting the dramas of homegrown characters in southern settings was so crucial to short fiction by Chesnutt,

Hurston, and Wright. The presentation of native southerners gave these writers' opportunities to explore local dimensions of the region. They composed narratives that incorporate Black vernacular speech and conflicts between a variety of characters. Telling stories that featured southern culture and locales empowered Chesnutt, Hurston, and Wright to create enriching compositions. Their stories testify to the power of homegrown characters and southern landscapes.

Chapter 3, "The Paradox of Homegrown Outsiders: Ralph Ellison, Alice Walker, and James Baldwin," explains why southern outsider characters are vital components of short stories by Ellison, Walker, and Baldwin. They composed short fiction that showed how social mores and local customs influenced internal thoughts of characters. Ellison's first-person stories about Black male characters show them struggling to fit into shifting and sometimes troubling southern environments. Ellison and Baldwin ventured into rarely charted territory for major Black writers by taking on the first-person perspectives of white male characters who witnessed the lynching of Black males. They explore the possibilities of Black storytellers passing as white narrators. Walker's stories illustrate the experiences of southern women homegrown characters. Her stories reflect her interest in celebrating Black culture and addressing internal conflicts.

Chapter 4, "New York Cityscapes: James Baldwin and Toni Cade Bambara," explains why New York City as a setting is integral to multifaceted short stories by Baldwin and Bambara. Their stories depict a diverse set of sights and sounds linked to one of our most famous cities. Their homegrown characters exhibit keen awareness of their environments as they navigate urban terrains. Baldwin's "Sonny's Blues" shows two brothers reconciling and gaining a deeper understanding of one another. Baldwin's references to city landmarks and descriptions of navigation routes reveal him in the process of crafting a story that utilizes the urban environment as a dynamic background. "Sonny's Blues," as the title suggests, takes the transformative power of song seriously. Baldwin, as well as Fisher, Dumas, and Baraka, demonstrates that musical gathering places can operate as captivating settings in short fiction. For Bambara, New York City serves as a defining setting. She showcases the experiences of Black girl characters, thus shifting the conventional kind of protagonist that appeared in short fiction.

Chapter 5, "Up South: Geo-Tagging DC and Edward P. Jones's Homegrown Characters," demonstrates how Jones preserves and extends the tradition of African American short fiction. Despite the long history and dense population of Washington, DC, the predominantly Black quadrants of the District have a relatively small presence in the scholarship on African

American literature. Jones depicts homegrown characters with acute knowledge about the geographies of the city. Accordingly, his stories offer intricate portrayals of streets, intersections, apartment buildings, walking and driving routes, neighborhoods, city landmarks, and quadrants in the nation's capital. His meticulous city narratives constitute an outstanding achievement in the production of African American short stories and warrant critical attention.

The conclusion first highlights the value of utilizing data in courses on African American and American literature. The uses of data motivated my students and me to engage short fiction in new and exciting ways based on what we discovered. Identifying and quantifying interrelated factors about dozens of stories prompted us to consider the importance of numerical information derived from literary art. Second, the conclusion reaffirms the significance of cultural geo-tagging as a method for exploring African American short fiction. An approach that focuses on geographic settings and the positionality of characters presents us with special opportunities for considering vital elements that make short stories such captivating compositions.

Chapter 1

LOCATING THE BIG 7

One Hundred Anthologies and the Most Frequently Anthologized Black Short Stories

Anthologies constitute one of the most important ways to examine the histories of Black short fiction. These collections, which contain multiple modes of writing, shape as well as reinforce views of African American and American literature. Literary canons, as well-known anthologist M. H. Abrams describes it, consist of "authors who, by cumulative consensus of critics, scholars, and teachers, have come to be widely recognized as 'major,' and to have written works often hailed as literary classics."[1] He continues, "The literary works by canonical authors are the ones which, at a given time, are most kept in print, most frequently and fully discussed by literary critics and historians, and most likely to be included in anthologies and in the syllabi of college courses." Anthology editors provide a platform for keeping writers and literary works in circulation. At the same time, editors necessarily filter and exclude works.

In the spring 1997 issue of *Callaloo*, Kenneth Kinnamon's essay, "Anthologies of African-American Literature from 1845 to 1994," offers an extensive historical account of the development of African American literature anthologies. Kinnamon examined collections that spanned more than eighty years and included comprehensive to genre-specific anthologies. He explained the structure of the collections in order to analyze the framing techniques of editors and document the multiple contexts through which Black writers circulated over several decades.[2]

Whereas Kinnamon focused solely on African American literature anthologies, a consideration of a variety of collections, including general primarily white anthologies and specialized books, reveals how stories appear in numerous kinds of collections. Editors of Harlem Renaissance collections highlight prominent and lesser-known works by writers of that particular era. Black women's collections such as *Black-Eyed Susans/Midnight Birds: Stories by and about Black Women* (1990) and *Revolutionary Tales: African American Women's Short Stories, from the First Story to the Present* (1995) include short story writers Ann Petry, Gayl Jones, Octavia E. Butler, Terry McMillan, and others who do not regularly appear in comprehensive Black or American collections. Ultimately, recognition of the multiple anthology types reveals the many contexts through which Black short fiction has circulated over several decades.

Editors of American literature anthologies accentuated the value of select Black writers by reprinting their stories more frequently than various other Black writers. African American collections presented a large group of Black writers, at least in comparison to American literature collections. *African American Literature: An Anthology of Nonfiction, Fiction, Poetry, and Drama—Vol. 2* (1993) reprints twenty short stories by Black writers, while *Harper American Literature, Vol. 2* (1993) includes six stories. An analysis of short fiction presented in anthologies over the decades reveals that editors collectively constructed, solidified, and altered historical periods, thereby creating cohorts of writers, sometimes arbitrarily, organized around key themes and social concepts.

Projects in the field of African American literary studies increasingly concentrate on truncated time periods. However, we can learn much about canonical history by observing the transmission of literary works over nearly a century. We additionally gain an understanding of framing practices by taking a closer look at the work of editors, an important but often overlooked group of contributors to the transmission of African American literature. Quantifying reprints clarifies how editors shaped canonical histories. While conventional bibliographies remain important, we can further advance African American literary studies by taking advantage of datasets, which greatly assist in exploring and quantifying multifaceted publishing histories.

This chapter offers a look at African American literary history by analyzing a dataset of one hundred anthologies published between 1925 and 2017. The first section addresses how editors established seven Black writers as the most consequential anthologized short story writers. The second section explains the importance of women's anthologies for promoting short fiction by Black writers, especially during the 1990s. The third section explains how the tendency of editors to present Black writers along a chronological continuum contributed to the formation of distinct literary periods.

THE FORMATION OF THE BIG 7

There is no shortage of short fiction. In "The Black Short Story Dataset," there are a total of 632 unique short stories by 297 Black writers. There are hundreds, if not thousands, more stories that were never selected for inclusion in collections. Individual stories rarely appear in three or more collections. In fact, only fourteen individual stories appear in ten or more anthologies. Chesnutt, Hurston, Wright, Ellison, Baldwin, Bambara, and Walker wrote twelve of those fourteen stories.[3]

These writers—the Big 7—are outliers for four main reasons. For one, their stories appear more frequently than 290 other short story writers whose works have been anthologized. Second, they are among a relatively small number of Black writers whose stories appear in different kinds of anthologies—general short story collections, comprehensive literature anthologies, and special topics collections. Third, each of the Big 7 has at least one signature story that has appeared in more than ten anthologies. Finally, since 1990, each of these writers has had their stories published in more than twenty-five anthologies. The only Black short story writers who meet those four criteria are Chesnutt, Hurston, Wright, Ellison, Baldwin, Bambara, and Walker.

Editors of African American and American comprehensive collections are especially important in the case of the Big 7. These anthologies make up forty-four of the collections in the current dataset. These types of collections, which are primarily used in survey courses, offer a historical survey of authors and a variety of literary work. Stories by all of the Big 7 writers appear together in *The New Cavalcade: African American Writing from 1760 to the Present* (1991), *The Norton Anthology of American Literature, Vol. 2* (1998), *The Heath Anthology of American Literature, Vol. 2* (2002), and the first, second, and third editions of *The Norton Anthology of African American Literature* (1997, 2003, 2014).

Editors ensured the visibility and widespread circulation of stories by Chesnutt, Hurston, Wright, Ellison, Baldwin, Bambara, and Walker by continually including their compositions. Repeated selections kept the stories in print. Moreover, American and African American literature anthologies circulated the stories in different contexts. On the one hand, American literature anthologies placed stories by Hurston, Wright, and Walker, for instance, in conversation with prominent white writers such as William Faulkner, Robert Frost, F. Scott Fitzgerald, John Steinbeck, Flannery O'Connor, and Sylvia Plath. African American literature anthologies, on the other hand, presented Hurston, Wright, and Walker in relation to Rudolph Fisher, Ann Petry, Ernest Gaines, and other Black writers.

The *Heath* anthology edited by Paul Lauter was one of the first major anthologies that set out to deliberately diversify the literary canon by including Black writers consistently in subsequent editions of the anthology during the late 1980s.[4] By 2002, the Big 7 had all appeared together in three editions of the *Heath*. In addition, Paule Marshall and Gaines had stories reprinted in the 1998, 2000, 2002, and 2006 editions. Ann Petry's stories also appeared in the 1998 and 2002 editions of the *Heath*. Although Gaines, Marshall, and Petry each have over twenty stories in the dataset, those stories are mostly reprinted in Black collections. Even though they are included in various editions of the *Heath*, their works do not appear in other general anthologies such as *The American Tradition in Literature, Shorter 10th Ed.* (2002) and *The Bedford Anthology of American Literature, Volume Two* (2014).

Editors have republished Chesnutt works in thirty-three comprehensive American and African American literature anthologies. His stories have been included in more comprehensive anthologies than any other Black writer. When editors sought short fiction from the late nineteenth century to include in anthologies, they often selected works by Chesnutt, whose successful career and prominence as a literary artist made his stories preferred choices. Chesnutt was not the only Black writer publishing short stories at the turn of the twentieth century. Various publications included stories by Frances E. W. Harper, Mary Weston Fordham, Booker T. Washington, and W. E. B. Du Bois. Chesnutt's stories, however, published in *The Conjure Woman* (1899) and *The Wife of His Youth and Other Stories of the Color-Line* (1899), are the favorites of editors who seek to include Black writers. Chesnutt's two collections of short stories depict Black southern characters living between approximately 1850 and the turn of the twentieth century.

Chesnutt's stories appear more than any other writer in the dataset as editors have collectively republished eleven of his stories in forty-eight anthologies. In eighteen instances, editors included at least two of Chesnutt's stories in the same anthology, which helped elevate the total number of reprints of his stories. His stories are included in comprehensive anthologies such as *Black Writers of America: A Comprehensive Anthology* (1972) and *American Literature: A Prentice Hall Anthology, Vol. 2* (1991), general short story collections like *The Oxford Book of American Short Stories* (2013) and *Great Short Stories by African-American Writers* (2015), and special topic readers, including *African-American Classics: Graphic Classics* (2011) and *Black Noir: Mystery, Crime, and Suspense Stories by African-American Writers* (2009). Five stories—"The Goophered Grapevine," "The Wife of His Youth," "The Passing of Grandison," "Po' Sandy," and "The Sheriff's Children"—became the stories most often selected to represent Chesnutt. In the introduction to *Cavalcade*'s "Accommodation and Protest: 1865–1910" section, Davis and Redding explain that Chesnutt was "the first Negro novelist of imposing stature," and the writer's "special theme was the Negro of mixed blood, the 'tragic mulatto': he was the first black author to deal in depth with the problem of the 'color line' within the Negro race, and the first to make imaginative capital of racism's consequences to the white man."[5] For Davis and Redding, Chesnutt's racial firsts were important, and those achievements likely contributed to the basis for his inclusion.

Chesnutt's plantation stories and use of Black southern vernacular gained popularity among majority white reading audiences during the late nineteenth and early twentieth centuries, similar to the popularity of the commercially successful poet Paul Laurence Dunbar and author of the Uncle Remus series Joel Chandler Harris.[6] All of their compositions dramatized events in southern locales offering readers a glimpse into rural landscapes. According to Matthew R. Martin, "Chesnutt undertook the difficult task of conquering the literary marketplace by selling plantation tales which refused his readers the expected pleasures of paradisaical settings or happy slaves."[7] He continues, "At the same time, he used a literary form whose appeal lay almost wholly in its romanticization of slavery and the plantation South as a means of revising public perceptions about those institutions." In these stories, Chesnutt is not so much interested in critiquing the cruelty of slavery, but instead focuses on contrasting the characterizations of his recurring protagonist Uncle Julius's beliefs and those of his northern counterparts.

Even though Chesnutt is the most frequently anthologized writer, Baldwin has the single most republished story. Editors chose to reprint "Sonny's Blues" in thirty-three anthologies, more than any other story in the dataset. The story has been republished in comprehensive African American collections such as *Dark Symphony: Negro Literature in America* (1968) and *The New Cavalcade: African American Writing from 1760 to the Present* (1991); the Black short story collections *From the Roots: Short Stories by Black Americans* (1970) and *Children of the Night: The Best Short Stories by Black Writers, 1967 to the Present* (1995); the general short story collections *The Riverside Anthology of Literature* (1996) and *Fiction 100: An Anthology of Short Fiction* (2012); and comprehensive American collections like *The American Tradition in Literature, Shorter* (1985) and *Harper American Literature, Vol. 2* (1993). "Sonny's Blues" has appeared in every comprehensive anthology in the dataset since 1972.

Baldwin's story, however, was not always so prominent. Anthology editors included a variety of Baldwin's stories such as "The Outing" and "This Morning, This Evening, So Soon." Gradually however, "Sonny's Blues," along with select essays by Baldwin, became the preferred choice of editors. With Chesnutt, editors decided between "The Goophered Grapevine," "The Wife of His Youth," and, to a slightly lesser extent, "The Passing of Grandison." With Hurston, editors made decisions between "The Gilded Six-Bits" and "Sweat." For Baldwin, they almost always went with "Sonny's Blues." It has become his signature short story.

"Sonny's Blues" first appeared in *Partisan Review* in 1957. The following year, Martha Foley and David Burnett selected Baldwin's story for inclusion in the *Best American Short Stories of 1958*. Their selection of "Sonny's Blues" for the collection represents the beginning of a long-standing choice made by editors. Since its initial appearance, the story has come to define much of Baldwin's reputation as a short story writer. James Nagel noted in the biographical sketch on Baldwin for *Anthology of the American Short Story* (2008) that "Sonny's Blues" is the writer's most famous short story and the composition addresses "the complexity of racial identity and the ways in which it impinges upon artistic expression."[8]

Critically acclaimed novelists are often represented by their short stories. Such was the case with Wright. The acclaim generated by *Native Son* as well as his autobiography, *Black Boy*, prompted editors to include the author, though they selected his short stories far more than excerpts from either of his most well-known books. In October 1938, Wright's literary agent, Paul Reynolds Jr., capitalized on the national media attention of *Uncle Tom's Children* and submitted a draft of *Native Son* to Ed Aswell, an editor at Harper and Brothers. In 1940, the Book-of-the-Month Club, which had five hundred thousand members, showcased Wright's debut novel as a selection, thereby ensuring that *Native Son* would exceed sales of two hundred thousand copies within the first three weeks of publication and greatly expanding his reading audience.[9] The reception of *Native Son* immediately secured Wright's prominence and prompted editors to begin to include new and previous works by him in anthologies. In 1940, Harper and Brothers reissued his short story collection *Uncle Tom's Children* with a new story "Bright and Morning Star" as well as Wright's essay "The Ethics of Living Jim Crow" as the book's introduction. *Uncle Tom's Children* paved the way for *Native Son*; in turn, the success of that novel created reasons for anthology editors to select Wright's short fiction.

Although Wright is widely known for his depictions of urban contexts in his work, his short stories reveal his facility in writing rural landscapes. Wright's stories appear in general short story collections like *Major American Short Stories* (1994), *The Best American Short Stories of the Century* (1998), and *The Norton Anthology of Short Fiction* (2006), as well as the comprehensive African American collections *The Negro Caravan: Writings by American Negroes* (1941) and *Black Voices: An Anthology of African-American Literature* (1968) and the comprehensive American collections *American Literature: The Makers and the Making, Vol. 2* (1979) and *The Norton Anthology of American Literature* (1989). Since 1941, editors have routinely included four of his stories, all set in primarily southern environments, in literary collections: "Bright and Morning Star," "Long Black Song," "Big Boy Leaves Home," and "The Man Who Was Almost a Man" (also known as "Almos' a Man"). The stories are presumed to be set in Mississippi during the 1910s and 1920s.[10] Robin Lucy describes Wright's short fiction as being "defined by geographical location, class, and gender—as southern and rural, poor, and most often male—and that this construct underwrote a discourse of black difference and, therefore, of racial identity."[11] Those combinations of factors highlight Wright's tendency to place southern Black characters at the center of his stories. Moreover, his stories demonstrate his interest in depicting experiences that might lead rural Black people to leave the South.

Similar to Wright, Ellison is better known as a novelist. Since the publication of *Invisible Man* (1952), the critically acclaimed novel has gone through more than three dozen printings, and there has been a Modern Library edition. The novel won the National Book Award for Fiction in 1953, and in 1998, the Modern Library ranked *Invisible Man* nineteenth on its list of the one hundred best English-language novels of the twentieth century. According to Herbert Mitgang, "in 1965, some 200 authors, editors and critics, polled by the *New York Herald Tribune*, picked *Invisible Man* as the most distinguished novel written by an American during the previous 20 years."[12] The novel was largely responsible for Ellison's reputation as a dominant force in African American and American literature. Accordingly, editors selected his short fiction as a preview for *Invisible Man*.

Ellison's stories appear in African American and American comprehensive collections like *Crossing the Danger Water: Three Hundred Years of African-American Writing* (1993), *Literature Across Cultures* (1998), and *The Heath Anthology of American Literature, Vol. 2* (2002), as well as short story collections like *The Art of the Short Story* (2005) and *The Oxford Book of American Short Stories* (2013). The repeated appearances of authors in different types of anthologies indicate that editors have come to a general consensus about the most essential Black short story writers. Editors have been especially inclined to include "Battle Royal," the first chapter of *Invisible Man*, in anthologies as a stand-alone story. Frank Taylor, Ellison's editor at Random House, prompted interest in *Invisible Man* by promoting excerpts of the book as a short story years before the novel's release. Unbeknownst to

Ellison, Taylor offered the first chapter of the novel to *Horizon* magazine's editor, Cyril Connolly, for a special issue on art in America to be published in 1947. The story was so well received that John Hersey of *'47: The Magazine of the Year* purchased the rights to publish the composition, and the following year, the story appeared in *'48: The Magazine of the Year*.[13] Among the most frequently anthologized Black writers, Ellison is the only one who had a chapter from his greatly lauded novel originally published as a short story.

Langston Hughes deserves special mention in a consideration of African American short story writers frequently chosen by anthology editors. More than forty of his stories were selected by editors in the dataset, yet he is primarily known as a poet. No single story by Hughes appears frequently in anthologies. The fact that no single short story by Hughes appears in more than six anthologies suggests that editors did not come to a consensus on Hughes's stories. Editors of African American comprehensive anthologies tend to present Hughes as a multigenre writer including his poems, essays, plays, novel excerpts, and short stories.

Comprehensive Black anthologies routinely include Hughes's Jesse B. Semple stories—short stories from his newspaper column that ran in the *Chicago Defender* from 1942 to 1962. *American Literature: Tradition & Innovation* (1969), *A Gift of the Spirit* (1971), *The Norton Anthology of African American Literature* (1997), and *Great Short Stories by African-American Writers* (2015), for example, all include Hughes's Semple stories. For the most part, Hughes's short stories only show up in comprehensive African American collections, while comprehensive American anthologies and special topics collections tend to only include his poetry and occasionally his essays. The lack of a consensus on Hughes's stories implies that his status as a short story writer was overshadowed by his reputation as a poet.

The absence of signature short stories by Hughes as well as his reputation as a poet places him at a distance from the Big 7. Hughes and, for that matter, Alice Dunbar Nelson, Jessie Fauset, and Chester Himes were all prolific short story writers. Nevertheless, editors did not come to a consensus about works by those writers. Instead, multiple stories by them were selected for inclusion. Moreover, Hughes's short fiction, similar to other writers, primarily appears in collections that include only Black writers. Most Black short story writers in general only appear in limited contexts such as Black special topics collections or theme-specific anthologies.

The thirty-six anthologies in this dataset published prior to 1990 offer contrasting views of the leading Black short story writers. During that time, editors most frequently chose to reprint short stories by Chesnutt, Hughes, Wright, Baldwin, and Ellison.[14] Noticeably absent was a consistent representation of women writers. Hurston, Bambara, and Walker became more frequently anthologized during the 1990s. Without the rise of collections devoted to literary art by women and without the feminist imperative to redress the exclusion of women writers in American and African American literature canons, stories by Black women would have received far less consideration.

BLACK WOMEN SHORT STORY WRITERS

Among Black women short story writers, we might view Hurston, Bambara, and Walker as an "essential 3." Editors chose stories by these three literary artists more than any other Black women writers. A chronological approach that emphasizes initial publication dates of writers and stories, however, inadvertently glosses over the importance of editorial selections made years and sometimes decades later. Since the mid-1990s, Hurston's "The Gilded Six-Bits" and "Sweat" became two of the most frequently anthologized short stories by a Black woman writer, despite the stories' being published nearly eighty years ago. Bambara first published "The Lesson" in 1972, and Walker published "Everyday Use" in 1973. However, those stories weren't reprinted several times until the 1990s and 2000s. The decisions by Mary Helen Washington, Pat Crutchfield Exum, Judith Musser, Bill Mullen, Marcy Knopf, Nellie Y. McKay, and other editors to include works by Hurston, Bambara, and Walker make them the most well-represented Black women short story writers.

Within my dataset of one hundred anthologies, there are twelve collections devoted exclusively to women writers. Six collections—*The Black Woman: An Anthology* (1970), *Keeping the Faith: Writings by Contemporary Black American Women* (1974), *Women Working: An Anthology of Stories and Poems* (1979), and *The Norton Anthology of Literature by Women* (1985)—presented large numbers of Black women short story writers. Those anthologies, including Lorraine Elena Roses and Ruth Elizabeth Randolph's *Harlem's Glory: Black Women Writing, 1900–1950* (1996) and Florence Howe's *Almost Touching the Skies: Women's Coming of Age Stories* (2000), increased reprints of stories by Hurston, Bambara, Walker, Octavia Butler, Jamaica Kincaid, and Gwendolyn B. Bennett. Even though these anthologies account for a small number of texts in the dataset, they expanded the circulation of short fiction by Black women, especially Hurston, Bambara, and Walker.

Feminist efforts to promote women writers, which began gaining heightened attention during the late 1960s and 1970s, encouraged editors to be mindful about including Black women writers. In the introduction to *The*

Black Woman (1970), Bambara, the editor, writes, "I don't know that literature enlightens us too much. The 'experts' are still men, Black or white. And the images of the woman are still derived from their needs, their fantasies, their second-hand knowledge, their agreement with the other 'experts.'"[15] Bambara's collection included poetry, short stories, and essays by Nikki Giovanni, Audre Lorde, Alice Walker, and Paule Marshall, among others. Bambara critiques the lack of African American women writers, and she sees evidence that publishers will have to soon start taking Black women writers and readers more seriously. "Throughout the country in recent years," she writes, "Black women have been forming women's workshops on the campuses, women's caucuses within existing organizations, Afro-American women's magazines" (4). Bambara saw her fiction illuminating "the struggles that women must confront to exist as people in their own right, apart from the men in their lives" (ii).

In the introduction to *Black-Eyed Susans/Midnight Birds: Stories by and about Black Women* (1990), editor Mary Helen Washington notes that *Black-Eyed Susans* (1975) and *Midnight Birds* (1980) "have been in print fifteen and ten years" and calls the endurance of this literary collection "a testament to the persistence of a literary tradition of black women."[16] It was imperative, stated Washington, that we acknowledge Black women's contributions to arts and letters because, through the creation of complex women characters, "these writers have chosen to tell their stories and to use language in certain ways, and in doing so have produced art, writerly designs, which constitute a unique literary tradition" (6). Washington's collection, which includes Sherley Anne Williams's "Meditations on History," Paulette Childress White's "The Bird Cage," Gayl Jones's "Asylum," and Paule Marshall's "Reena," contributes to the processes of expanding reprint possibilities for Black women short story writers.

Several editors contributed to expanding the circulation of Black women's writing. Bill Mullen's *Revolutionary Tales: African American Women's Short Stories, from the First Story to the Present* (1995) also includes stories by Hurston, Bambara, and Walker alongside a diverse array of contributors. Similar to African American or American comprehensive collections that attempt to comprehend the entirety of American literature, this collection places well-known and less popular works by Black women together in chronological order. The collection begins with Frances Harper's "Two Offers," the first short story believed to ever be published by an African American author. Mullen also reprints stories by Alice Childress, Grace W. Tompkins, Hazel V. Campbell, Anita R. Cornwell, Jessie Fauset, and Maxine Clair. Of course, *Revolutionary Tales* includes works by Hurston, Bambara, and Walker.

Hurston was perhaps one of the most important beneficiaries of the shift to acknowledging the artistic contributions of Black women writers. Robert Hemenway's *Zora Neale Hurston: A Literary Biography* (1977) and Alice Walker's writing on Hurston in *Ms.* magazine in 1975 stimulated interest in the writer and her life. In 1978, Harper and Row reissued *Their Eyes Were Watching God*, which sold nearly seventy-five thousand copies in less than a month.[17] The renewed attention that Hurston received during the 1970s for her novel encouraged future editors to include her short fiction in anthologies and collected works. *Revolutionary Tales: African American Women's Short Stories* (1995), *Cornerstones: Anthology of African American Literature* (1996), *The Wiley Blackwell Anthology of African American Literature* (2014), *Great Short Stories by African-American Writers* (2015), and other collections republished short stories by Hurston. Consequentially, comprehensive collections regularly included her works, ensuring that her short fiction became familiar in American and African American literature.

Even though Hurston is a central figure of the Harlem Renaissance during the 1920s, she was not the only woman writing during the period. Marcy Knopf-Newman's *The Sleeper Wakes: Harlem Renaissance Stories by Women* (1993) includes stories by Hurston, Jessie Fauset, Nella Larsen, and Dorothy West. The collection also reprints short fiction by Eloise Bibb Thompson, Ottie Beatrice Graham, and Anita Scott Coleman—writers who are typically overlooked in discussions of African American short stories. More than just publishing less popular writers alongside canonical works, this collection republished stories by well-known writers that are otherwise not reprinted—in this case, Hurston's previously unpublished story "The Bone of Contention."[18] Henry Louis Gates Jr. noted that Hurston discovered and recorded this folktale in her hometown of Eatonville, Florida.[19]

Judith Musser's *"Tell It to Us Easy" and Other Stories: A Complete Short Fiction Anthology of African American Women Writers in "Opportunity" Magazine (1923–1948)* (2008) also expanded conventional definitions of the Harlem Renaissance era and presented a less widely known story by Hurston. Whereas the Harlem Renaissance is believed to have ended the decade following the stock market crash of 1929, women writers associated with the cultural movement were still publishing short fiction nearly a decade after the era is supposed to have ended. The stories in this collection first appeared in *Opportunity* literary magazine, which ran monthly from 1923 to 1942 and then quarterly through 1949. Few of the many women who published in the magazine became widely known beyond that period. The collection includes Anita Scott Coleman's "Cross Crossings Cautiously" and "The Eternal Quest," Marian Minus's "Half-Bright: A Short Story" and "The Fine Line: A Story of the Color Line," Cordelia T. Smith's "Black Brother," and Elizabeth Walker Reeves's "Not in the Record." The collection also includes another story by Hurston, "Drenched in Light," that circulates less frequently than her other works. By 2008, Hurston was a prominent, critically acclaimed author, and eight of her stories—"Drenched in Light," "The Bone of Contention," "Spunk," "Sweat," "The Gilded Six-Bits," "The Conscience of the Court," "The Back Room," and "John Redding Goes to Sea"—had been republished.

While scholars worked to recenter Hurston's work during the 1970s, her stories appeared in a large number of collections after 1990 as the number of anthologies increased. Hurston is one of the relatively few Black short story writers whose works appeared in anthologies during multiple decades. During the late twentieth and early twenty-first centuries, editors framed Hurston as a literary foremother and cited her as an influence for later generations of Black women writers. In the "Introduction" to Hurston's edited collection, *The Complete Stories*, Henry Louis Gates Jr. and Sieglinde Lemke remark how Black feminists "seized upon Hurston as the canonical black foremother."[20] In *The Prentice Hall Anthology of African American Literature*, editor Rochelle Smith explains how Hurston "has been viewed as a literary foremother by many African American women writers."[21] The presentation of Hurston as a foremother may have inadvertently erased or at least diminished those Black women who proceeded her.

Anthologists have actively advanced the link between Hurston and Walker, suggesting a sense of continuity, if not artistic lineage, between the writers. In 1967, Langston Hughes had included Hurston's "The Gilded Six-Bits" and Walker's "To Hell with Dying" in *The Best Short Stories by Negro Writers*. Over the decades, editors have continuously linked Walker with her apparent literary foremother, Hurston.

Editors included stories by Walker in forty-four anthologies. Her appearances in so many collections indicate her status as one of the most widely anthologized African American writers. "Everyday Use" has become Walker's most famous story, appearing in twenty collections between 1973 and 2016. Editors have also included Walker's "Nineteen Fifty-Five," "To Hell with Dying," and "Advancing Luna and Ida B. Wells," though far less frequently than "Everyday Use." Her stories have been reprinted in *Tales and Stories for Black Folks* (1971), the fourth edition of the *Anthology of American Literature, Realism to Present, Vol. 2* (1989), *Cornerstones: Anthology of African American Literature* (1996), *The Prentice Hall Anthology of African American Literature* (2000), *The Story and Its Writer: An Introduction to Short Fiction* (2011), and *40 Short Stories: A Portable Anthology* (2016). "To Hell with Dying," a story about a young girl who recalls a man, Mr. Sweet, constantly evading death, appeared in anthologies from the mid-1970s until present day. Since 1973, "Everyday Use," a story of intergenerational conflict between a mother and her two daughters, has been Walker's most frequently reprinted short story. Unlike other Black women short story writers such as Bambara and Paule Marshall, Walker concentrates on Black women in rural southern settings, not the urban North. The routine reprinting of Walker's "Everyday Use" solidified her reputation as a southern writer.

With the growing interest in stories by and about Black women during the 1970s, editors seemed to find three of Toni Cade Bambara's stories featuring Black girl protagonists particularly useful for filling a void in their collections. Her work has appeared in twenty-nine anthologies since 1966. In 1972, Bambara released her first collection of short stories, *Gorilla, My Love*—a fifteen-story collection featuring Black female protagonists. She would go on to release two other collections of short stories and a novel over the course of her lifetime, but editors have primarily reprinted selections from *Gorilla, My Love*. Although Bambara published over twenty-eight short stories between 1955 and 1977, anthologists have selected just eleven of those works for their collections.[22] Of those eleven, three of her stories, "Gorilla, My Love," "Raymond's Run," and "The Lesson," are the most popular. Bambara's stories appeared in *Tales and Stories for Black Folks* (1971), *Women Working: An Anthology of Stories and Poems* (1979), *Breaking Ice: An Anthology of Contemporary African American Fiction* (1990), *Literature Across Cultures* (1998), *American Short Stories Since 1945* (2001), and *The Norton Anthology of Short Fiction* (2006), among others. The young Black girls featured in Bambara's stories provide alternatives to the abundance of adult male protagonists in the majority of anthologized short fiction.

New York City served as the setting for what became Bambara's most widely anthologized stories, "Gorilla, My Love," "Raymond's Run," and "The Lesson." Bambara credits New York City as contributing to her literary accomplishments. In a 1982 interview with Kay Bonetti, Bambara explained, "I grew up in New York. I grew up with people who were interested in books. They eventually went into publishing and became copy editors, or editors, or journalists, or something. And since I was right there—I couldn't miss."[23] In New York, Bambara came to know prominent literary editors and up-and-coming writers. Not surprisingly, the city was central to her short fiction.

Hurston, Bambara, and Walker round out the Big 7. They are routinely included in African American and American literature anthologies as short story writers. Dozens of anthology editors were responsible for keeping these writers in print. Editors made these three women the most frequently anthologized Black women short story writers. Including stories by Hurston and Walker ensured that anthologies would have differing views of southern terrains published at different points in history. Bambara's stories diversify representations of female characters by showcasing girl protagonists. While at least 164 Black women published short stories in anthologies between 1925 and 2017, editors settled on Hurston, Bambara, and Walker as favored choices for reprinting stories. This essential three would join Chesnutt, Wright, Ellison, and Baldwin, becoming the most visible group of African American short story writers.

THE PERIODIZATION OF BLACK SHORT FICTION

In 1971, Arthur P. Davis and Saunders Redding published *Cavalcade: Negro American Writing from 1760 to the Present*, declaring that the collection accounts for the "entire two hundred years of Negro American literature."[24] The editors noted that "There have been several collections of Negro American writing in recent years, but an anthology of writings by any national, cultural, time-contained, or ethnic group should serve a pedagogical function for students." Davis and Redding were articulating the educational role of anthologies in classrooms during a time of unprecedented growth of Black enrollment in colleges and universities.[25] The organization of materials in *Cavalcade* emphasized a chronological approach to the presentation of African American literary works. Such an approach adhered to a linear view of publishing and presented short fiction along a historical continuum.

Chronological, thematic, and alphabetical orders are all approaches editors use to organize literary collections. The arrangement of anthologies chronologically, however, is most pervasive. In my dataset of one hundred anthologies, sixty-one are organized chronologically. The repeated presentations by editors of authors and literary works based on chronological order or author birthdate solidified perceptions that the Big 7 and other fiction writers belonged to distinct historical eras or literary periods.

In *Cavalcade*, Davis and Redding used a chronological approach to define the parameters of African American writing with publications spanning from 1760 to 1954. They organized the collection to highlight four general periods: "Part I: Pioneer Writers: 1760–1830," "Part II: Freedom Fighters: 1830–1865," "Part III: Accommodation and Protest: 1865–1910," and "Part IV: The New Negro Renaissance and Beyond: 1910–1954." The anthology suggested that Black literary history began in 1760, the year that the supposed first African American poem was published with Jupiter Hammon's "An Evening Thought: Salvation by Christ, with Penitential Cries." Later editors would readjust the beginnings of African American literature. Davis and Redding offered a concluding point in 1954, the year of the US Supreme Court's ruling in *Brown v. Board of Education*.

Comprehensive African American literature anthologies contribute to the crucial task of temporal place-making in Black literary history. Time period designations are unstable, or at least contested, as new anthologies routinely displace start and end dates offered by previous collections. Richard Barksdale and Kenneth Kinnamon's *Black Writers of America: A Comprehensive Anthology* (1972), published shortly after *Cavalcade*, presented the beginning of African American literature without a specific starting year as "The Eighteenth-Century Beginnings." Later still, *Call & Response* (1997) shifted those dates and offered 1619 as a beginning. The variety of beginnings represented in African American anthologies indicate multiple entry points into Black literary history proposed by editors. The variety also reveals that there was no clear consensus about when African American literature begins.

As one of the most influential collections, the *Norton Anthology of African American Literature* (1997, 2004, 2014) was particularly important for solidifying a chronological approach to the presentation of Black literature and to the designation of subsections for authors. The first two editions of the anthology were compiled by general editors Henry Louis Gates Jr. and Nellie McKay and eight section editors: William L. Andrews, Houston A. Baker Jr., Frances Smith Foster, Deborah E. McDowell, Robert G. O'Meally, Arnold Rampersad, Hortense Spillers, and Cheryl A. Wall. After the death of McKay in 2006, Valerie Smith was brought on as general coeditor with Gates for the 2014 edition, which was divided into two volumes. Kimberly Benston and Brent Hayes Edwards were brought on as section editors as well. Theodore Mason Jr. argues that because this anthology, published by W. W. Norton & Company, "signifies a certain 'insideness' hard to ignore . . . this is a volume whose very title signals an idea of mainstream acceptance and canonization."[26] The importance of Norton as a publisher, the prominence of its editors, and the availability of the book in three editions evidence its significance.

Editors arrange anthologies to make expansive time periods and large bodies of works manageable. The third edition of the *Norton Anthology of African American Literature* (2014) organizes Black writing into six historical periods: "The Literature of Slavery and Freedom, 1746–1865," "Literature of the Reconstruction to the New Negro Renaissance, 1865–1919," "Harlem Renaissance, 1919–1940," "Realism, Naturalism, Modernism, 1940–1960," "The Black Arts Era, 1960–1975," and "The Contemporary Period" (in previous editions called "Literature Since 1970" when the prior section ended in 1970).

Like previous anthologists who have used chronological approaches, the editors of this Norton anthology applied label names prior to the years, suggesting that literature of various time periods adhered in some way to general themes or topics (e.g., "Literature of Slavery," "Literature of the Reconstruction").

The decisions of editors to present compositions and authors in designated literary periods shed light on the importance of framing practices. The *Norton Anthology of African American Literature* editors situated the Big 7 across five literary periods. No signature stories by these writers appear in "The Literature of Slavery and Freedom" section. Chesnutt and his stories are positioned as "Literature of the Reconstruction." Zora Neale Hurston is a leading figure in "Harlem Renaissance," while Richard Wright, Ralph Ellison, and James Baldwin are presented in "Realism, Naturalism, Modernism." Toni Cade Bambara's stories are included in "The Black Arts Era," and Alice Walker is included in "The Contemporary Period." The presentation of the Big 7 across five time periods conveniently highlights an expansive time span of Black short story writing.

The designation of literary periods by the editors situated writers within distinct micro-histories of American and African American literature. The time periods in collections are of varying lengths of time. In the *Norton Anthology of African American Literature*, one section, "The Literature of Slavery and Freedom," covers 119 years. On the other hand, "Realism, Naturalism, Modernism" and "The Black Arts Era" represent fifteen and twenty years, respectively. "These competing narratives of American literary history," explained Sandra Gustafson, "translate into numbers of pages and volume divisions in anthologies, as well as defining the parameters of survey courses."[27] Gustafson further noted that the historical arrangements and setup of anthologies "have the potential to shape scholarship at a deeper level." After three editions, the *Norton Anthology of African American Literature* has shaped chronological framing of Black literary history. The varying start and end dates, on another level, have gave countless teachers and students ideas about the writers in each period.

The name designations for time periods in anthologies are not static. Many anthologies published prior to the 1980s identified the "New Negro Renaissance" or, more commonly, the "Harlem Renaissance" as a major literary period that sometimes covered more than three decades. *Cavalcade* designated the "New Negro Renaissance and Beyond" as taking place between 1910 and 1954; *Black Writers of America* included it in "Renaissance and Radicalism: 1915–1945"; and *Afro-American Writing* designated this period as taking place between World War I and World War II, 1914–1945. The editors of the *Norton Anthology of African American Literature*, as noted, defined the Harlem Renaissance as taking place in 1919–1940. The changes reflect an evolving consensus among scholars.[28] "Literary history is messy" and "movements don't just replace each other in succession," explain Cody Marrs and Christopher Hager; they contend that literary periods "coexist, buckle, or veer off in strange directions. Authors fade or get rediscovered."[29]

The alterations to the timeline of the Harlem Renaissance had consequences for the presentation of two of our most prominent authors. Up until the 1970s, Hurston and Wright appeared in the same section. Since then, they have been most often presented in separate time periods. That separation corresponds to their apparently contrasting ideological positions.[30] Hurston's and Wright's major works—*Their Eyes Were Watching God* (1937) and *Native Son* (1940)—were published only three years apart, yet the appearances of these writers in different sections suggest a much wider gap. In this regard, the designation of historical periods and positioning of writers therein accentuates divisions.

In the introduction to the *Norton Anthology of African American Literature*'s "Realism, Naturalism, Modernism: 1940–1960" section, Deborah McDowell and Hortense Spillers explain that although "literary historians are fond of subdividing and punctuating artistic periods with references to war," the publication of Wright's *Native Son* prompted a change, at least in African American literary history.[31] According to McDowell and Spillers, Wright's novel "almost single-handedly birthed and shaped a radically new agenda and established for African American writing a new center of gravity, one pitched toward the gritty realities of urban living for black Americans" (1358). For these editors, that meant utilizing the publication date of *Native Son* as the start of a historical-literary period.

The publication of Margaret Walker's collection of poetry *For My People* (1942), Chester Himes's *If He Hollers Let Him Go* (1945), Ann Petry's *The Street* (1946), Lorraine Hansberry's *A Raisin in the Sun* (1959), and others secures the plausibility of 1940–1960 as a discrete literary period.[32] Ellison and Baldwin are central figures in this section, and they represent yet even another iteration in African American literary history. Anthology editors describe their works as being in opposition to Wright. In the *Norton Anthology of African American Literature* (2014), McDowell and Spillers note that Ellison and Baldwin contributed to liberating "those African American writers already chafing under the narrative straitjacket of realism and naturalism thus breaking free of the pressures to protest injustice."[33] Here the editors are highlighting how writers of a common subsection might notably differ.

Anthology editors are often aware that linear views of literary history are imperfect. In the introduction to *Trouble the Water: 250 Years of African*

American Poetry (1997), Jerry W. Ward Jr. notes that since poets are subversive, "they may or may not write works that conform to the dominant ideas of a period and their works may defy convenient periodicity."[34] He goes on to explain that some poets gain notice later in life and as a result are distanced from their peers in literary collections. Ward adds, "This should remind us that poets are productive over the years that span divisions" (xxii). Do the points that Ward makes about poets apply to short story writers as well?

Designating literary periods creates groups of writers whose short stories are commonly associated with significant moments in American history. The arrangement of authors based on chronological order, however, has limits. Even if writers started publishing short stories across a long career, anthology editors tended to classify them in literary eras when their most prominent works were published. Cody Marrs and Christopher Hager note in *Timelines of American Literature* that "periodization flattens or falsifies the very textures that make literary culture interesting and meaningful."[35] Wright's "Long Black Song" from 1938 appears in the 1940–1960 section of the *Norton Anthology of African American Literature*. In the second edition of the anthology, Walker is presented in the "Literature Since 1975" section, even though her most well-known short story, "Everyday Use," was first published in 1973. The republication of short stories outside the time periods in which their authors appear should be a reminder that literary history is not as organized or coherent as anthologies suggest.

So far, scholars and editors of African American literature have not yet defined the parameters of the current contemporary era. The *Prentice Hall Anthology of African American Literature* (1999) includes literature from 1970 through the present; *Call & Response* (1998) designated 1960 through the present; and the *Wiley Blackwell Anthology of African American Literature* (2014) and the *Norton Anthology of African American Literature* indicate 1975 to the present. Paule Marshall was born in 1929, Maya Angelou in 1928, and Ernest Gaines in 1933, nearly forty years before Edwidge Danticat and Colson Whitehead, who were born in 1969. Nevertheless, all of these writers appear together in the *Norton Anthology of African American Literature*'s "The Contemporary Period." Gene Jarrett points out that "periodizing literary works according to authorial birthdates also bodes poorly for those who had written multiple literary works across multiple historical periods," continuing, "The birthdate periodization of literature also threatens to mischaracterize authors who released their best literature not exactly when their generational contemporaries were most productive and publicized."[36] The presentation of writers based on their birth year does not account for the variety of times when authors published their works and when they became prominent, which could be years and decades later.

Put another way, arrangements based on chronology sometimes mask the variances of individual writers. In the second edition of the *Norton Anthology of African American Literature*, the editors included two stories by Wright, "Long Black Song" (1938), set in the South, and "The Man Who Lived Underground" (1944), set in New York City. But of course, Wright's "The Man Who Was Almost a Man" (also entitled "Almos' a Man" and "The Man Who Was Almos' a Man") has been an anthology favorite since 1980, appearing in thirteen collections. A version of Wright's story initially appeared as part of novel that he wrote in 1936. After that project was rejected for publication, Wright transformed two sections of the longer work into what became "Almos' a Man." It was rejected by *Story* magazine in 1936, but was revised and eventually published by *Harper's Bazaar* in January 1940. Wright made slight revisions to the story toward the end of his life, and that version appeared in *Eight Men* (1961) a year after Wright's death.[37] The republication of "Almos' a Man," "The Man Who Was Almos' a Man," or "The Man Who Was Almost a Man" with no mention of the multiple versions could erase an important history of the story.

There are several ways to organize short fiction aside from a chronological approach. Throughout the dataset, anthologies use themes, author last names, and genre-specific collections as organizing methods. Chesnutt is a key figure to think about when considering multiple ways that a writer can be constantly reframed and republished. He is the most frequently anthologized Black short story writer, and his stories have become popular placeholders for the post-Reconstruction era in America. At the same time, editors have published him in varied contexts, including collections focusing on Black men, mystery, and speculative fiction.

Brotherman: The Odyssey of Black Men in America (1995) offers an alternative to chronological collections. Herb Boyd and Robert L. Allen describe their collection as being a variety of responses portraying the experiences of Black men. In the introduction, they explain, "*Brotherman* is both a literal and metaphorical map of the Black man's quest for self-affirmation reflected through the multifaceted prism of his fiction and nonfiction writings."[38] Boyd and Allen reprinted stories by Chesnutt along with works by Chester Himes, Walter Mosley, Kalamu ya Salaam, and Melvin Dixon, whose stories have been infrequently republished in anthologies. Chesnutt's "The Wife of His Youth," Edward P. Jones's "A New Man," Henry Dumas's "Strike and Fade," and Amiri Baraka's "The Screamers" are organized into the same section of *Brotherman*. The presentation of short story writers, whose works are often arranged based on their birth years, together in a common section highlights the possibilities of organizing authors and literary works based on criteria beyond chronology.

Chesnutt and Jones also appear in the collection *Black Noir: Mystery, Crime, and Suspense Stories by African-American Writers* (2009). The collection's editor, Otto Penzler, explains that "While many novels and short stories by black Americans had been published during the twentieth century, very few were detective novels."[39] Whereas he mentions W. Adolphe Roberts, Rudolph Fisher, and Chester Himes as exceptions, Penzler notes that the focus in African American literature largely centered around other issues. *Black Noir* includes Chesnutt's "The Sheriff's Children" and Jones's "Old Boys, Old Girls." Both stories contain prison scenes and low to mild violence. The thematic focus of Penzler's anthology creates an occasion to reprint works by Chesnutt and Jones that were published over one hundred years apart. A thematic approach for collections can link works that are chronologically disparate.

Anthology arrangement based on major historical events could explain the exclusion of topics that do not conform to conventional narratives and themes in American literature. Genre fiction such as science fiction, detective fiction, and street literature are often overlooked in standard historical surveys of the field. However, compositions in those genres have become increasingly popular in the twenty-first century. *Dark Matter: A Century of Speculative Fiction from the African Diaspora* (2000) and *Dark Matter: Reading the Bones* (2004), both edited by Sheree Thomas, represent notable efforts to showcase a variety of speculative compositions, including short stories by Black writers. In the introduction to the first *Dark Matter* collection, Thomas explains that, for the most part, "literary scholars and critics have limited their research largely to examinations of work by authors Samuel R. Delany and Octavia E. Butler, the two leading black writers in the genre."[40] Her motivation for compiling the works was to show how "black writers have been offering distinctive speculative visions to the world far longer than is generally thought" (9). The inclusion of science fiction short stories by Chesnutt, W. E. B. Du Bois, Henry Dumas, and others, along with those by Delany and Butler, indicates a long-running tradition. Nonetheless, comprehensive anthologies rarely foreground genre fiction, suggesting that it exists on the periphery of canonical works.

Anthology editors have been undoubtedly constrained by issues of space, which has prevented them from publishing a larger number and variety of short fiction, not to mention other works. With simply no room to publish all the many enjoyable and educational short stories published by Black writers, editors have been inclined to make choices that were inevitably selective, limited, and subjective. The habitual presentation of African American literature along a historical continuum has prompted editors to regularly choose key short story writers from distinct time periods and from the region of the country with the largest number of African Americans.[41] Consequently, those editors have chosen seven short story writers far more than others, and three—Chesnutt, Hurston, and Wright—of those seven writers stories often relied on African American Vernacular English and rustic settings in their stories about the South.

WRITING THE SOUTH

Charles Chesnutt, Zora Neale Hurston, and Richard Wright

Scholars such as Henry Louis Gates Jr., Claudia Roth Pierpont, and Ayana Mathis and Pankaj Mishra have noted the unfavorable reviews that Richard Wright and Zora Neale Hurston gave of each other's works.[1] In an assessment of *Their Eyes Were Watching God*, Wright claimed that Hurston's writing was "cloaked in that facile sensuality that has dogged Negro expression since the days of Phillis Wheatley."[2] In a charge against *Uncle Tom's Children*, Hurston wrote that Wright's short stories were "so grim that the Dismal Swamp of race hatred must be where they live. Not one act of understanding and sympathy comes to pass in the entire work."[3] The critiques that Hurston and Wright presented, along with the long-standing interest among scholars in those viewpoints, suggest the existence of competing, not merely complementary, African American approaches to representing the South. Their personal differences aside, both Hurston and Wright explored distinctive components of Black life, which necessarily resulted in widely varying perspectives. Consequently, their competing visions of the South created fairly expansive parameters for understanding how Black writers depict the region.

Hurston, Wright, and Charles Chesnutt represent the American South as the most frequently anthologized Black writers whose stories first appeared prior to 1940. These writers create southern landscapes that are largely devoid of specific geographic details. Even though precise descriptions of places in towns are not central to their stories, the types of settings are crucial to their representations of the South. Chesnutt's stories are usually set on plantations depicting scenes at the homes of various characters. Hurston's stories focus on predominantly African American communities in a moderately populated Florida town, and she uses local businesses and family homes as the settings. Wright, however, focuses on sparsely populated rural areas and uses the natural landscape as the backdrop for violent and deadly interactions between Black and white characters. Their stories demonstrate regional diversity within the South, showcasing snapshots of North Carolina, Florida, Arkansas, and Mississippi. Taken together, this trio of Black short story writers offer contrasting views of southern geographic sceneries.

Homegrown characters play an important role in highlighting the values, tensions, superstitions, and local color of southern regions in stories by these writers. Chesnutt, Hurston, and Wright create characters that represent distinctive qualities of the South. Southern African Americans "have drawn upon all these lores, and added materials from their own environment and experience to produce a highly diversified and culturally independent folk tradition," notes Houston Baker Jr.[4] Chesnutt, Hurston, and Wright reflect multiple approaches to depicting this "southern tradition" in short fiction. Chesnutt, for instance, frequently presents interactions between Black southerners and white northerners. He considers passing, folk culture, and Black people in the aftermath of slavery. In her stories, Hurston highlights the various layers of an all-Black Florida community and contrasts the differences within a seemingly similar cast of characters. And Wright illustrates how the South represents the site of tense racial interactions between Black and white characters.

The representation of African American Vernacular English (AAVE) is a unifying thread among short stories by Chesnutt, Hurston, and Wright. These writer-storytellers rely on common words such as "dat" (that), "ah" (I), "yuh" (you), and "en" (in) to signal the speaking styles and sounds of Black southerners. Even though they represent the oldest and most republished writers among the Big 7, we must resist grouping them together in a single neat category. Chesnutt uses AAVE to contrast southern and non-southern characters. Hurston uses vernacular dialogues to drive the action of stories and to showcase the wonder and amusement of colorful language among Black speakers. And Wright uses AAVE to represent dialogue as well as the internal thoughts of his characters. The works by Chesnutt, Hurston, and Wright are indeed set in the South and utilize AAVE; however, there are variations regarding the types of events they focus on across stories, how they portray characters, and how they depict different locales in the South.

The discussion of cultural geo-tagging in this chapter will largely focus on the significance of homegrown characters to highlight a variety of concerns and customs depicted across different southern terrains and distinguishing features of AAVE within a given story. The first section of this chapter describes how Chesnutt challenged conventional plantation narratives that presented African Americans as simple-minded. Chesnutt presents culturally and intellectually adept southern Black characters as a way of envisioning a double-voiced Black plantation tradition. The second section focuses on how Hurston depicted dramatic intraracial conflicts in a small Black community. Doing so allowed her to show a variety of private and all-Black communal settings, including kitchens, bedrooms, general stores, town roads, front yards, and front porches. These communal and familial locales gave Hurston opportunities to create entertaining and sometimes troubling narratives about interactions among Black people. The third section explores how Wright composed short stories that emphasize the disturbing conflicts that emerge when southern racial boundaries are crossed. The tensions and unsettling events that occur in the stories offer possibilities for why Wright and so many other Black people from the region felt obligated to flee. The representation of distinct settings and characters, along with the employment of AAVE, constitutes the southern-based cultural geo-tagging that defines the most widely circulated short fiction of Chesnutt, Hurston, and Wright.

CHARLES CHESNUTT AND THE PLANTATION SOUTH

In 1887, Thomas Bailey Aldrich, editor of *The Atlantic Monthly*, accepted Chesnutt's short story "The Goophered Grapevine" for publication—unaware that Chesnutt was African American.[5] After receiving positive reviews from readers and editors alike, the following April, Aldrich accepted Chesnutt's second story, "Po' Sandy." Biographer Frances Keller noted, "At last the door was open; the younger writer could get consideration from an important publisher."[6] Chesnutt's appearances in *The Atlantic Monthly* greatly raised his visibility. Over the next several decades, these two stories, along with "The Wife of His Youth" and "The Sheriff's Children," would become Chesnutt's most commonly appearing compositions in anthologies.

An approach that takes cultural geo-tagging into account reveals Chesnutt's interest in depicting various locales across the Midwest and South. His stories take place in Ohio, Kentucky, and North Carolina. Presented across a broad time frame either leading up to the Civil War or in the years immediately following known as Reconstruction, his stories feature plantations as recurring settings. Even though Chesnutt spent some of his boyhood and teenage years in Fayetteville and Charlotte, North Carolina, he was born in Ohio and spent the majority of his adult life in Cleveland, not the South. Barbara Baker explains that Chesnutt "in no way considered himself part of Southern black culture, but instead considered himself an artist who would shape the raw materials of this culture into marketable matter."[7] The South apparently appealed to Chesnutt's artistic sensibilities in ways that the Midwest did not.

Chesnutt does not offer vivid descriptions of rustic landscapes or incorporate specific landmarks. Instead, he creates a strong sense of place by tagging these settings with cultural facets reminiscent of a plantation. In particular, Chesnutt's homegrown southern characters constitute an essential geo-tagging feature of his short fiction. Plantations present an opportunity to combine several different types of characters—formerly enslaved characters and servants as well as white slave owners and wealthy characters. For some characters, Chesnutt establishes a sense of place through his use of phonetic spellings that resemble southern drawls. The practice of representing regional vernaculars was integral to the southern settings that Chesnutt depicted in his stories.

Chesnutt's homegrown southern characters constitute an essential cultural signifier in his short fiction, deploying AAVE in dialogues to create scenes of the plantation South. "The Goophered Grapevine" and "Po' Sandy," from his first collection, feature stories within stories. Julius McAdoo, more commonly known as Uncle Julius, is a recurring character who is southern and homegrown and who speaks entirely in AAVE. Chesnutt "used dialect not merely to demonstrate class and intellectual divisions within and among social groups," points out Gene Jarrett, but also "to deliver subtle moral and political messages that elevated the sensibilities of whites on race and racism."[8] Uncle Julius recounts local incidents of the plantation to transplanted northerners.

In "The Goophered Grapevine," the first story of the collection, the external narrator, John, and his wife, Annie, travel to North Carolina shortly after the Civil War ends to investigate the possibility of buying a rundown and abandoned vineyard. While walking around the plantation, the couple encounter Julius, the internal narrator, who is also a fanciful storyteller. Uncle Julius advises the couple against buying the plantation in their initial encounter. He tells John and Annie the story of Henry, an enslaved man who fell victim to a cursed grapevine: "Well, I dunno whe'r you b'lievs in cunj'in er not . . . but de truf er de matter is dat dis yer ole vimya'd is goophered."[9] According to Julius, the property was cursed. "'I wouldn' spec' fer you ter b'lieve me 'less you know all 'bout de fac's," Julius says to the couple. But he reassures them, "I kin 'splain to yer how it all happen." Julius warns John that even though most of the vines are dead, a few of the cursed ones remain. Against Julius's advice, John buys the vineyard and later finds that Julius owns a cabin nearby and has been making a profit from making and selling moonshine from the leftover grapes on the plantation.[10]

Chesnutt contrasts the interactions between a Black southern homegrown character and two white northern outsiders to highlight how their different regional personalities contribute to a scene on an abandoned North Carolina plantation. By doing so, Chesnutt builds suspense by creating tension between the internal narrator, Julius, and the external narrator, John. Julius is deceptive, and John questions the veracity and motives of his stories. Even though the reliability of Julius's stories is in doubt, as northern outsiders, John and his wife remain entertained by the tall tales from the days of slavery at the vineyard. According to John, Annie "takes a deep interest in the stories of plantation life which she hears from the lips of the older colored people" (18). He continues, "Some of these stories are quaintly humorous; others wildly extravagant, revealing the Oriental cast of the negro's imagination." Julius is a homegrown trickster figure of sorts—coming across on the surface as an entertaining, kind, enduring, and seemingly trustworthy figure.

Julius once again creates a fanciful story to northern outsiders in "Po' Sandy." In this story, when John and Annie decide to use lumber from an old schoolhouse to build a kitchen, Julius tells them about Sandy. Growing frustrated at being separated from his wife, Tenie, Sandy implores her to use her "conjuring" to help him spend more time with her since Master Marabo constantly loans Sandy for labor. Reluctantly, Tenie transforms Sandy into a tree during the day and back to his original state periodically so that they can be together. However, when there is no one left to watch Sandy in tree form, he is cut down and used as lumber for a kitchen at the Marabo home. Uncle Julius informs the northerners that Sandy's spirit thereafter haunts the Marabo kitchen, and since no one wanted to work there, it was eventually dismantled and the lumber donated toward the building of a school. John and Annie decide to purchase new lumber to construct their new kitchen. Later on, Annie gives Julius permission to use the abandoned schoolhouse for his church services. When John inquires about it, Annie replies, "Uncle Julius says that ghosts never disturb religious worship, but that if Sandy's spirit should happen to stray into meeting by mistake, no doubt the preaching would do it good" (26). Similar to "The Goopered Grapevine," Julius masks his true intentions and plays upon the trust of John and Annie in an attempt to achieve some sort of economic payoff.[11]

Part of what makes the geo-tagging in this story and Chesnutt's other plantation stories so notable is his decision to cast a gifted Black storyteller and showcase the rhetorical abilities of a rural and formerly enslaved Black person. Chesnutt positions Uncle Julius to drive the action by providing an oral history of the environment. Even though John serves as the overall narrator, the stories are primarily told from the perspective of Julius. According to Donald M. Shaffer Jr., "Uncle Julius emerges as a trickster figure whose ability to effectively manipulate others through language belies his racially proscribed status"; as a result, "His storytelling becomes a means of securing his own interests and place on the vineyard recently purchased by his new employer."[12] Rarely does John interject and interrupt Julius's story, even if he questions the truthfulness. Julius serves as an important connector to the history of slavery at the North Carolina plantation. Through Uncle Julius's tales of days gone by, Chesnutt shapes the tone and scenery of the setting.

Chesnutt's "The Wife of His Youth," which first appeared in *The Atlantic* in 1898, also appears frequently in anthologies. Chesnutt's collection *The Wife of His Youth and Other Stories of the Color-Line* (1899) includes two stories, "The Sheriff's Children" and "The Passing of Grandison," which appear to lesser extents in anthologies as well. Unlike his earlier conjure stories in which Uncle Julius was the only Black character, in *The Wife of His Youth* collection Chesnutt incorporates a wider variety of Black characters. This collection includes enslaved, formerly enslaved, and free-born Black southern characters and midwestern middle-class biracial people. Tanfer Tunc explains that Chesnutt's "color lines characters" illustrate how class hierarchy among Black characters perpetuates "an internalized racism in the black community which created intraracial conflict and marginalized the inclusiveness of hybridity."[13] "The Wife of His Youth," in particular, confronts the inherent tensions among a small and select group of middle-class Black Americans at the turn of the century as Chesnutt addresses the problemed aspects of upward racial mobility.

In "The Wife of His Youth," the main character, Mr. Ryder, is a free-born biracial man and a prominent member of the Blue Veins Society, a social organization for light-skin, biracial, and presumably well-to-do Black people. The name of the society comes from an "envious outsider" who proclaimed that, to join the society, one's skin had to be so white that blue veins could show.[14] At the next Blue Vein ball, Mr. Ryder plans to give a speech and propose to a widowed light-skinned woman from Washington, DC, named Molly Dixon. Before the ball, however, he encounters an older Black woman, Liza Jane, a former slave from the South who asks for his help in finding her husband, whom she has not seen in twenty-five years. At the ball, he begins to tell Liza Jane's story and her search for her husband. At the end, he asks the attendees if her long-lost husband should come forward and acknowledge his wife after all these years. Everyone says yes, and Mr. Ryder brings out Liza Jane and introduces her as the "wife of his youth," telling the attendees that he is indeed the man she sought.

Take notice of geo-tagging in this story. Chesnutt created circumstances within the story to bring together different types of characters from different geographic origins, to intensify potential conflicts and drama, and to bring attention to class differences in a midwestern Ohio town. Mr. Ryder, Molly Dixon, and Liza Jane are contrasting characters who allow Chesnutt to emphasize the diversity among Black people immediately after the Civil War in America. The narrator explains that Mr. Ryder's appearance "was such as to confer distinction" as "his hair was almost straight," "he was always neatly dressed," and "his manners were irreproachable, and his morals above suspicion" (4). In comparison to Mr. Ryder, the widow, Molly Dixon, is "whiter than he, and better educated" and "had moved in the best colored society of the country, at Washington, and had taught in the schools of that city" (5). Liza Jane, however, is described as looking "a bit of the old plantation life, summoned from the past by the wave of a magician's wand," who was in fact so Black "that her toothless gums, revealed when she opened her mouth to speak, were not red, but blue" (10). In addition, her heavy vernacular English connects her to the South and serves as a contrast to the erudite speaking styles of Mr. Ryder and Molly Dixon. The linguistic variety of the story rests on Chesnutt's placement of distinct characters from dissimilar regions together in the unnamed Ohio town.

Chesnutt began presenting a more diverse set of words in his later writings than in his earlier short fiction. This contributed to the regional and class diversity apparent among his characters. An excerpt from a poem by nineteenth-century British poet Alfred Lord Tennyson; the language of the story's middle-class, African American protagonist, Mr. Ryder; the vernacular speech of a formerly enslaved Black woman, Liza Jane; and the standard English of the narrator—all account for the relatively high word density and variety of language in "The Wife of His Youth." Liza Jane is the only other character with a substantial speaking part. Her heavy dialect serves as a contrast to Mr. Ryder and the narrator, making her rural and southern characteristics stand out and further highlighting her status as an outsider in the Ohio town where the story is set. She simultaneously represents the wife and life of Mr. Ryder's youth in Missouri. Liza Jane is a reminder and relic of a region from whence many Black midwesterners and northerners originated. The inclusion of African American characters who display different speaking styles evidences the linguistic diversity of Chesnutt's writing and his intent to bring together characters from different geographic regions and social classes.

In "The Passing of Grandison," Chesnutt again opts to narrate the story in Standard English and from the perspective of a white narrator in the South. Set in Kentucky during the early 1850s, the story follows Dick Owens, an irresponsible and lazy son of a wealthy plantation owner, Colonel Owens. Dick's love interest, Charity Lomax, disapproves of the institution of slavery and is impressed by the actions of abolitionists across the South. Determined to impress Charity and ask for her hand in marriage, Dick concocts a plan to free one of his father's enslaved persons. Carrying out the plan, Dick takes one of his father's field workers, Grandison, to Canada, leaves him there, and returns to Kentucky, telling his father an elaborate story about how abolitionists stole and freed the enslaved man while in free territory. Weeks later, however, to Dick's surprise, Grandison reappears at the Kentucky plantation in bad shape. He is welcomed with open arms by Dick's father, the Colonel, as Grandison is promoted to a household servant and granted permission to marry Betty, an enslaved girl with whom he is in love. Within a matter of weeks, however, Grandison and his wife, along with his parents and siblings, have all gone missing. Grandison, a trickster figure, seemingly liberates his loved ones from the confines of slavery. They're last seen on a boat passing into Canada, where they will be free.

Movement and travel constitute a vital element of cultural geo-tagging in "The Passing of Grandison." For this story, rather than bring characters from different regions together, Chesnutt presents those from a common region who are altered by their experience of traveling. Movement matters. By having Dick venture out of the South with Grandison to New York City, Boston, and Niagara Falls, Chesnutt contrasts the slavery territory of Kentucky with free territories of the North. According to Charles Duncan, "The Passing of Grandison" includes "an element of Northern life (before the Civil War) not found anywhere else in Chesnutt's short fiction: the influence of abolitionists."[15] Abolitionists add another element to the story as they represent a threat to slavery and southern slaveholders in their ability to influence and aid enslaved Black people to escape to free territories. The assorted types of environments and characters Chesnutt introduces in the story increased the likelihood that Grandison would encounter people who could encourage and assist him in his pursuit of freedom. Leaving the South, Grandison gains access to resources denied to him in his immediate environment on the plantation, even though this fact is not made apparent throughout the dialogues within the story.

This story does not contain a considerable amount of AAVE dialogue and instead relies more on Standard English as the narrator relates the story primarily from the perspective of Dick. The lack of AAVE character dialogue on the part of Grandison and the other enslaved people on the plantation alerts readers to the covert nature of plantation life. Grandison and the rest of the Black people on the plantation seem dutiful and respectful when speaking with white characters. In actuality, they do not make their true intentions known and are patiently waiting for an opportunity to escape. Dick Owens and the narrator drive the action of the story in Standard English, all while the thoughts and motivations of the enslaved community are gone unnoticed. AAVE is used minimally in this story, and readers are not exposed to the inherent feelings and even worldviews of the Black southern characters.

In "The Sheriff's Children," Chesnutt again introduces diverse characters, a way of enlivening his tale and using language as a social marker to represent the South. In the story, set in the small rural town of Troy, North Carolina, the town's beloved Civil War hero, Captain Walker, has been murdered. The white townspeople, who speak in southern vernacular styles, waste no time in blaming a biracial man who was seen near the captain's house the previous night. "Hangin' air too good fer the murderer," said one onlooker; "he oughter be burnt, stidier bein' hung" is the response of another white townsperson talking to the sheriff.[16] When word reaches Sheriff Campbell that the townspeople intend to lynch the prisoner for unsubstantiated crimes, he intervenes by going to the jail to calm the tempers of the angry mob. While at the prison, Sheriff Campbell learns that the prisoner, Tom, is his illegitimate son from a love affair he had as a young man with a field worker, Cicely. Tom attempts to kill his father with a gun he has stolen, but his plans are thwarted as Polly—the sheriff's daughter—arrives just in time. She saves her father's life by delivering a nonfatal shot to the suspected prisoner, her half-brother. The next morning, the sheriff returns to find that Tom has ripped off his bandages and bled to death in what appears to be a suicide.

Chesnutt uses vernacular to connect characters—Black, white, and biracial—to southern geographic regions. He also uses character dialogues to create notable distinctions and distances between characters. In "The Sheriff's Children," the Black servants and white townspeople are represented by vernacular speech, but Sheriff Campbell and his daughter speak in Standard English and represent a level of separation from the townspeople. The narrator of the story notes, "The sheriff of Branson was a man far above the average of the community in wealth, education, and social position" (71). Tom, who is biracial, also speaks in Standard English as his father, the sheriff, notes: "the mulatto [Tom] spoke more eloquently and used better language than most Branson County people" (86). Taken together, their speaking patterns unite them and distinguish them in terms of speech, making them different from other characters in the story.

Representations of speaking style constitutes a mode of cultural geotagging for Chesnutt. Furthermore, his character dialogues are embedded with regional and class markers. Chesnutt's use of phonetic spellings to signify southern speech patterns connects his stories to a particular region and historical era. When other, non-southern characters are introduced, they offer a contrast because they speak in Standard English. The representation of southern vernacular English plays a significant part in marking the settings in his stories.

HURSTON'S ALL-BLACK SOUTH

On May 1, 1925, *Opportunity: A Journal of Negro Life*, whose editor was Charles Johnson, hosted a large banquet where Zora Neale Hurston's short story "Black Death" won second place in its category.[17] According to Deborah Plant, the after-party that Hurston attended that night proved important as well, as she met author and Barnard College founding trustee Annie Nathan Meyer, novelist Fannie Hurst, and author and "man-about-town" Carl Van Vechten.[18] Plant continues that "Charles Johnson's award ceremonies were designed to bring about such happy consequences." In short, Johnson facilitated Hurston's interactions with supporters who would play vital roles in advancing Hurston's career. These invitations to parties and other social functions typically go undocumented in anthology biographical sketches. However, Hurston's social interactions guaranteed her a place in the emerging literary scene in Harlem during the 1920s and would later contribute to her legacy as one of the most visible and endearing figures of that era. Decades later, when anthologists assembled collections, her stories would be frequently reprinted as representative literature from the Harlem Renaissance.

Whether set in a private home or a public communal setting, Hurston's southern tales revolve almost exclusively around Black homegrown characters. Similar to Chesnutt, Hurston incorporates AAVE to connect the setting to southern terrains and dramatize portrayals of characters in the region. Hurston relies heavily on her characters, not the narrator, to discuss the sequence of events in her stories and to describe their emotional responses. Henry Louis Gates Jr. and Sieglinde Lemke explain in their introduction to a collection of Hurston's short stories that, "Above all else, Hurston is concerned to register a distinct sense of space—an African-American cultural space" and capture "the nuances of speech or the timbre of voice that give a storyteller her or his distinctiveness."[19] Hurston effectively links Black speech and southern narratives, thereby creating a distinct sense of culture, space, and storytelling.

Hurston is consistent with her cultural geo-tagging. She uses the same Florida as the setting for her most famous stories, thereby underlining her interest in depicting Black communities that are outside the purview of white mainstream representations. Hurston's attention to geography is evident, based on her acknowledgment of key places and character types in a close-knit Florida community. She sets her stories during what is perhaps the 1900s in an unnamed town much like Eatonville, Florida, where Hurston lived until the age of thirteen.[20] While not urban, the settings are moderately developed and home to a predominantly Black community. Hurston does not provide specific addresses and descriptions of the places in the town; but what does stand out is that she takes readers into private spaces of Black characters. The plots of her stories unfold through marital disputes in a bedroom, women doing domestic work in a kitchen, and conversations on the front porch at convenience stores and other social settings. Hurston's stories were entertaining and revealed drama that took place mainly among Black people and especially in intimate conflicts between a husband and wife.

In "The Gilded Six-Bits," Hurston uses a private home setting in the South as the primary setting to dramatize marital conflict and forgiveness between the two main homegrown characters, Missie May Banks and her husband, Joe Banks. Joe has reconciled with Missie May, who betrayed him after she slept with a newcomer in town, an outsider named Otis Slemmons, who appears to be rich. Otis convinces Missie May to sleep with him in exchange for money. It is later revealed, however, that he is not what he appears as his money is fake. Through Missie May and Joe's conflict, Hurston highlights conflicts that occur within a home in an all-Black Florida town.

Hurston utilizes the bedroom as a focal point of the story to present private interactions and intimate moments in the story. Beyond showcasing drama, Hurston displays a moving, intimate scene of a Black woman in this setting. Readers first encounter Missie May bathing herself in a washtub in the couple's bedroom while waiting for her husband, Joe, to come home from work. Hurston describes how Missie May's "dark-brown skin glistened under the soapsuds" and how her "stiff young breasts thrust forward aggressively, like broad-based cones with the tips lacquered in black."[21] The scene is fleeting, but it represents a rare moment in popular short stories in which a writer describes a woman bathing. The presentation of African Americans in private settings gave Hurston this special opportunity to artfully depict a Black woman's glistening body.

The bedroom is also the stage for the story's high point. One Saturday evening, Joe comes home early from work, excited to surprise his wife. When he gets in the room, he thinks he sees an intruder in the dark, but quickly realizes Otis is in bed with his wife. Joe goes into a rage and "grabbed at Slemmons with his left hand and struck at him with his right" (1047). After Slemmons leaves, Missie May cries and pleads, "Oh Joe, honey, he said he wuz gointer give me dat gold money and he jes' kept on after me," to which

Joe replies, "Well, don't cry no mo', Missie May. Ah got yo' gold piece for you" (1048). After a while Joe's anger subsides, but he still takes a long time to fully forgive his wife for cheating on him. Joe constantly reminds Missie May of her infidelity by paying her for massages and meals as a means of making her feel guilty about her betrayal. Perhaps Missie May slept with Slemmons in hopes of giving her husband the gold coin? Even though Missie May says she is not impressed with Slemmons, the money certainly had an effect on her. Missie May's betrayal of her husband in this particular setting heightens the sense of deception and represents the ultimate violation and sanctity of their bedroom.

Racial tensions, especially those in southern environs, constitute an important source of conflict in many works by Black writers. For Hurston, though, deception is the driving force in this Florida town. Trudier Harris writes that, "More often than not, in depicting this duality of attraction and repulsion, African American writers place their characters in situations where there is a profound fear of the South."[22] That is not the case for Hurston, whose characters are quite comfortable with southern living. The conflicts are based on Hurston's explorations of trouble with money, love, and sex. She creates drama by having a husband unexpectedly find his wife in an intimate situation with another man. A short story about love, betrayal, violence, and money no doubt carried high entertainment value.

This story underscores Hurston's interest in representing intraracial conflicts in majority Black private settings—a Black wife cheating on her Black husband in their home. According to Nancy Chinn and Elizabeth E. Dunn, "'The Gilded Six-Bits' signaled Hurston's arrival as an author capable of building multi-faceted characters with deceptively simple prose and dialogue—a talent she would soon put to use as a novelist."[23] The drama of a tale about a cheating woman who is discovered by her husband having an affair might explain why "The Gilded Six-Bits" remains Hurston's most anthologized short story. In other frequently anthologized stories by Hurston, Black households, and specifically Black marriages, are a central site for exploring and embellishing conflicts. Through marital couples, Hurston can expose the inner workings and local dramas in the unnamed Florida town.

In Hurston's "Sweat," a married couple's home also serves as a central setting. This story follows Delia and her abusive marriage to Sykes. For fifteen years, Delia has supported herself and her husband as a domestic worker washing clothes for white families. Sykes, seemingly bitter, chastises his wife for washing the soiled clothes of white people and considers her job an embarrassment. Sykes threatens her with physical abuse. He even parades around town with his girlfriend Bertha and announces his plans to leave his wife for his mistress. Sykes exploits his wife's fear of snakes and one day tries to frighten her by adopting a rattlesnake. One evening, the snake escapes from its cage and takes up residence in a laundry basket. Delia happens upon the basket and manages to escape the wrath of the rattler. When he returns home, Sykes is attacked by the snake and dies a slow and painful death as he calls out for Delia, who is hiding out of fear in the barn.

For Hurston, cultural geo-tagging involves presenting and exploring interactions in private settings, not only public ones. Accordingly, the most consequential events in her story "Sweat" take place within a couple's home. Interactions between the married couple, Delia and Sykes, constitute the main source of conflict and entertainment, displaying dramatic verbal and physical conflict in the story. The couple hurl harsh and amusing insults at each other during an argument. Early on in the story, Delia and Sykes have an argument, filled with name-calling and insults. Sykes tells his wife, "Look at yuh stringey ole neck! Yo' rawbony laigs an' arms is enough tuh cut uh man tuh death"; and Delia responds, "Yo' ole black hide don't look lak nothin' tuh me, but uh passle uh wrinkled up rubber."[24] The verbal assaults of the couple highlight the tense marital discord between them. At the same time, the invectives confirm Hurston's facility with bawdy language and wordplay. It is unusual for canonical short stories to show Black people expressing so much ill will toward each other. Hurston was not interested in creating images that showed Black people in perfect racial harmony. Instead, she created a scene in which a husband and wife engaged in playing "the dozens," launching a volley of colorful insults at each other.

Language, especially character dialogues, contributes to Hurston's ability to create a strong sense of place and connect her stories to the South. According to Tiffany Ruby Patterson, "Hurston documented black communities as places inhabited by complicated individuals, where humor and conflict as well as violence and discrimination are facts of life," even though Patterson insists that Hurston's "communities are also graced with unique cultural beauty."[25] Hurston's characters employ a diverse set of phrases in their animated exchanges with each other, and even the communities of onlookers, who speak in the vernacular, contributing to the originality of words that appear in the stories. Hurston was, after all, a folklorist and anthropologist. The presence of considerable dialogue from her characters indicates her reflections on childhood as well as her training in documenting first-person narratives of Black people. The many days and months she spent listening to Black oral histories shaped her understanding that these individuals were quite capable of framing their own stories.

Even though the climax of "Sweat" happens at Delia and Sykes's home, public settings also play a crucial part in the story. At one point, a group of onlookers gossip and offer key background information about the couple. The use of vernacular phrases in the character dialogues contributes to how Hurston constructs the townspeople and portrays the marriage of Delia and Sykes. The porch in Hurston's stories is a central and recurring setting where characters gather to talk and provide some perspective on other characters and actions. Her use of the front porch would later become a hallmark of her novel *Their Eyes Were Watching God* and also the setting of famous scenes in works by Alice Walker, Ernest Gaines, and other writers.[26]

Part of what makes this story powerful is the cultural geo-tagging enacted when Hurston utilizes groups of men, gathered in a common space, to offer commentary about local affairs in their community. The insider knowledge displayed by the characters in "Sweat" strengthens the sense of place in the story. Hurston's Elijah Mosely tells a group on the porch of a store that "Too much knockin' will ruin any 'oman" as he sees Delia passing by on the street and then observes that Sykes "done beat huh 'nough tuh kill three women, let 'lone change they looks" (1034). In another scene, after Skyes leaves the store with his mistress, Elijah says, "She don't look lak a thing but a hunk uh liver wid hair on it." Another character, Dave Carter, adds, "When she gits ready tuh laff, she jes' opens huh mouf an' latches it back tuh de las' notch. No ole grandpa alligator down in Lake Bell ain't got nothin' on huh" (1036). Hurston uses this setting to provide extended commentary from the locals who gossip about Delia and Sykes and add a layer of humor to the story.

In a brief, seemingly inconsequential, scene in "Sweat," a group of minor characters makes a significant contribution to the overall word diversity of Hurston's story that contributes to how we conceive of southern settings. This group of men gathered on the porch generates 460 or 33 percent of the total 1,406 unique words in the story.[27] The originality of the group's conversation indicates that Hurston was interested in showing diverse representations of the speaking styles of Black folks. The presentation of multiple characters gives her a chance to suggest the range of people who might comprise a Black community. Hurston's stories reveal the cultural competency of southern characters through amusing dialogues.

Representing the sights and sounds of a small Black town during a time when artists and observers were discussing and debating aspects of African American art and culture likely gave Hurston a deep sense of purpose. Philip Joseph points out that "Hurston became more conscious of these residues as she committed herself to the method of knowledge acquisition embraced by the Eatonville porch talkers."[28] Joseph contends that, "In the world of porch talking, all participants take part in maintaining the openness of the discourse, as they mock their own attempts and those of others to finalize judgments" (467). The porch is a site for characters to gather and swap stories about events that take place in their town. The porch gave Hurston the chance to showcase the diverse and colorful language of her homegrown characters and reinforce the sense of place.

In "Spunk," the homegrown supporting cast of Elijah Mosley, Joe Clarke, Dave Carter, Jim Merchant, and Walter Thomas also contributes to the setting and drives the action in the story. The characters evidence Hurston's interest in portraying local interactions, and their colorful dialogues in AAVE contribute to shaping impressions about the setting. The men gather to discuss events that unfold in town from the porch of and inside Joe Kanty's store. In the story, Joe has become the subject of gossip and ridicule as community members mock him in private for his inability to stand up to the figure Spunk, who carries on a public affair with Joe's wife, Lena. Fed up, Joe announces to the group of gathered men at the store his intent to get even with Spunk by challenging him to a fight. Joe confronts Spunk, only to be shot and killed. Spunk is later acquitted of murder, clearing the way for his marriage to Lena. In the story's conclusion, Spunk dies by accidentally falling on a saw. In Spunk's dying words, retold to everyone by Elijah, "It was Joe, 'Lige—the dirty sneak shoved me . . . he didn't dare come to mah face . . . but Ah'll git the son-of-a-wood louse soon's Ah get there an' make hell too hot for him. . . . Ah felt him shove me . . . !"[29] Joe, or at least his ghost, reigns victorious in this instance, but Spunk's dying words suggest the battle is far from over.

For Hurston, characters are representative of the southern setting. In "Spunk," the homegrown characters gather at a local store and narrate the events of the story from the porch. The entire story is relayed by second- and third-hand accounts, over several days, by the local men passing through the store. As the story progresses, each male character interjects his opinion about the central conflict in AAVE. After Spunk's untimely death, one of the characters remarks, "If spirits kin fight, there's a powerful tussle goin' on somewhere ovah Jordan 'cause Ah b'leeve Joe's ready for Spunk an' ain't skeered any more yes, Ah b'leeve Joe pushed 'im mahself" (31–32). The men suggest that Joe's death was only a precursor to his ultimate revenge upon Spunk. Through their dialogues, the homegrown characters share aspects of their worldview and give insight into local customs within the Florida community.

Hurston infuses her story with references to supernatural elements to reveal cultural components of the town and how the characters view other-worldly beliefs as valid. After Lena and Spunk move in, Spunk spots a bobcat lurking around the house and proclaims, "Joe done sneaked back from Hell!" (31). Through their dialogue, Hurston introduces supernatural elements to demonstrate the Eatonville community's belief in a system of law and order that is more powerful than the worldly court system that found Spunk innocent. Sharon Lynette Jones writes, "The black cat—a traditional symbol of doom and death—lends a sense of the supernatural to the story, as Spunk believes that Joe's soul has been reincarnated into the body of the black bobcat"; she continues, "The cat may also be considered a manifestation of Spunk's guilty conscience for killing Joe."[30] Hurston is clearly captivated by the perspectives that might emerge as groups of men gather in a town and share their opinions about fellow townspeople. Within this community, even though the residents are a practical and sensible people, they also accepted superstition as another way of knowing things and understanding the world.[31] Hurston chooses to geo-tag her stories using local customs as a vital part of the story to describe communal knowledge and, ultimately, explain the death of Spunk Banks.

While Hurston seems to privilege male characters in terms of dialogue, she uses apparently deceptive southern Black women to generate drama in her stories. At the close of "Spunk," Lena is alone as both of the men who quarreled over her are dead. At the repast for Spunk, "the women ate heartily of the funeral baked meats and wondered who would be Lena's next. The men whispered coarse conjectures between guzzles of whiskey" (32). The men and women of the town take it as a given that Lena will find another partner or additional ones. Conjectures about who she would become involved with next occupy everyone's interest. In "Sweat," Bertha has an affair with a married man, accentuating the problems of a couple. In "The Gilded Six-Bits," Missie May has an affair with a man to improve her financial situation. Bertha, Lena, and Missie May all participate in extramarital affairs, which, to varying degrees, intensify conflict in the stories. These presentations of adulterous Black women in the South are fairly uncommon among the thirty most-anthologized African American short stories.

Hurston's reliance on characters in short stories reflects her interest and faith in the perspectives of southern Black people. According to Anna Storm, "Many of her stories are drawn directly from Eatonville 'porch talk' or 'lying sessions.'"[32] Eatonville, one of the first places in the United States to be incorporated as an all-Black town, was home to a vibrant and proud African American community. Storm explains that Hurston's literary representation of characters in an all-Black Florida town was a "distinct contrast to popular depictions of black folk culture (most often by whites) that reduced and distorted black cultural representations to a supposedly 'authentic' expression of inherent racial and biological characteristics" (149). In an example of the differences between Hurston and Wright, while Hurston was concerned with highlighting tensions within Black communities, Wright was interested in addressing interracial conflicts.

WRIGHT'S DEADLY SOUTH

When First Lady of the United States Eleanor Roosevelt reviewed Wright's *Uncle Tom's Children* in 1938, she wrote that the stories were so "beautifully written and so vivid that I had a most unhappy time reading it," adding, "What impressed me most is the tragedy of fear portrayed. If only there had been no fear, the outcome of these stories might have been so very different."[33] Throughout the collection, Wright depicts intense, fatal violence to dramatize racial conflicts between Black and white people. No wonder that Roosevelt described the reading experience as "most unhappy." Nevertheless, Roosevelt's review of *Uncle Tom's Children* assisted, as Jennifer Jensen Wallach noted, in bringing Wright's collection "to the attention of many Americans who might not otherwise keep abreast of the latest literary news."[34]

In Wright's stories, Black and white homegrown characters take center stage when engaging in confrontations with each other in southern settings. Interracial conflicts are common in his stories and usually result in a horrific death. According to Adam Gussow, Wright's southern stories embody "Blues expressiveness," or what he describes as a literary work "grounded in, and significantly shaped by, the encounter of working-class black folk with violence in the Jim Crow South."[35] White characters in Wright's stories enact what Gussow calls a "disciplinary violence" that "consists primarily of lynching, police brutality, and related forms of white vigilantism" for the sole purpose of keeping "the Negro in his place" (143). Wright showed the explosive eruptions that could occur when racial boundaries are crossed in the South.

Scholarly articles on Wright's short stories have highlighted the deadly conflicts that occur between Black and white characters.[36] But perhaps we have not given enough attention to Wright's vivid depictions of rural landscapes, especially in his short fiction. His renderings of southern landscapes are notable, especially since he is so often presented as an urban writer based on *Native Son*. He uses rural landscapes as the backdrop in stories that are frequently anthologized, while also depicting the dangers associated with these settings. He does not specify the town names and addresses of locations in his stories. Still, the physical landscape figures prominently in his renderings of southern settings. His stories incorporate descriptions of open fields, wooded areas, ponds, and front yards, demonstrating his awareness of rustic scenery.

In "Big Boy Leaves Home," Wright illustrates the dangers of southern territories when Black teenage characters trespass on a white man's property. Big Boy and his friends—Lester, Buck, and Bobo—go to a swimming hole on the private property of a noted racist, Old Man Harvey. As the boys are swimming, a startled white woman happens upon them and screams, prompting a white man in a soldier's uniform to appear with a rifle and immediately shoot Buck and Lester on sight. In self-defense, Big Boy takes the gun, kills the uniformed man, and flees the scene with Bobo. Big Boy's family agrees he has to leave town to avoid a lynching, so he goes into hiding. However, Bobo is eventually captured by the white mob and tarred, feathered, and hung. In the end, Big Boy escapes on a truck bound for Chicago.

Wright utilizes AAVE as a way of identifying or geo-tagging the distinct cultural and social location of his southern characters. Wright's stories depart from Chesnutt's and Hurston's works, however, as he presents the inner thoughts of his characters. As Big Boy makes his escape to the woods to wait until the next morning, the narrator explains, "Suddenly a thought came to him like a blow" as Big Boy "recalled hearing the old folks tell tales of bloodhounds, and fear made him run slower."[37] Wright then shifts the narration from Standard English to AAVE as he reveals Big Boy's innermost thoughts: "Why hadnt Pa let im take the shotgun?" (100). Big Boy stops and thinks, "He oughta go back n git the shotgun" (101). Wright takes an approach that involves varied narrative modes to adequately account for the psychological or mental traumas brought on by intense interracial conflicts in the South.

An analysis that takes cultural geo-tagging into account highlights how Wright uses AAVE to connect Big Boy to southern terrains. The passages that describe Big Boy's internal thoughts are written in AAVE, while the descriptions of character actions are written in Standard English. Ralph Ellison pointed out that Wright sought "to reveal to both Negroes and whites those problems of a psychological and emotional nature which arise between them when they strive for mutual understanding."[38] For Wright, those problems involve illustrating how racism and violence affect mental well-being. Disclosing innermost thoughts of his characters, he illustrates how violent racial disagreements stoke fear, anger, and hostility. The combination of English variations—standard and vernacular—allow Wright to deploy multiple narrative styles in the context of a single story and further emphasize the characters' connection to the South.

Wright sets his story in a rural environment, allowing him to depict the social and physical interactions among Black and white people as well as nature in southern settings. Melissa Ryan explains, "Big Boy raises fundamental questions about access to nature, or how one can interact with or make use of nature."[39] For Wright, Old Man Harvey's swimming hole represented an area that was off limits, and held fatal consequences, especially for Black trespassers.[40] The story exemplifies Wright's interest in representing the dangers of southern racial boundaries. "Naw buddy naw!" is Big Boy's response in the story when his friends suggest going to take a swim in old man Harvey's swimming hole (65). When his friends chastise him about his reluctance to go swimming, Big Boy retorts, "N git lynched? Hell naw!," anticipating the deadly conflicts to come.

The physical landscape at the onset of the story seemed refreshing when the boys decided to swim in the cool waters of the pond. Wright initially describes the boys as "laughing easily" as they "came out of the woods into cleared pasture," walking in "bare feet, beating tangled vines and bushes with long sticks" (60). Later, as Big Boy makes his escape, he hides in a hole described as "fringed by the long tufts of grass" (104). While in the hole, Big Boy encounters a "six foot of snake" (102). Big Boy "beat till the snake lay still; then he stomped it with his heel, grinding its head into the dirt" (103). By setting his story in a rural southern environment, Wright draws on and confirms popular views of the South as a racially volatile space.

In his story "Long Black Song," Wright also incorporates pastoral descriptions and uses a rural setting for a deadly final conflict on southern soil. This story deals with issues of infidelity between a married couple, Silas and Sarah. One day, a white salesman comes to Sarah's door to try to entice her to buy a musical device, a graphophone. When she declines to purchase the device, she still seems to gain pleasure from entertaining the salesman. Despite Sarah's better judgment, she ends up sleeping with the stranger and later seems to regret her part in what transpired. After Sarah has sex with the salesman, he leaves the graphophone with her and tells her he will come back the following day to collect the money. Silas returns home and sees the musical device and believes that Sarah cheated on him in return for the graphophone. He unleashes his rage on Sarah and beats her, prompting her to flee from the house. The next day, when the salesman comes to collect the money, Silas shoots and kills him. Soon after, a mob of white people shoot at and burn the house. As Sarah watches from a distance, Silas kills as many of the mob as he can before the house goes up in flames.

In this story, Wright troubles popular notions about racial interactions in the rural South by depicting a consensual sexual relationship between a Black woman and white man. At least two scholars have viewed the white man's actions as a sexual assault of a Black woman.[41] In Trudier Harris's reading of the story, however, Sarah was not raped, but instead the white salesman piqued her sexual interest.[42] Harris contends that "absolutely nothing in the description suggests that Sarah has been raped" and notes, "The white man touches, kisses, and chases her; he does not force her onto the bed or pry her legs apart" (195). Harris points out that Sarah "merely uses him to quell the sexual urges that neither her absent husband Silas nor her equally absent previous lover Tom is available to satisfy" (189). In this view, Sarah was an active and willing participant in the sexual encounter.

Silas's jealous and violent rage stems from his sense of betrayal and perhaps social position in the South. "As a black man in America," Harris argues, "his diatribe suggests, he [Silas] was doomed from the beginning."[43] She continues, "It did not matter if Sarah were unfaithful, or if his crops failed, or if he had enough money to pay his debts" because "He was doomed to failure." On the one hand, Silas decided to kill the white man as retribution for making physical advances on his wife. On the other hand, the history of racial tensions in the South added another element of anger and contempt of the white men that caused Silas to react as he did. Silas was offended and enraged that physical boundaries were crossed: a white man entering his home and bedroom. Silas was also furious by the betrayal of his wife, who crossed a boundary: the sanctity of their marriage.

After Silas kills the white man, he instructs Sarah to run to safety in a wooded area: "Yuh git on fo they ketch yuh too!"[44] Wright weaves descriptions of the landscape into the narrative as he describes Sarah "Blind from tears," as she is running away "across the swaying fields, stumbling over blurred grass." Wright again uses the rustic scenery of the woods as a setting for a fatal confrontation. The scene is important to consider because it demonstrates the salesman, as an outsider, invading a private home space. Silas dies fighting against white people at his home. Whereas in "Big Boy Leaves Home," a group of Black boys were attacked for trespassing on the private property of a white man, in "Long Black Song," a white man is attacked for his trespasses against a Black man.

In "Bright and Morning Star," Wright uses a rural wooded area as the setting for yet another violent conflict. Once again, he demonstrates his commitment to incorporating pastoral descriptions into stories about interracial southern clashes. After a local communist branch is infiltrated by the local sheriff, the story's protagonist, Sue, is confronted and beaten by the sheriff for refusing to tell the whereabouts of her son, Johnny-Boy, and name other members of the organization. Realizing that she may have compromised her fellow comrades by unintentionally revealing information to her white fellow communist member Booker—who is also the sheriff's informant—Sue commits herself to saving her son and comrades from danger.

Wright's descriptions of the weather play a pivotal role in heightening the sense of danger in this story's climax. After Sue realizes Booker was an informant to the sheriff and betrayed the other comrades, she is determined to avenge her son and his associates. Sue sets off through "the wind and the driving rain" to kill him as she carries a concealed weapon, "sagging cold and heavy in her fingers."[45] When Sue finds the sheriff and others assembled in the woods, she sees the men torturing her son as he is "lying in a trough of mud" (401). Sue initially pretends as if she has brought the white sheet to cover up her son after the white men kill him. Once she sees Booker, she fires her gun, flinging him to the ground as she watches him "lying sprawled in the mud, on his face, his hands stretched out before him" (406). After Sue shoots Booker, prompting the sheriff's men to shoot first Johnny-Boy and then Sue, she lies dying on the cold damp ground, feeling "the heat of her own blood warming her cold, wet back" (408). In her last thoughts, Sue says to herself, "Yuh didnt git whut yuh wanted! N yuh ain gonna nevah git it!" (452). Sue dies with a feeling of triumph, content that she has stood up for her beliefs. The weather descriptions amplify the story's dramatic conclusion and complement the countryside setting.

The Deep South and troubled interactions between white people and Black people figure prominently in Wright's settings. Given his own background, readers can assume that Wright's stories were inspired by his memories of the South and impressions of southern racism.[46] In his 1971 essay, Blyden Jackson argues that Wright's background as a southerner is of "utmost importance in understanding the growth and peculiarities of his artistic imagination."[47] Wright's development undoubtedly stems from his harrowing experiences as a boy growing up in the Jim Crow South.

Stories that Wright heard growing up in Mississippi and Arkansas appeared in "Bright and Morning Star." Notably, the scene of a Black woman attacking a group of white men was likely inspired by a story that Wright heard as a child. In his autobiography *Black Boy*, Wright writes, "One evening I heard a tale that rendered me sleepless for nights."[48] A Black woman's husband had been killed by white men, and she went to collect the body. "The woman, so went the story," recalled Wright, "knelt and prayed, then proceeded to unwrap the sheet; and before the white men realized what was happening, she had taken the gun from the sheet and had slain four of them." Wright could not verify the story, but for him, the tale "was emotionally true," and he determined that "I would emulate the black woman if I were ever faced with a white mob." With the character of Sue, Wright created a Black woman southern heroine committed to a militant by-any-means-necessary response to racial oppression.

Novelist and literary critic Sherley Anne Williams described "Bright and Morning Star" as "one of the most deft and moving renderings of a black woman's experience in the canon of American literature."[49] Wright depicts Sue as a female character claiming her agency and overcoming inner conflicts to support her son and her larger community of communist associates. As a Black southern woman living in the Jim Crow South, Sue defies social norms and takes an active role in avenging those who have wronged her and her family. Rarely are women characters portrayed as taking a violent role in exacting revenge. Wright's portrayal of Sue contributes to the diverse landscape of homegrown character portrayals and is a testament to southern women who become heroines.

As in "Big Boy Leaves Home," Wright weaves in Sue's internal thoughts in "Bright and Morning Star" while also using an external third person narrator to diversify the linguistic variety. At the beginning of this story, Sue is nervous and wondering about her son Johnny Boy's whereabouts. The narrator describes the setting: "She heard the clock ticking and looked. Johnny-Boys a hour late!" (351). Sue thinks, "Ever time they gits ready to hol them meetings Ah gits jumpity," adding that "Ah been a lil scared ever since Sug went t jail." Wright does not use quotation marks to make a distinction between Sue's internal thoughts and those of the narrator. He uses quotation marks for characters only when they are talking to one another. He creates a separation between the characters speaking in AAVE and the third person narrator speaking in Standard English. Wright's vernacular usage highlights Sue's inner musings and how she makes sense of the unfolding events. With Sue, Wright shows the internal negotiations southern Black people endure while contending with racist forces.

In his later short fiction, rural landscapes and homegrown characters are still prominent to the configuration of Wright's southern settings. His story "Almos' a Man" appeared in his collection *Eight Men*, published posthumously in 1961.[50] In this story, Dave, a young boy, is a sharecropper growing up in rural Mississippi who thinks a gun will help him to gain the respect and power so closely associated with manhood. Dave pleads with his mother, asking her if he can buy a gun. She reluctantly gives in and tells him after he buys the gun to bring it back to her so she can keep it. After buying the gun, Dave is excited to fire the weapon. He takes the gun to work and accidentally shoots his boss's mule, Jenny. His boss proposes that Dave work off his debt, and his father severely scolds Dave. Embarrassed by the shame that comes from his accident, Dave runs away by stowing away on a train headed towards Chicago.

Wright's story illustrates how a southern Black boy navigates his sense of manhood and independence. Unlike Wright's other stories, "Almos' a Man" does not feature intense violence and tragic deaths. Dave wants a gun to gain and assert more power. In the opening, he thinks to himself, "Ahm going by ol Joe's sto n git that Sears Roebuck catlog n look at them guns."[51] Later, when Dave begs his mother for permission to buy the gun, she says, "Whut yu wan wida gun, Dave? Yuh don need no gun. Yuh'll git in trouble. N ef yo pa jus thought Ah let yuh have money t buy a gun he'd hava fit" (9). From Dave's perspective, a gun is necessary for becoming a man since he associates the weapon with ideas of power and respect. His fascination with guns suggests that he equates the weapon with a symbol of protection. Dave wants freedom from the rules of his parents. He also wants the privileges that come along with power, which includes freedom from being the victim of violence or freedom from restraints.

Would "Almos' a Man" have prompted a different response from Hurston than Wright's stories in *Uncle Tom's Children*? Dave's story is not "so grim" or a "Dismal Swamp of race hatred" as she says about those stories.[52] But the story does reflect Wright's interest in depicting southern environments. And perhaps Wright would have had different responses to Hurston if he was aware of her short fiction, which anticipated the kind of marital conflicts he explored in "Long Black Song." Their works use settings as "a metaphorical and symbolical basis for making the Deep South analytically and aesthetically accessible as a signpost of a larger geographical region," explains Thadious Davis, while also not "excluding the significance, individuality, distinctiveness, or specificity of other Deep South states."[53] The widespread circulation of the stories by Chesnutt, Hurston, and Wright discussed here gives us opportunities to unsettle the broad category of the South in their varied depictions of southern characters navigating various terrains. Another group of frequently anthologized short story writers, discussed in the next chapter, would extend these depictions.

Chapter 3

THE PARADOX OF HOMEGROWN OUTSIDERS

Ralph Ellison, James Baldwin, and Alice Walker

In her article "Expanding the Limits: The Intersection of Race and Region," Thadious M. Davis wrote that "race and region are inextricable in defining a Southern self, society, or culture."[1] With its idyllic landscapes and southern charm, the South is a region that people often refer to fondly, invoking images of peacefulness and down-home hospitality. On the other hand, we also recognize the many troubles of the area. Slavery, lynching, Jim Crow, and poverty are all associated with the South. People may speak admiringly of southern hospitality, while remaining silent about the fact that states with the highest murder rates and perilous health standards are in the South.[2] The rich histories, contradictions, and sometimes tense Black-white interactions of the region have drawn considerable interest from African American writers.

Ralph Ellison and Alice Walker, two of the most prominent post-1940 short story writers, represent a departure from the works of Chesnutt, Hurston, and Wright. Unlike their predecessors, Ellison and Walker do not use phonetic spelling to represent southern speakers. Ellison and Walker depend on their characters, not precise descriptions of geographic landscapes, to describe the settings. Similar to Wright, Ellison and Walker probe the interiority of characters, accounting for the psychological or mental traumas brought on by intense interracial conflicts in the South. However, they employ different narration strategies to depict southern landscapes and characters interacting with those environments.

Flashbacks constitute an integral feature of southern stories by Ellison and Walker. Their characters are native to a particular landscape but are at a distance from their surroundings. Flashbacks such as dream sequences and sometimes even hallucinations interrupt the linear narrative and transport characters to virtual settings. Their internal thoughts, narrated in the first person, reveal how memories inform relationships with a given setting. These memories reveal intimate internal thoughts that explain how the setting shapes the social dispositions of protagonists and sometimes puts them at odds with their surroundings. Ultimately, Ellison and Walker present characters who are estranged from their immediate environments, thus creating conflict to drive the story's plot.

A consideration of short fiction by Ellison and Walker that takes account of their geo-tagging reveals how their stories are especially dependent on southern homegrown outsiders. A seeming contradiction, homegrown outsider characters are native to a particular region, but, for a variety of reasons, struggle to relate to others in their local environments. Ellison and Walker reveal the dramas that unfold when people become strangers in their home settings. Exposure to different places and ideas is a driving source of discontent for these types of characters. In some instances, southern homegrown outsiders leave and return to their local environments unable to fully reintegrate themselves. And sometimes, characters develop alternative views or learn something that puts them at odds with their immediate environs. The use of homegrown outsider characters allows writers to present settings usually reserved for insiders and at the same time move beyond the social norms of those places.

The concept of a homegrown outsider becomes even more interesting to consider when analyzing Ellison and James Baldwin as short story writers. Neither author is from the South, yet they assume the narrative voice of a white lead character regarding incidents of southern lynching. Their stories utilize white men as protagonists but differ in terms of how the lead characters relate to their immediate surroundings. Ellison presents a midwestern protagonist who travels south and becomes greatly disturbed by the local customs, notably a lynching. Baldwin, on the other hand, presents a southern sheriff who reminisces about his childhood and recalls the excitement he experienced when going to his first lynching. By assuming the personalities of white characters, Ellison and Baldwin explore lynching from different perspectives. From this vantage point, these writers explore the varying emotional impact that lynching has on non-Black onlookers. Their white characters' experiences with lynching leave them marked and thus at a distance from their immediate peers. These stories by Ellison and Baldwin use white male homegrown outsiders as central characters to drive the plot.

The presentation of seemingly out-of-place main characters in short fiction is integral to the practice of geographic or spatial referencing. In this chapter, section one explains how Ellison's homegrown outsiders reflect his interest in highlighting underexplored aspects of African American thought. A consideration of how Ellison navigates varied interior perspectives in three of his most anthologized works—"Battle Royal," "Flying Home," and "King of the Bingo Game"—reveals how he charted new or uncommon territory in the presentation of Black male characters in short fiction. The second section focuses on explorations of white perspectives of lynching in stories by Baldwin and Ellison. Their stories expand our views of how Black writers depict racial violence in the South from unusual positions. The third section examines four of Alice Walker's most popular short stories—"Everyday Use," "To Hell with Dying," "Advancing Luna and Ida B. Wells," and "Nineteen-Fifty-Five"—and explains how she makes Black women the focal point of her stories. In these stories, Walker incorporates both homegrown and homegrown outsider characters to illustrate how generational differences among women shape perceptions about the South and relationships with the setting.

RALPH ELLISON'S HOMEGROWN OUTSIDERS

Literary scholars routinely cast Ralph Ellison as a southern writer. Robert O'Meally explains that "in Ellison's fiction one hears a voice as deeply southern as Faulkner's—a voice as rich and as quick with exalted southern lies, told with conversational jam-session style as well as with poetic eloquence."[3] Other scholars have also noted the comparison to Faulkner. John Callahan writes that, in Ellison's fiction, he had "accepted the challenge of William Faulkner's complex literary image of the South."[4] In *Ralph Ellison and the Genius of America*, Timothy Parrish describes Ellison as the most important American writer since William Faulkner.[5] Despite efforts to align Ellison with southern-born writers such as Hurston, Margaret Walker, Jean Toomer, Tennessee Williams, and William Faulkner, he was, in fact, from Oklahoma.

In *Heroism and the Black Intellectual*, Jerry Gafio Watts explains, "When reading Ellison's perceptions of the South, one must remember that he did not experience the South from the vantage point of a native black southerner"; instead, "Ellison's sense of possibility was decidedly that of a black raised outside the Deep South."[6] Beyond not being a southerner, Ellison spent relatively little time in the South: only while attending Tuskegee University in Alabama from 1933 to 1936 before moving to New York to study sculpture. Still, the southern region of the United States was a source of inspiration for Ellison's short fiction. Ellison's own distance from the South may have further inclined him to construct such a memorable homegrown outsider.

An examination of Ellison's short fiction that takes geo-tagging into account sheds light on his deep interest in depicting the experiences of Black southerners, despite the fact he himself was a relative outsider to the region.

The protagonists in Ellison's stories are central to his representations of southern regions. The unnamed narrator of "Battle Royal," Todd in "Flying Home," and the unnamed protagonist in "King of the Bingo Game" are all from the South. Ellison avoids naming specific towns, addresses, and geographic markers in his stories. Moreover, like Wright, Ellison incorporates the inner thoughts of his characters, and those inner thoughts become portals to alternative virtual settings.

After his recent graduation from high school, the narrator of "Battle Royal" has been invited to give a speech to the leading white male citizens in an unnamed Alabama town. Unbeknownst to him though, he will first be required to participate in a battle royal—a boxing match with nine other Black teenage boys who must compete blindfolded for the amusement of the white men. After the fight ends, the boys are given the chance to collect gold coins from a carpet. But, again, the boys are fooled as the protagonist leaps for a coin only to be met with a violent shock because the rug has been electrified. The men in the room find this extremely comical and are thoroughly amused before finally giving the boys money and dismissing them, but not before allowing the protagonist to deliver his speech. Bruised and bloody, the protagonist finally begins to give his speech. The men gathered seem uninterested until the protagonist accidentally says the words "social equality," a suggestion that he is critiquing the Jim Crow requirement that Black people abide by the status quo of "social responsibility."[7]

Ellison's story exposes the town's leading white men who demean Black boys for entertainment and suppress African American social and political interests. According to Bhoendradatt Tewarie, "The Battle Royal episode can, consequently, be seen as an allegorical presentation of power relationships in Southern American society."[8] Tewarie continues, "Ellison uses the Battle Royal episode, therefore, to depict the peculiar character of the political, economic, and social system which prevails in the South and to show where the Negro stands in relation to that system." Ellison's story was groundbreaking for its display and treatment of the internal consequences of racism and social isolation experienced by a southern Black boy. Ellison drew on the troubled racial history of the South and used the internal thoughts of the narrator to inform the social dynamics of the setting.

Ellison's unnamed protagonist in the story is something of an outsider. He is a native of the South, yet he grapples with whether he truly belongs there. "All my life I had been looking for something and everywhere I turned someone tried to tell me what it was," he observes (264). The narrator considers himself different from his classmates who are participating in the boxing match, explaining that he had "some misgivings over the battle royal" because he "didn't care too much for the other fellows who were to take part" (265). In relation to his peers, the protagonist "felt superior to them in my way," but the powerful white townsmen subject him to the same demeaning treatment as the other Black teenagers (266).

Ellison incorporates flashbacks or dream sequences to disrupt the linear construct of time by showing how past and imagined events can intrude upon the narrator's current thoughts, thereby influencing his relationships with other characters. In the final scene, the protagonist explains that he is haunted by an ominous dream in which he and his grandfather go to a circus. While watching the clowns perform and hearing the reactions of the crowd, the protagonist's grandfather refuses to laugh. The grandfather tells the boy to open a briefcase and several envelopes stamped with a state seal, until he gets to a final letter that says, "To Whom It May Concern . . . Keep This N----r-Boy Running" (274). The protagonist awakens with his deceased grandfather's "laughter ringing in my ears." The constant memory of his grandfather makes the narrator conscious of how his personal lineage is directly connected to the histories of slavery and the South.

Dream sequences allow Ellison to explore alternative realms. The protagonist in "Battle Royal" moves from a private, intimate setting where he reflects on his grandfather's dying words to a public space dominated by the influence of white men. The white men consider the protagonist inferior, causing him to feel uncomfortable. Also, the haunting memory of his grandfather serves as an ominous warning that things are not totally what they appear to be, which further exacerbates the protagonist's discomfort. In this instance, dream sequences allow Ellison to explore additional spaces beyond the protagonist's immediate environment.

The grandfather that Ellison presents also fantastically exhibits qualities of a homegrown outsider with an attitude. "I have been a traitor all my born days, a spy in the enemy's country," says the grandfather on his deathbed (264). Although he is a native of this country, he views himself at the same time as a defector and infiltrator. The grandfather is an outsider, and he wants others to follow. He encourages his grandson to "overcome 'em with yeses, undermine 'em with grins, agree 'em to death and destruction, let 'em swoller you till they vomit or bust wide open" (264–65). By presenting such a figure, Ellison reveals his interest in the interplay of character and geography. Ellison uses the grandfather as a contrast to the protagonist, depicting how, despite the generational distance between the two characters, remnants of the South's troubled history would forever haunt the protagonist.

Like his grandfather, the protagonist sees himself as estranged from Black people in his home environment, though also not at home among white people. Despite the title of Ellison's well-known novel, the main character is not invisible within his community. His intellect makes him noticeable. After all, he was invited to the hotel under the pretense of delivering his graduation speech, as he was recognized as a top African American pupil. The protagonist believes he stands out from his peers and that his invitation to deliver his speech was "a triumph for our whole community" (265). The protagonist is "praised by the most lily-white men in town" and "considered an example of desirable conduct." This puts the narrator at a further distance from others, making him think he is exceptional and a credit to his race. According to the narrator, his peers "were tough guys who seemed to have no grandfather's curse worrying their minds." His introspection, however, places him in opposition to other people in his surroundings.

One of the factors that makes "Battle Royal" so compelling concerns its geo-tagging. In particular, the convergence of several disparate settings in this one story is quite fascinating. The venues mentioned include the bedroom of an elderly dying Black man, an elevator, a ballroom populated by white men, a boxing ring populated by Black boys, and a circus. The presentation of those diverse spaces in a single story further illustrates how environment shapes the social disposition of the narrator. The combination of those spaces also signals Ellison's creativity—his ability to weave a captivating narrative that has his Black male protagonist traversing eclectic spaces.

In "Flying Home," Ellison also uses a flashback or dream-like sequence. Once again, the flashback provides a way for Ellison to incorporate multiple types of settings into a narrative in which the story's main action is contained in one central location. Narrated from the third-person perspective, the story is focused on Todd, a young Black man who is training to be a pilot in Alabama and has just crashed his airplane in the middle of a field in Macon County, Alabama. A Black man named Jefferson and his son, Teddy, see Todd is badly injured and offer to get help. Jefferson sends his son to get Dabney Graves, the owner of the land and a noted racist. To distract Todd from the pain he's in while they wait, Jefferson tells a story about how he was kicked out of heaven by the other angels for wanting to fly freely without a harness. Todd thinks Jefferson is mocking him and goes into a rage until, eventually, he succumbs to his pain, passes out, and reverts to his early childhood when he developed his fascination with airplanes. While passed out, Todd is transported to a different time and place.

The flashbacks or dream sequences that follow contextualize Todd's emotions and explain how his fascination with airplanes has led to his estrangement from other characters. Even though the story is narrated in the third person, during the dream sequences Todd offers a first-person account: "I was four and a half and the only plane that I had ever seen was a model suspended from the ceiling of the automobile exhibit at the state fair."[9] After the fair, Todd was a nuisance, constantly asking people questions about airplanes as he became fixated on them, wanting a plane "more than I wanted the red wagon with rubber tires, more than the train that ran on a track with its train of cars" (216). Todd is adamant about his love for planes even though there are no Black pilots. The flashback separates Todd from the immediate action in the story and contributes to his position as an outsider.

The history of Jim Crow figures prominently in Ellison's representation of the South and contributes to Todd's position as a homegrown outsider. As a pilot, he stands out in relation to most characters in other short stories by Black authors. Ellison depicts a formally educated Black male character who aspires to transcend racial barriers based on his professional achievements. Todd embodies the sentiments of a burgeoning Black middle class, with its members' insistence on becoming full participants in American society. On the one hand, his identity as a Black man differentiates him from other pilots, who are primarily white. The US armed forces were segregated until 1948, based on the racist belief that Black soldiers were inferior to their white counterparts and could not learn to adequately operate military machinery.[10] On the other hand, Todd's identity as a pilot differentiates him from Black characters, who are primarily not pilots. These dueling qualities contribute to Todd's estrangement from the southern Alabama setting.

Todd's position as an outsider shapes his initial perspective and orientation to other characters in the story, particularly Jefferson. While on the ground in pain after the plane crash, Todd thinks to himself: "The closer I spin toward the earth the blacker I become" (222). As a pilot, Todd thinks he can earn respect and social status. Jefferson represents what Todd does not want to be. On the Alabama soil, Todd feels restricted; so, in this sense, flying liberates him from societal confines most Black people face. Todd is also ambitious. And for him, flying a plane in the US Air Force is an achievement in itself that sets him apart from Black and white people alike.

Todd's ambition to become a pilot both takes him away from a Black figure like Jefferson and frustrates a white person like Dabney Graves. Jefferson, a sharecropper who speaks in AAVE, serves as a contrast to Todd, a flight school candidate who speaks in Standard English. Robin Lucy explains, "Todd lies injured on what is, in this historical context, the common ground of southern soil: soil on which Jefferson labors under the system of sharecropping and debt-peonage."[11] She continues, "these material conditions largely determined the economic, political, and cultural category of the black folk." Despite the apparent social and class differences between Todd and

Jefferson, Dabney Graves fails to acknowledge the dissimilarities between the two characters. Long-standing racist views of Black people shape Graves's views of Todd and Jefferson.

Ellison and other Black short story writers are ever mindful of the Great Migration. In many stories, authors have cast characters who migrated away from the South. In Rudolph Fisher's "City of Refuge," the action takes place in Harlem, but the protagonist, King Solomon Gillis, is from North Carolina. The conclusions of Wright's "Big Boy Leaves Home" and "The Man Who Was Almos' a Man" show southern characters headed north. Edward P. Jones has characters in "All Aunt Hagar's Children" living in Washington, DC, and reminiscing about their migration from Alabama. Ellison's unnamed protagonist of "King of the Bingo Game" is from Rocky Mount, North Carolina.

In *The Warmth of Other Suns*, a history of the Great Migration, Isabel Wilkerson explains that the millions of Black people migrating northward "would seep into nearly every realm of American culture, into the words of Ralph Ellison and Toni Morrison, the plays of Lorraine Hansberry and August Wilson, the poetry and music of Langston Hughes and B. B. King, and the latter-day generation of Arrested Development and Tupac Shakur."[12] The presence of southern migrants in African American short fiction corresponds to the movement of millions of African Americans from the South to the Midwest, West, and North. Those southern migrant characters in short stories also reflect an interest among writers in cultural geographies or, more specifically, the travel patterns and activities of Black people. Ellison, among others, was intrigued with what it meant for southern Black men to adjust to the North. Ellison had firsthand knowledge about the struggle to adjust to new places, based on his own movements from Oklahoma to Alabama to New York.

In Ellison's "King of the Bingo Game," the unnamed protagonist has not been able to secure a job because he does not have a birth certificate. He has come to the theater—the setting of the story—to play a bingo game that takes place at the end of the feature film. The protagonist hopes to win the jackpot in order to take his sick wife to the doctor. The man plays five bingo cards, wins, and has a chance to spin the bingo wheel to win the day's jackpot. As the bingo king remains on the stage, he refuses the bingo caller's demand for him to release the button and stop the wheel from spinning. The protagonist feels powerful and thinks that, as long as he pushes the button and the wheel keeps spinning, he will maintain control and win the game. As the audience and the bingo caller get increasingly angry, two guards manage to wrestle the button from the protagonist. The wheel lands on the double zero as the curtain comes down on stage and the protagonist is hit in the head. The protagonist's southern upbringing determines his personal outlook and makes him feel out of place.

The protagonist is an outsider. He views his peers in the North as detached and not as hospitable as people in the South. While watching the film, the protagonist's stomach begins to growl, but he is reluctant to ask the people sitting next to him for any peanuts. He contrasts this with his experiences growing up in the South, thinking, "If this was down South . . . all I'd have to do is lean over and say, 'Lady, gimme a few of those peanuts, please ma'am,' and she'd pass me the bag and never think nothing of it."[13] He adds, "Folks down South stuck together that way. They didn't even have to know you. But up here it was different." Ellison contrasts "up here" to the Deep South, and by doing so, he further highlights geographical differences or, in this instance, the lack of southern hospitality. The unnamed protagonist feels a sense of coldness from the people he is surrounded by in the theater, a feeling he believes is uncommon to his southern home.

Despite the tension with his urban environment, the narrator longs for his southern home. Similar to his practice in his other two stories, Ellison uses flashbacks as a way of presenting multiple types of settings and creating distance between his main characters and their immediate surroundings. As in "Flying Home," even though the story is narrated from the third-person perspective, the main character interjects in the first person. The main action of the story occurs in a single setting, but Ellison's incorporation of a dream sequence allows him to transport the narrator back to his southern home environment. The artistry of flashbacks shines through as Ellison uses this technique to create other spaces. The intense emotions the protagonist experiences in his dreams and flashback contribute to how he responds to people in the story's present moment. Ellison probes the interior of this character's mind and uses virtual settings to show how geography influences personality.

Even though the character finds his new northern home inhospitable, his recollections of his southern home suggest it's an oppressive environment. While in the theater, the narrator drifts off to sleep and dreams that he is a young boy being chased by a train. He jumps off the tracks to escape, but the train follows him onto the highway and down the street, while he notices all of the white people pointing and laughing as he is screaming. According to Patricia Chaffee, even though the narrator "contrasts the hostility of the North with the camaraderie of the South," his dream suggests that the South, for him, is "as inescapably oppressive" at least on the subconscious level.[14] After all, the main character, Ellison, and millions of other African Americans left the South because better opportunities were presumably available elsewhere.

CHAPTER 3

WHERE WHITE CHARACTERS AND BLACK WRITERS MEET

The recurring presentation of the South in works by southern-born Black writers seems expected. Hurston's and Wright's writing about their region of birth and rearing seems fitting. But how do we explain the prevalence of the South in the works of so many non-southerners? The region is haunting but also alluring for Black creative writers. In *The Scary Mason-Dixon Line*, Trudier Harris wonders, "How does geography shape literary imagination?" and considers how Black writers, regardless of where they are born, "align a crucial portion of their identities with the site on American territory, that is, the American South."[15] Indeed, Toni Morrison (who is from Ohio), Octavia Butler (who is from California), Charles Johnson (who is from Illinois), and dozens of others have all published fiction with southern settings. In 2017 and again in 2020, Colson Whitehead, a New York City-based writer, was awarded the Pulitzer Prize for Fiction for novels set primarily in the South.

Inspired by a history of terror and violence, Baldwin and Ellison, two non-southerners, each wrote stories that vividly illuminate the innermost thoughts of white male characters to reveal how racism influences their thinking. Baldwin's "Going to Meet the Man" and Ellison's "A Party Down at the Square" are both about the public execution of Black men in the Deep South as told from the perspectives of white men. The stories illustrate how the brutal killing of Black men in the South might affect white male characters. Baldwin's character, Jesse, is a homegrown southern white male who is stimulated by the thought of violence inflicted upon Black people. Ellison's unnamed character, on the other hand, is a non-southerner—an outsider from Ohio who has reservations about the violent experience of a lynching. In both stories, the mob of people who gather as onlookers are enthralled rather than shocked by the killing of a Black person.

The homegrown protagonists in each story play a vital role in illustrating attitudes and sentiments within each setting. The stories could conceivably be anywhere in the South since Baldwin and Ellison provide sparse details about the exact locales, but then the writers were trying to connect the idea of lynching to the entire region. According to Davis, "Within the regime of segregation, place is a spatial marker conveying quite specific meanings."[16] She explains, "Place is a powerful signifier of identity that cannot be overestimated, particularly in terms of the South with its specific history and sociology," and as a result, "No section of the United States has taken on so contested but persistent an identity or role in the creation of an image as the South" (15). Consequently, the protagonists' first-hand accounts of events unfolding and precise descriptions of sights and sounds they encounter become all the more crucial for how we make sense of the story's settings. Ultimately, how each character is positioned in relation to the lynch mob provides insight into the setting.

Sites of lynching constitute horrifying yet memorable places in history but also in the realm of African American literature. In *Lynching: Violence, Rhetoric, and American Identity*, Ersula Ore explains how a major feature of lynching in the South involved the aid of law enforcement. Not only did lynching accounts "frequently implicate law enforcement and other branches of the justice system as agents of the mob," but "Despite the public nature of spectacle lynchings, lynchers were rarely ever indicted or tried, and in the event they were, were rarely ever convicted for their crimes."[17] Dozens of writers, including Paul Laurence Dunbar, Claude McKay, Langston Hughes, Lucille Clifton, and Wright, have written about this vicious and racist practice. Ellison and Baldwin move into fairly uncharted territory by presenting lynching scenes from the perspectives of white characters.

Published in a collection of the same name in 1965, Baldwin's "Going to Meet the Man" takes place in an unidentified southern town and revolves around Jesse, the town's sheriff. As Jesse lies in bed, he begins contemplating having sex but, becoming frustrated after not being able to get an erection, reflects on his day. He tells his wife about having to contain a civil rights protest and says the incident reminds him of a boyhood memory when his parents took him to a lynching of a Black man. The father, who was the former sheriff of the same small southern town, took Jesse as a young boy to witness the event. Jesse recalls the man being tied to a tree, with his hands chained above his head as his genitals were cut off. Even though Jesse is somewhat disturbed by the horrifying event, he takes pride in knowing that his parents trusted him enough to allow him to view the gruesome killing. At the story's end, Jesse becomes aroused and tells his wife, "Come on, sugar, I'm going to do you like a n----r, just like a n----r, come on, sugar, and love me just like you'd love a n----r."[18] His coupling of arousal and racism underscores his perverse preoccupation with Black males.

As a homegrown character, Jesse plays a crucial role in highlighting cultural aspects of the setting. His position as sheriff becomes all the more important when making sense of this setting so indelibly intertwined into the fabric of the southern town. As the sheriff, he is duty bound to uphold white privilege and maintain segregation. Harry L. Jones explains, "'Going to Meet the Man' points to the increasing internalization of racism that is as much a killing sickness as externalized racism."[19] From a young boy until adulthood, Jesse has witnessed Black people in pain. He follows in the footsteps of his father and becomes the town's sheriff. As Jesse grows older, he has internalized the brutality of lynching, and the thought of extreme violence underscores the idea that lynching is integral to law and order in the South.

Flashbacks are essential for adding depth to the story and showcasing different types of settings outside the couple's bedroom. The scenes Baldwin incorporates into "Going to Meet the Man" are reminiscent of the civil rights era in America as he depicts protestors clashing violently with police officers. Jesse mentions beating protestors, throwing them in the paddy wagon, and locking them up in jail cells, while failing to stop them from singing. Jesse then shouts in anger: "You all are going to stop your singing . . . you are going to stop coming down to the court house and disrupting traffic and molesting the people and keeping us from our duties and keeping doctors from getting to sick white women and getting all them Northerners in this town to give our town a bad name—!" (422). The context of the civil rights movement makes a setting like this possible in which Baldwin could incorporate a scene where Black protestors and policemen clash. And Jesse's role as a law enforcement officer makes a more revealing viewpoint.

Baldwin, a native New Yorker, explores the nuances of southern racism in his work. According to Kevin Birmingham, "Baldwin's South was more menacing than mythical because he imagined reality as a space of dangerous depths rather than sublime heights, and he saw the reality of art in the same way."[20] The history of lynching in the South shaped Baldwin's impressions of the region and influenced his fictional renderings. Baldwin challenged himself artistically by taking on the interior thoughts of a homegrown southerner, someone who would have been racially and geographically distant from the author.

Ellison also extends his artistic sensibilities by focusing on the perspective of a white male protagonist. He presents a somewhat sympathetic portrayal and shows a white character evolving beyond the racist traditions of the South. Published posthumously in 1997, three years after Ellison's death, "A Party Down at the Square" is about the burning of a Black man in the center of town. Ellison's collection of short stories, *Flying Home and Other Stories*, published posthumously in 1997, is the most-taught volume of his work. Many of these stories, including "A Party Down at the Square," however, were actually written in the late 1930s and early 1940s. Raymond A. Mazurek explains, "Perhaps the strongest of the previously unpublished stories in *Flying Home*, 'A Party Down at the Square' is the lynching story Ellison never published in his lifetime, and it illustrates Ellison's adeptness at writing in the protest traditions of the thirties."[21] The story is narrated from the first-person perspective of an unnamed young white man. Even though the story is set in the South, the narrator is a transplant from Ohio and an outsider of sorts. The day after the Black man was killed, the narrator was too disturbed by the events to leave the house, leading his uncle to chide him by calling him "the gutless wonder from Cincinnati."[22] While his Uncle Ed assures his nephew that they must "always have to kill n----rs in pairs to keep the other n----rs in place," the narrator senses the tension among the Black townspeople (55).

After the tension has died down in the community and the Black people begin to re-emerge around town, the narrator observes, "They all came back, but they act pretty sullen" (55). From his perspective, "They look mean as hell when you pass them down at the store." As an outsider, the narrator is disgusted by what has transpired, though he does not take action or disavow the lynching. He encounters a local sharecropper in the store a few days after the lynching who believes "it didn't do no good to kill the n----rs 'cause things don't get no better."

Mazurek explains that "Ellison frames the issue of lynching in the context of the forces impoverishing both black and white sharecroppers in the South."[23] Moreover, according to Mazurek, this story hints at the potential for "people like the white sharecropper to acquire the beginnings of a radical analysis and comprehend how racial divisions function to divide the working class." By the story's end, the differences between the narrator, the sharecropper, and the rest of the community are magnified. The narrator and sharecropper are notable because, unlike the other white townspeople, they are not yet beyond redemption. Their attitudes about lynching diverge from many others in their environments.

Ellison reinforces the racist sentiments of the white townspeople by incorporating symbolic images within his story. According to the narrator, the lynching occurs "right in front of the courthouse" where a "bronze statue of the general standing there in the Square was like something alive" so much that "The shadows playing on his moldy green face made him seem to be smiling down at the n----r" (46, 47). The narrator's impression of the statue smiling in front of the courthouse reinforces the public approval of the townspeople killing the victim. In this instance, white supremacy is supported and upheld by symbols of power. According to Jennifer Lieberman, Ellison's story "ridicules the United States for its monstrous devaluation of African American humanity."[24] In particular, writes Lieberman, Ellison casts judgment on the South as his story "elicits reflection about human rights by leaving the reader to process disturbing, violent scenes without authorial interjection" (12). Ellison's story highlights the subtle and overt power of dynamics of southern racism. The site of the lynching is a symbol of how racism is engrained into the social and political fabric of this southern community.

Both Ellison and Baldwin align Christianity and racial terror with the South in their stories, as described by Donald G. Mathews.[25] They reveal how religion and the ritual of lynching were intertwined to illustrate the hypocrisy of southern racism. Mathews explains that "Religion permeated communal lynching because the act occurred within the context of a sacred order" (63). He continues, "Holiness demands purity, and purity was sustained in the segregated South by avoidance, margins, distances, aloofness, strict classification and racial contempt in law and custom." Even though Black people were lynched in the North and Midwest, the higher numbers of lynching in the South make the region more known for its brutal history.

In Baldwin's story, Jesse feels that he is only doing his duty and obeying the rules cast down from a higher being, and "it wasn't his fault if the n----rs had taken it into their heads to fight against God and go against the rules laid down in the Bible for everyone to read!" (329). In Ellison's story, while the flames are heating up and death is imminent for the Black man, he begs the townspeople to have sympathy on him: "Will somebody please cut my throat like a Christian?" (52). One of the white people responds: "Sorry, but ain't no Christians around tonight. . . . We're just one hundred percent Americans."

Stories about lynching provided writers with the opportunity to create vivid and gruesome scenes in which mobs of white people ferociously tortured and killed Black victims. Ellison and Baldwin incorporate gory details to illustrate the violence and erratic behavior of the mob. Fire is a crucial image in these stories, as it is ever-present in the background. In both stories, the men are not just hung, but their bodies are set on fire. Even though the exact locales of the stories are vague, the the sounds and scenes at the public lynchings are described in gaudy detail. The characters are important figures because they describe what they witness first-hand. The accounts add another heinous element to the overall idea of lynching, illustrating just how extreme the communal act was during that time.

From the vantage point of Jesse in "Going to Meet the Man," Baldwin illustrates how certain prejudices and stereotypes that were rampant in the South shaped perceptions about Black people's sexuality. Baldwin offers vivid portraits of the lynching party to illustrate how sights associated with this southern ritual affected the protagonist. In his recollection of the lynching, the young Jesse marvels at the sight of the naked man, who is "a bigger man than his father, and black as an African jungle cat" (346). Jesse describes the victim as "the most beautiful and terrible object he had ever seen till then" as he becomes fixated on his genitals and notes that "the n----r's privates" were "huge, huge, much bigger than his father's, flaccid, hairless, the largest thing he had ever seen till then, and the blackest" (348). Jesse notices the reactions of people around him—most notably, his mother who "was more beautiful than he had ever seen her" and he "began to feel a joy he had never felt before" (347). Through Jesse, Baldwin highlights how the racist practice of lynching has psychological effects on all those involved in the act.

As a young and impressionable character, the young Jesse is forever traumatized socially and sexually by the incident. According to Sara Taylor, "The image of the lynched man's testicles" was linked to "white patriarchy's false construction of a hypersexualized black masculinity, as well as its subsequent attempts to repress and destroy that very construction."[26] This scene provides a window into the early childhood events that shaped Jesse's race consciousness as it relates to Black people and the South. Furthermore, Jesse's reflection on the lynching of the Black man, by the story's end, arouses him enough to have sex with his wife.

Ellison also emphasizes the spectacle of a Black body burning in "A Party Down at the Square." As the narrator is fixated on the flames, he explains, "The n----r was bleeding from his nose and ears, and I could see him all red where the dark blood was running down his black skin" (53). As the ropes burn and the victim falls into the fire, the Black man "started jumping and kicking about like he was blind, and you could smell his skin burning." The narrator gets an up-close look at the victim's body and thinks, "Every time I eat barbeque I'll remember that n----r. . . . His back was just like a barbecued hog" and "I could see the prints of his ribs where they start around from his backbone and curve down and around." May Anderton explains how the structure of this story allows "readers to coexperience and reconsider through wiser eyes a similar 'place' of inner conflict as the narrator: between watching and walking away."[27] Because he does not think of the Black man as human, he has a hard time reconciling his own morality and totally disavowing the practice of lynching.

As a Midwesterner and thus an outsider, the narrator in "A Party Down at the Square" has no direct connection to the South and is thus unfamiliar with the lynching rituals of the region, describing the experience as "my first party and my last" (55). The repulsive scene of the Black man burning troubles the narrator so much that he vomits. Even though he considers himself to be forever scared by the horrific sights and smells, he never turns away from the gruesome scene or condemns any of the perpetrators and onlookers. So far, most outsider characters discussed in this book and most characters in short stories by African Americans are Black. However, Ellison's protagonist is white, and he questions the motivations and usefulness of lynching, which places him at odds with many of the white people he encounters in the South. The presentation of a white outsider allows Ellison the possibility of discussing lynching from a fresh perspective, at least in the context of Black short stories.

By composing narratives about white people conducting public executions of Black men, Baldwin and Ellison contribute to an expansive, horrifying realm of cultural geo-tagging: the presentation of lynching scenes. Such depictions of mob violence are rare among widely anthologized African American short stories. However, Baldwin and Ellison join a wide variety of poets, novelists, filmmakers, visual artists, historians, and journalists who have sought to present these gruesome and distressing acts in their works.[28] The act of presenting or tagging lynching scenes gives Baldwin and Ellison opportunities to situate these terrible deeds on the map of American cultural memory and at the same time align their works with many others who sought to do so.

In these stories, Ellison and Baldwin bring a new perspective to the idea of outsiders. On the one hand, the writers hail from Oklahoma and New York, respectively. Ellison and Baldwin are Black writers who take on the first-person perspectives of white protagonists, which was not done often in the history of African American short story writing. The ever-present memory of Jim Crow led these men to confront the South and represent the terror and trauma associated with the region through fiction.

ALICE WALKER'S HOMEGROWN OUTSIDERS

Walker grew up in Eatonton, Georgia, a rural farming town, and later, she spent time in Georgia and Mississippi doing voter canvassing.[29] Walker sometimes blurs the lines between her real-life experiences and fictional representations, thus underscoring the importance of the South to her literary imagination. The women characters in her stories also have southern origins and sometimes reflect the growing consciousness of Black people who came of age during the 1960s, similar to Walker. Like several other writers, Walker is contemplative about the South after leaving the region. Understandably, her short stories, and homegrown women characters, exhibit same internal negotiations.

Walker's most well-known stories are set in the South and focus on intraracial conflicts. Those conflicts are not violent, but they do signal subtle and overt tensions that exist among groups of southern Black characters. In this regard, Walker is extending the kinds of conflicts that Hurston introduces—conflicts among Black people. Furthermore, like Hurston and other short story writers who depict the South, Walker chooses to be vague about her rural southern settings and instead uses the characters to create a strong sense of place. Her stories, like Hurston's, demonstrate what it means for a southern-born writer who left the region to return through her literary art. As a writer, Walker was something of a homegrown outsider.

Unlike Hurston who featured primarily male characters, Walker chose women as focal points and narrators. According to Thadious Davis, scholars typically overlook Walker's "fictional examination of racial and regional identity, along with gender identity, and her portrayal of a contemporary need to reinstate a black southern experience into cultural and historical contexts despite the reality of pain that a truthful reinstatement necessarily bears."[30] Scholars have discussed Walker's explorations of gender; however, considerations of Walker as a southern Black short story writer are less evident even as anthologies regularly include "Everyday Use." Walker's story is one of the few widely read short stories to include only Black women characters. That those Black women are southern testifies to Walker's interest in composing narratives about the region.

In "Everyday Use," Mrs. Johnson (also called Mama) has to reconcile tensions in her family and the relationship between her two daughters—Maggie and Dee. The story opens as Mama anxiously waits in her front yard for the arrival of Dee. When Dee finally arrives home, she is accompanied by her boyfriend, Hakim-a-barber. Maggie and Mama learn Dee has converted to a Black Islamic faith and changed her name to Wangero Leewanika Kemanjo. Dee revels in the down-home, folksy nature of her mother's home and exclaims to her mother, "Oh, Mama . . . I never knew how lovely these benches are. You can feel the rump prints in them."[31] She begins asking her mother if she can have items in the house such as a butter churn and dash to use as decorative pieces in her own house. When Dee asks if she can have some quilts, her mother protests, "I promised to give them quilts to Maggie, for when she marries John Thomas." Dee responds derisively, "Maggie can't appreciate these quilts. . . . She'd probably be backward enough to put them to everyday use" (1193). Dee tries to defy her mother and take the quilts, but her mother stops her and gives the quilts to Maggie. The story ends with Dee storming off with her boyfriend as Mama stands with Maggie.

The sparse geo-tagging that Walker uses in "Everyday Use" is fitting given Mama's limited mobility. The house and the front yard, which is "like an extended living room," are the only settings for the story (1188). The placement of Mama in this one place accentuates her distance from Dee, who is on her way to becoming an experienced traveler. While some writers identify several different places in a single story, Walker uses minimal locales. She instead devotes time to exploring the interiority of her protagonist and the struggle with her daughter.

As a narrator, Mama reveals her thoughts as she considers the challenges of raising two different kinds of daughters. Susan Farrell writes, "Dee seems to attain almost mythic stature in Mama's imagination" and "inspires in Mama a type of awe and fear."[32] Mama and Maggie are homegrown characters, and the once-familiar Dee makes them feel uncomfortable. Walker uses Mama and Maggie as representations of an old, rural southern way of life in contrast to Dee. In the story, Mama, "a large, big boned woman," describes herself as a laborer "with rough, man working hands" (1189). She explains, her "fat keeps me hot in zero weather" enabling her to "work outside all day, breaking ice to get water for washing." She describes Dee as "lighter than Maggie, with nicer hair and a fuller figure." Walker calls attention to Dee's appearance to further illustrate her distance. By upholding her word and giving Maggie the quilts, Mama validates her younger daughter as an equal to her sister.

Mama portrays Dee as both a source of frustration and admiration. Farrell explains that even though Dee is cast as "self-centered and demanding," she is also "a determined fighter" who will "do whatever is necessary to improve her circumstances."[33] In the story, Mama describes Dee as a woman who "would always look anyone in the eye" since "Hesitation was no part of her nature" (1189). Dee's disdain for her humble origins is made readily apparent. Nonetheless, Mama is in awe of Dee's confidence and ability to confront seemingly insurmountable odds. Mama longs to have a made-for-TV reunion in which her daughter embraces her "and leans across the table to tell how she would not have made it without their help." But Mama realizes it's all a fantasy.

Although Walker seems to have more in common with the character Dee, she narrates the story from the perspective of Mama. Walker pushes herself as an artist to consider the changing landscape of rural southern culture and reflect these shifts through character portrayals. "The first-person narrative voice, the fact that Mrs. Johnson is both narrator and character," according to Matthew Mullins, "has an immediate and forceful effect upon our perception of Dee."[34] As the sole narrator, Mama drives the action of the story and sets up the initial contrast between herself, Maggie, and Dee. Mama may lack formal education, but Walker presents her as an enduring and trustworthy source with wisdom that escapes her daughters. Walker's decision to take on the perspective of a character who was in some respects very different from her personal background reflects her interest in experimenting or at least extending herself artistically in short fiction.

Mama is portrayed as a sensible and credible woman, a homegrown character who is accustomed to rural southern living. Dee is presented as troubling. After their house burned down when the girls were teenagers, Mama recounts how Dee reacted, describing "a look of concentration on her face as she watched the last dingy gray board of the house fall in toward the red-hot brick chimney. Why don't you do a dance around the ashes? I'd wanted to ask her. She had hated the house that much" (1189). When Dee returns to visit her family, Maggie seems nervous to greet her sister upon her arrival and tries to run off before Mama intervenes. Dee, exuding the sense that she is above her family, is intimidating to them.

Walker's personal experiences leaving her rural home first to attend Spelman College in Atlanta and then to Sarah Lawrence in New York likely gave her insight into the familial tensions that might arise when a Black daughter departs and later looks on her home environment from a new college-educated, urban perspective. Walker offers a critique of shifting values to reveal how Dee has determined that her home and its people are out of touch with a changing world. The tension is more than generational since Dee and Maggie are siblings. Instead, Dee has become a homegrown outsider based on her travels and college experiences. The story thus highlights a growing divide within a family of Black women.

The idea of a Black female character who leaves for college and returns appears in another popular short story by Walker. In "To Hell with Dying," presented through a flashback that takes place over many years, the unnamed narrator is away in the North working on her doctorate. As a child, the narrator and her family had participated in the reviving of Mr. Sweet Little—"a diabetic and an alcoholic and a guitar player."[35] Many times throughout the story, a doctor comes to Mr. Sweet's bedside and declares that he is dying. Each time, the narrator's father proclaims, "To hell with dying," and the children instantly surround Mr. Sweet with affection and bring him back from the brink of death (156). When the narrator is away at graduate school, Mr. Sweet gets sick again, but after she rushes home to his bedside, he finally dies. She then realizes that the "revivals" in which she participated as a child hid from her that death was permanent. After Mr. Sweet's death, the family celebrates him, and the narrator accepts the gift of his guitar, which she plays in his memory.

Michael Hollister describes Walker's story as being in the "mainstream oral tradition of pastoral writers such as Mark Twain, Sherwood Anderson, and most specifically, Zora Neale Hurston, who developed the technique of sustaining a tension between two voices."[36] Walker's childhood upbringing had a profound impact on her and also served as a source of continued inspiration that she said in an interview "will probably always be there in the work."[37] In that interview, Walker acknowledges, "In my own life I have had the kind of mobility that has taken me not just all over the South but all over the country." But even still, she explains, "When I go back to Eatonton, Georgia, I get these new reverberations of things, new enlightenment" that makes her "understand on a deeper level." Walker projected the fondness of her upbringing onto the unnamed protagonist of "To Hell with Dying" to demonstrate how, even though far away from home, the memories of Mr. Sweet still touched her. The narrator had left the South, yet she remained connected to her home through those who remained there.

The protagonist of the story has become a homegrown outsider based on her travels and academic trajectory. When she returns to see Mr. Sweet one last time, she notes, "The house was more dilapidated than when I was last there, barely a shack," and even describes how she "felt strange walking through the gate and up the old rickety steps" (164). Her time away from her rural farm has changed her perspective on the home environment of which she was once a part. Even though she does not initially realize it, she has grown distant from once-familiar people. As a young girl, she played a special role in the revivals of Mr. Sweet and always was able to bring him back from the brink of death. Reality has set in as she, as an adult, contemplates the time that has elapsed between her childhood and the present moment. She begins to fully acknowledge how she imagines her home and childhood as a fantasy of sorts. Her ideas associated with home are formed by memories from throughout her childhood and fond memories of Mr. Sweet's revivals.

For Walker, distance from the South also affords characters the opportunity to question long-held beliefs about the region. Her story "Advancing Luna and Ida B. Wells" is about the friendship of two civil rights workers—the narrator, an unnamed Black woman, and her friend Luna, a white woman—and a moral comprise the narrator makes. The two women first meet in the summer of 1965 in Atlanta at a political conference; soon after, they work together on a voter registration drive in a "small, rigidly segregated South Georgia town."[38] A year after graduating from Sarah Lawrence, the college Walker herself attended, the narrator is evicted from her Brooklyn Heights apartment, and Luna offers to share her two-bedroom flat on East 9th Street. While living together, Luna tells the narrator she was raped by a Black civil rights worker, Freddy Pye, during the summer they registered Black people to vote in rural Georgia. Horrified and angered, the narrator confronts her and asks why she did not scream, to which Luna replies: "You know why" (1198).

The majority of the action is set in New York, but the history of the South figures into the story literally and figuratively. Growing up in the South, whenever interracial rape is mentioned, the narrator explains, it is "so clear that the black men accused of rape in the past were innocent victims of white criminals that I grew up believing black men literally did not rape white women" (1199). Luna's revelation places the narrator in an uncomfortable position as a Black woman. As a white woman, Luna's accusing Freddy of rape would almost certainly lead to life in prison and even possibly death. She remembers seeing the famous photo of Emmett Till and countless pictures of white people celebrating the lynching of other Black men. The narrator begins to consider what justice could look like for Luna, especially given the taboo nature of race and sexual assault in the South.

Later, the narrator seems conflicted on whether she should include a fictional account of the rape in a novel she is writing, so she rereads Ida B. Wells's autobiography to channel the spirit of the early civil rights leader and anti-lynching crusader. She envisions Wells telling her to "Write nothing. Nothing at all. It will be used against black men and therefore against all of us" (1199). The title of the story raises the challenge of acknowledging sexual assault and at the same time remaining mindful of false accusations against Black men. Even if Luna never achieves justice, the story signals a sense of hope as the narrator begins to question long-held beliefs about interracial rape.

Walker's story is one of the few well-known short stories by an African American writer that considers a friendship between a Black woman and white woman. The two women meet in the South, and their friendship develops in New York. Walker's story demonstrates how physical and social distance from southern terrains can lead to different perspectives and relationships. Tense racial strains between Black and white characters permeate southern short fiction, but Walker opts to showcase a level of understanding between her Black and white characters. Her exploration of interracial friendship enables her to chart new or rarely traveled territory in the larger context of short stories by African American writers. Walker's stories reconfigure popular impressions of the South by showing how moments of understanding can occur between Black and white characters.

Walker presents another unusual, interracial alliance in "Nineteen Fifty-Five." In this story, Walker's narrative invokes the connection between Elvis Presley and famed blues singer Big Mama Thornton.[39] Elvis made Thornton's "Hound Dog" a hit. In Walker's story, the fictional characters Traynor and Gracie Mae Still have a similar relationship. The story, which begins in 1955, chronicles Gracie Mae's life as a retired singer living in the rural South. Gracie Mae had local and regional acclaim, but she never became a mainstream success. One day, a young singer, Traynor, and his manager come to visit Gracie Mae to offer to buy one of her songs for the young artist's exclusive use. Gracie Mae gladly accepts the extra cash—more than she ever thought the song was worth. She makes a connection with the singer even though he is shy and reserved. The rest of the story is told in dated episodes as Gracie Mae follows the young singer's career. Even though southern stories are often riddled with interracial conflict, Walker presents a Black woman and white man who have a healthy and enduring friendship. Gracie Mae and Traynor's interactions represent a departure from violence and interracial strife found in stories by Wright. The relationship between Walker's two characters over several years informs the setting.

Over the years, Traynor ponders the meaning of Gracie Mae's song and returns to her several times to understand the lyrics. Traynor explains, "I've sung it and sung it, and I'm making forty thousand dollars a day offa it," but "I don't have the faintest notion what that song means."[40] On various visits, Traynor gives Gracie Mae a car, a farm, a house, and other presents in an attempt to return some of the wealth her song has brought him. One night in 1977, she tells her partner, Horace, that the boy's in trouble. And she is right: in 1977, the successful yet unhappy singer dies. Though his fans make a show of mourning him, only personal friends like Gracie are sad for his troubled life.

Walker explores multiple dichotomies between Gracie Mae and Traynor such as gender, race, and economic status. The friendship between Gracie Mae and Traynor is unusual given the setting and historical era. Walker depicts Gracie Mae as a homegrown character. She's down-to-earth, honest, endearing, and true to her cultural heritage. Traynor, however, is an outsider and does not appear to have strong cultural or social roots in the South. The irony is that Traynor's fame is based on music he has bought and appropriated from Gracie Mae even though he does not understand the song's meaning. On the one hand, Traynor is an insider to his fan base, and Gracie Mae is an outsider. On the other hand, Traynor's inability to understand the song highlights his position as an outsider.

In the story, Traynor invites Gracie Mae to perform her song on the Johnny Carson show and announces to the audience, "The lady who wrote my first hit record is here with us tonight, and she's agreed to sing it for all of us, just like she sung it forty-five years ago" (27). Gracie Mae stands before the audience "singing my own song, my own way. And I give it all I got and enjoy every minute of it." By contrast, Traynor "sings it just the way he always did. My voice, my tone, my inflection, everything" (86). After they finish, the audience gives a tepid response to Gracie Mae, but cheers loudly for Traynor. Traynor has received critical acclaim because of the song, yet he still experiences internal strife because of his inability to claim ownership of the music. A deeper understanding of the song and culture eludes Traynor, while fame eludes Gracie Mae.

While never making it big as a major singer, Gracie Mae still possesses a distinctly southern, down-home quality, which counts for something. Maria V. Johnson believes Walker's story challenges strict racial and social classifications and offers the lesson "that these prescriptive definitions not only keep people from one another but, as exemplified in the case of Traynor, often tragically keep people from themselves."[41] Although Traynor is a tragic figure, unable to find himself or to find meaning in his life, he comes to understand a great deal about his own unhappiness from his association with Gracie Mae. His inability to comprehend the meaning of the song symbolizes his estrangement from other people. Even though Traynor is far more famous than Gracie Mae, she is a homegrown character who is grounded and self-assured. Walker bestows Gracie Mae with an innate wisdom that is beyond the grasp of Traynor.

We should take the notion of cultural geo-tagging seriously when analyzing short stories by Alice Walker to understand how the South plays a crucial role in her artistic sensibilities. Geography contributes to the outlook of her characters. Long-held cultural beliefs from their upbringing bear on each of the women characters in Walker's stories. Her background influences how they interact with other characters in each story. The perspectives presented in the stories offer readers considerations of lingering memories of the South and shape presentations of women in short fiction.

Chapter 4

NEW YORK CITYSCAPES

James Baldwin and Toni Cade Bambara

In *Writing New York: A Literary Anthology*, editor Phillip Lopate explains that "almost every major American author, if not a New Yorker, at least went through a New York phase . . . and countless distinguished visitors left a literary record of their sojourns."[1] Lopate's remarks seem especially relevant when considering place as a crucial factor in shaping the thematic and publication history of African American literature. Lopate's descriptions signal the significance of Harlem in the historical and artistic imaginations of Black people. New York City served as an important destination during the Great Migration and also the location for many cultural movements. The emphasis on Harlem, in particular, has contributed to that neighborhood's importance in African American literary and cultural history.

James Baldwin and Toni Cade Bambara extend the practice of geo-tagging New York City in short fiction. They present a variety of settings: Lenox Avenue, an apartment building, a jazz club, a movie theater, a toy store, a park, and a school yard. They have characters who travel in cars and taxis, and they reference people who gather on street corners and subway stops. As native New Yorkers, Baldwin and Bambara were quite familiar with city landmarks, buildings, informal gathering places, and routes of travel. The scenes they depicted and narratives they created derived from their geographical knowledge.

Baldwin and Bambara cast homegrown city dwellers in their stories, and those characters create opportunities for the writers to geo-tag multiple facets of New York City. The urbanites in these stories view and reference street corners, cross streets, residences, public gathering places, and other locales. They serve as guides and, to some degree, mapmakers of the city. Characters pass people on sidewalks, talk to others while walking to a subway stop, and look down on people from apartment windows. These are typical activities in a city, but somewhat rare in African American short stories, as many of the most canonical stories take place in southern towns and within relatively confined places.

In section one of this chapter, I explain how Baldwin makes use of the expansive New York City terrain to explore multiple locales and perspectives in the process of creating a compelling narrative. Baldwin's characters advance our views about homegrown characters by illustrating how familiarity with an environment facilitates movement and knowledge. Section two highlights how Baldwin and short story writers Rudolph Fisher, Henry Dumas, and Amiri Baraka use musical settings in urban environments to draw attention to outsiders. In section three, I explain how Bambara's stories contribute to shifting the conventional character paradigm in short fiction by showcasing the experiences of homegrown Black children in urban settings. The focus on Black girls makes Bambara's stories particularly important for diversifying views of characters in African American short fiction.

JAMES BALDWIN'S HARLEM

From the mid-1960s, editors frequently included Baldwin's stories "Going to Meet the Man," "The Outing," and "This Morning, This Evening, So Soon" in their anthologies. "Sonny's Blues," however, was by far the most frequently selected choice of editors. According to Richard N. Albert, the story became and remained popular because the story "is less polemical than many of his later efforts" and because it offers common themes such as "individualism" and "alienation."[2] James Tackach posits a strength of the story: "Like the parable of the Prodigal Son, 'Sonny's Blues' is a tale of sin and redemption. In both stories, the lost son ultimately returns to the family fold and is saved."[3] Whatever the case, the emphasis on brothers, the city, and music makes instances of cultural geo-tagging in this story particularly noteworthy.

Set in New York City, "Sonny's Blues" tells the story of an overprotective older brother as he worries about and tries to come to grips with his younger brother's desire to be a musician. The unnamed narrator is searching for a way to reconnect with his younger brother, Sonny, after losing contact when Sonny was arrested and sentenced to jail for his involvement with a drug scandal. Once Sonny is released, his older brother attempts to reconcile their differences based on "a pretty awful fight."[4] The narrator is frustrated by Sonny's love for music and inability to get a more socially acceptable and financially secure job. The protagonist's yearning to watch out for Sonny and care for him by planning his life is driving a wedge between the two brothers.

John Claborn explains, "What we get in 'Sonny's Blues' is a vision of the limitations of life in the northern city—limitations that . . . cause widespread anger and despair throughout the community."[5] Instead of writing a story that directly critiqued the systems of inequality that kept Black residents of Harlem in poverty for generations, Baldwin offers a portrait of how being poor and working class impedes the development of two brothers and causes tension. For instance, flashbacks in "Sonny's Blues" reveal the consciousness of the story's narrator. He recalls that every time his mother mentioned moving to a neighborhood that would be safer for children, his father would retort: "Safe, hell! Ain't no place safe for kids, nor nobody" (419). His father "was always on the lookout for 'something a little better,' but he died before he found it" (420). These memories inform how the unnamed narrator thinks about physical and social features of his Harlem neighborhood.

Cultural geo-tagging, especially the practice of incorporating actual locations into the plot of the story, is essential to Baldwin's representation of New York City. Its people, its buildings, its streets become integral to the story that Baldwin is telling. As a native New Yorker, the protagonist narrates his interactions from the perspective of someone who is quite familiar with the city. Accordingly, words such as "street," "sidewalk," "subway," "block," "corner," "walk," "window," and "park" appear at intervals throughout the story. The experience of living in and moving around a city motivates writers to use a broad but distinct body of words associated with an urban space like New York City. Many words and concepts associated with city life provide details about neighborhoods and give characters a sense of placement and direction.

Homegrown characters exhibit keen navigational instincts that demonstrate their familiarity with the settings. Characters in "Sonny's Blues" move from one location to another, allowing Baldwin to project the vibrancy and kinetic energy of the city while at the same time showcasing his knowledge of the environment. At the beginning of the story, the unnamed narrator is leaving the school where he teaches when he happens upon an old acquaintance. As they walk down a Harlem sidewalk, the acquaintance talks to the protagonist about a story in the newspaper detailing Sonny's arrest. The narrator notes that their conversation is so casual that "from his [the acquaintance's] tone we might have been discussing the quickest way to get to Brooklyn" (416). The casual reference to a route to Brooklyn confirms the narrator's familiarity with the city and area. Those who view navigational directions as regular casual conversation are, of course, knowledgeable city dwellers.

In at least one instance, references derived from place-based markers are employed to shape impressions of the setting by distinguishing the Harlem neighborhood in which the story is set. Reflecting on his old acquaintance, the narrator thinks to himself: "even though he was a grown-up man, he still hung around that block, still spent hours on the street corners, was always high and raggy" (415). The "block" and "street corners" allude to places where allegedly troublesome people, especially Black men, gathered and hung out together. Since lawbreaking sometimes occurs in these places, the narrator desperately wants Sonny to stop meeting people there. For some, a term like "block" or "street corner" suggests bad and unsavory connotations, while, for others, these words refer to communal spaces. By using language that draws on space, Baldwin shows that place-markers represent physical locales and connote social and emotional qualities.

At another moment, Baldwin really takes advantage of the scenic possibilities of the cityscape by using navigational routes. When the narrator meets up with Sonny, who has been released from prison, they take a taxi ride through their childhood neighborhood as they make their way through Harlem to the narrator's apartment where he lives with his wife and children. Riding in the car, the narrator notes the quickly shifting demographics of the people they see outside: "the cab moved uptown through streets which seemed, with a rush, to darken with dark people," and then "We hit 110th Street and started rolling up Lenox Avenue" (418–19). The presentation of a car ride scene, a rare depiction in canonical African American short stories, gives Baldwin a chance to chart a roving view of the city.

The narrator has come to see the familiar street as containing veiled hazards. "I'd known this avenue all my life," he thinks to himself, "but it seemed to me again, as it had seemed on the day I'd first heard about Sonny's trouble, filled with a hidden menace which was its very breath of life" (419). For Baldwin, a common activity like a car ride becomes an opportunity to explore physical landmarks and routes as well as different emotions about a place. This type of scene is common in urban contexts, but more importantly, it gives Baldwin an opportunity to show the variety and disparity that exist within a concentrated geographic space.

As the narrator and Sonny ride in the taxi, the narrator takes time to notice the physical surroundings of his decaying Harlem community. Even though the narrator notes, "Most of the houses in which we had grown up had vanished," in their place he observes how buildings now dominated the landscape and were populated with "boys exactly like the boys we once had been" who "found themselves encircled by disaster" (418–19). Baldwin offers vivid accounts of the urban landscape in order to capture the insufferable living conditions that plague Black people in New York City.

In his 1948 essay, "The Harlem Ghetto," Baldwin proclaims, "All of Harlem is pervaded by a sense of congestion, rather like the insistent, maddening, claustrophobic pounding in the skull that comes from trying to breathe in a very small room with all the windows shut."[6] Baldwin states that "Harlem, physically at least, has changed very little in my parents' lifetime or in mine," and now "the buildings are old and in desperate need of repair, the streets are crowded and dirty, there are too many human beings per square block." Baldwin depicts the attitudes that permeate Harlem and, in doing so, he dramatizes this famous New York City neighborhood. The settings in "Sonny's Blues" highlight how decades of compounded poverty took a toll on the physicality of Harlem as a whole.

In addition to presenting outside, public scenes of the city, Baldwin incorporates home settings, contributing to the diversity of setting types within the story. Unlike the stand-alone houses that appear in southern short stories, Baldwin mentions apartments in large building. "We live in a housing project," notes the narrator at one point; "A few days after it was up it seemed uninhabitably new, now, of course, it's already rundown" (419). Life in an urban context necessitates a distinctive type of representation that is unlike homes in southern stories. For instance, in a flashback describing a Sunday dinner at his parents' house, the narrator recalls hearing "the street noises every now and again, or maybe the jangling beat of a tambourine from one of the churches close by" (420). Cityscapes includes a variety of sounds, several of which Baldwin seeks to harness in "Sonny's Blues." Despite hearing these sounds beyond the house, the narrator adds, "it's real quiet in the room," suggesting a level of separation or division between the streets and their home (420). Baldwin uses the home as a barrier of protection—a small space or world unto itself.

Apartment buildings, particularly a room on an upper floor, also offer special lines of sight in the story. From the perspective of an apartment, characters can peer down at activities taking place on the street. The narrator notes, "On the sidewalk across from me, near the entrance to a barbecue joint, some people were holding an old-fashioned revival meeting" (428). Among all the people on the sidewalk, he notices, from high above, his brother as he "started across the avenue, toward the house" with "a slow, loping walk, something like the way Harlem hipsters walk, only he's imposed on this his own half-beat." The view from above grants the narrator another perspective on Sonny. From afar, the movements of the younger brother appear in a different light: "I had never really noticed it before" (429). So, in addition to descriptions of physical locations providing for distinct views, the outlook from a distinctly urban construction—the high-rise apartment building—opens up new venues for observing the environment.

When Sonny comes into the apartment, he joins his brother at the window as they look down on the Harlem street corner, and both watch the revival. As the revival ends, the narrator notes, "We watched the three women and the lone man walk slowly up the avenue" (429). Looking out the window from above gives Sonny and his brother the chance to consider their neighbors and the street from afar. "All that hatred down there," Sonny observes, "all that hatred and misery and love" (432). The elevated position of the characters establishes the occasion for Sonny's overarching assessment. The high-rise apartment constitutes yet another of the many vantage points that Baldwin makes use of in his panoramic story.

Baldwin's story takes on expansive terrains. His characters move across streets; they take a taxi through Harlem; they go into a high-rise apartment building; and they walk down neighborhood streets. "Sonny's Blues" primarily presents Harlem settings, but one of the most consequential scenes happens in Greenwich Village, outside of Harlem. Near the story's end, Sonny tells his brother, "I'm going to sit in with some fellows in a joint in the Village" and invites his brother to attend a jazz club to hear him perform (429). At first, the narrator is reluctant but then agrees to attend. Traveling outside the familiarity of his neighborhood shifts the social and spatial dynamics of the story up until this point. Even though the narrator is a native of New York City, he is most familiar with his Harlem neighborhood, a place where his brother, Sonny, does not fit and is restless.

The narrator describes the club where Sonny is playing as "the only nightclub on a short, dark street, downtown," where they "squeezed through the narrow, chattering, jampacked bar to the entrance of the big room, where the bandstand was" (432). The club is out of the purview of the main avenue. This locale is seemingly concealed within one of the many locales of the story and city. Yet, those in attendance are accustomed to the environment. The narrator's descriptions stand out because he is unfamiliar with his surroundings as he is navigating through the crowd. For much of the story, the narrator assumes the status of homegrown city dweller, but in the nightclub, he feels out of his element. Being knowledgeable about a city does not necessarily mean one is familiar with all its many facets.

The jazz club constitutes an alternative space within the larger metropolis of New York. Sonny is at home in this environment. "Here, I was in Sonny's world. Or, rather: his kingdom," observes the narrator. "Here, it was not even a question that his veins bore royal blood" (432). Similar to peering down at Sonny from his apartment window, the Village neighborhood gives the narrator a changed perspective on his younger brother. As an outsider character in the Village, out of his comfort zone, the narrator begins to understand Sonny in a way that he was previously unable to do in Harlem. Once in Sonny's world, the narrator begins to understand the motivations of his brother through the music that he hears. After hearing Sonny play, "Freedom lurked around us," he says, and he realizes his brother's music "could help us to be free if we would listen" (434).

In "Sonny's Blues," mobility and positioning matter. Physical movement constitutes an integral feature of the settings as the characters traverse their urban environs in taxis and on foot. Traveling to another environment facilitates the narrator's ability to come to a deeper and more meaningful understanding of Sonny's life as a musician. Only when the narrator decides to attend a jazz club to listen to his brother perform does he understand their dissimilar experiences have shaped both of their lives in profound ways. Apartment windows, in the case of "Sonny's Blues," provide insight into the larger Harlem community and facilitate Baldwin's ability to create panoramic scenes of a city. Only in urban contexts can you create scenes where characters can observe the interactions on a busy street from an elevated vantage point. Overall, "Sonny's Blues" presents worlds within worlds or subterranean, hidden environments. Through Baldwin, we gain views of Black New Yorkers who are a part of, and at times apart from, others in the city.

URBAN SETTINGS AND BLACK MUSIC

Musical environments are important locales for African American in storytelling. Settings like jazz clubs, theaters, and cabarets facilitate the gatherings of homegrown Black people. These settings create abundant possibilities for storytellers to showcase ideas and scenes concerning Black culture, conflicts, crime, and familial memories. Outsiders, with their conspicuous unfamiliarity with nightclubs and related spaces, become a good source of creative tension or unexpected revelation. The narrator of "Sonny's Blues" must take time to understand the properties of a place that is already quite familiar to his brother. Musical environments are important locales for African American storytellers to combine several types of characters and incorporate sensory details related to the sound of instruments and even singing. These scenes are distinctive because they allow for writers to focus on the central conflict regarding a small group of characters while also emphasizing the musical performance taking place.

The jazz club in Greenwich Village in "Sonny's Blues" connects two distant siblings, and Tracey Sherard explains that the story "deals not only thematically with the cross-roads between the blues and jazz but addresses the need for a new form of cultural narrative as a repository for the experiences of African Americans." She continues, "the 'blues' Sonny plays are a commentary on the historical context and function of the blues Baldwin suggests are inadequate to convey the 'sad stories' of urban Harlem."[7]

For generations, writers have highlighted the invigorating power of Black music. Poems by Langston Hughes, Sterling Brown, Jayne Cortez, Sonia Sanchez, Michael Harper, and dozens more have illuminated music and musicians. Novels by James Weldon Johnson, Gayl Jones, Toni Morrison, and many others have also underscored the interconnectedness of New York City and Black music.

What stands out when we take geo-tagging into consideration is how musical scenes showcase groups of people together. For Hurston's southern settings, the porch serves as a key place where Black people gather. In urban environments, clubs, dance halls, bars, and cabarets offer a variety of social settings that prominently feature music. Stories by Rudolph Fisher, Henry Dumas, and Amiri Baraka, in addition to Baldwin's, showcase the convergence of music and locations. These writers use New York City settings, or the nearby Newark in Baraka's case, to present scenes showing the transformative power of music.[8] Moreover, these stories reveal the gathering power of these spaces and how musical settings bring together an array of characters. These writers incorporate musical settings into their stories to diversify views of the city and thus highlight music as an integral part of urban short fiction.

The configuration of musical settings creates opportunities for writers to draw on and incorporate an array of topographies into the story. The crowded nature of the nightclubs prompts writers to present background characters in their stories. Musicians and club patrons populate the settings, where music is being played and songs are being sung. These nightclubs are key settings for some of the major ideas that writers want to present. Of course, while reading, we do not actually hear music. Still, the clubs give the writers opportunities to stage dramatic action.

Two of Rudolph Fisher's most frequently anthologized stories, "Miss Cynthie" and "City of Refuge," revolve around outsider characters. In both stories, southern transplants come to Harlem, and musical venues serve as crucial settings. The southern character traits inherent in the protagonists are contrasted with the urban music environment. The southern protagonists in both stories go to New York City but take southern cultural beliefs and behavior with them. Fisher utilizes scenes in a cabaret and a theater to draw a contrast between southern-born characters and the sensibilities of the city.

In "Miss Cynthie" (1933), an elderly woman comes to New York from the rural South to visit her grandson, Dave Tappen, whom she raised since he was a young boy. Unbeknownst to her, however, Dave has become a prominent entertainer in New York. One evening, Dave and his girlfriend, Ruth, take Miss Cynthie to the Lafayette Theater. When she sees her grandson dancing on stage, she laments that he has become a "tool of the devil, disciple of lust, unholy prince among sinners."[9] At the close of the show, Dave comes on stage, but before performing his final number, he acknowledges his grandmother as a source of inspiration and attributes his good manners and proper upbringing to her. He closes by singing a song that his grandmother taught him as a child. As a New York City and theater-scene outsider, Miss Cynthie immediately connects to the old southern song.

Miss Cynthie's opinions of the theater highlight her status as a southern outsider. For Miss Cynthie, "the theatre had always been the antithesis of the church" and "the stronghold of transgression" for undesirable and immoral people (104). Her relationship with her grandson, however, makes her reconsider her opinions of his involvement in secular life. Music is a driving force that connects Miss Cynthie to her grandson despite being separated by differences and social customs. The musical setting and geographical origins of Dave's final song make the resolution of the conflict between Miss Cynthie's and Dave's perspectives possible.

Fisher demonstrates how music is embedded with cultural and regional qualities that travel across time and space. He challenges the notion that New York and music automatically lead to a life of sin and degradation. As an outsider, Miss Cynthie is turned off by urban living; however, once she sees Dave perform the song from his childhood, she has a change of heart. Music serves as the connecting point for relatives who would have otherwise been quite distant. Similar to the musical setting for the unnamed narrator in "Sonny's Blues," the theater is where Miss Cynthie finally understands her grandson.

In "The City of Refuge" (1925), Fisher offers another perspective of a southern outsider in a musical environment. In the story, King Solomon Gillis flees North Carolina for Harlem to avoid being lynched. The details are left unclear, but in North Carolina, King Solomon accidentally killed a white man and fears punishment in the Jim Crow South. Upon arriving in Harlem, King Solomon is mesmerized by his perceptions of high-achieving Black people, commenting, "Done died an woke up in Heaven.... Cullud policemans... even got cullud policemans." King Solomon meets Mouse Uggam who plays on the southern outsider's naivety by enlisting him in a drug scheme. In the final scene, King Solomon is in a cabaret and is confronted by police officers for selling drugs. A brawl ensues between him and the officers as he tries to proclaim his innocence. Wrestling three white officers off him, suddenly he becomes transfixed at the sight of a Black officer. He surrenders as he says with a smile across his face, "Even—got—cullud—policemans."[10]

Fisher associates the city's unsavory and undesirable aspects with this particular club setting. The narrator explains that "Even the oldest and rattiest cabarets in Harlem have sense of shame enough to hide themselves under the ground—for instance, Edwards's" (1246). Tom Edwards, the owner, is described as someone "who stands in with the police, with the political bosses, with the importers of wines and worse" (1247). While Fisher does not specify the location of the club, he does offer enough descriptions to indicate that it is in a part of town where respectable people do not venture.

In this story, Fisher details the path to the underground world and offers views of the physical geography of the club setting. "To get into Edwards's," according to the narrator, "you casually enter a dimly lighted corner saloon" and "crouchingly descend a narrow, twisted staircase until, with a final turn, you find yourself in a glaring, long, low basement" (1246). The club is on the fringes and a haven for a discreet culture. After descending the stairs, "You see men and women seated at wire-legged, white-topped tables, which are covered with half-empty bottles and glasses," and "a tall brown girl is swaying from side to side and rhythmically proclaiming that she has the world in a jug and the stopper in her hand" as a "white-vested waiter hustles you to a seat and takes your order" (1246–47). The storyteller, likely a homegrown patron of the place, is quite familiar with the people who frequent this nightclub.

Fisher uses the narrator to describe the actions of various background characters, thereby providing a framework for the interactions in this club setting. The narrator describes seeing musicians—"a cornetist, and a drummer on a little platform at the far end of the room"—and hearing music as "The song's tempo becomes quicker; the drum and the cornet rip out a fanfare, almost drowning the piano" (1246–47). The narrator describes lyrics of the entertainer's song as "issuing an ultimatum to all sweet mammas who dared to monkey around her loving man" as "her audience was absorbed and delighted" (1248). The place and people that the narrator describes are out of view of the general public. Only the homegrown patrons have access. The fictional musical setting creates an opportunity for Fisher to bring together sensory details—sounds and sights—associated with a cabaret environment. He captures a historical social moment by incorporating contrasting types of music venues in his stories. Overall, Fisher illustrates the variety of settings where people might encounter music in New York such as the theater and cabarets.

Fisher's stories anticipate future writers like Baldwin and Henry Dumas who present memorable scenes where people gather to listen to music. For Baldwin and Dumas, musical venues serve as gathering places where people heal or make connections to loved ones. Dumas extends the practice of using a musical setting to emphasize the differences between characters. His story "Will the Circle Be Unbroken," set in New York City, incorporates a nightclub to dramatize the powerful effects of Black music. Dumas's story, which first appeared in *Negro Digest* in 1966, focuses on three white characters—Jan, Ron, and Tasha—who are trying to make their way into a Harlem jazz club to hear famed musician Probe Adams play. The doorman has forbidden their entrance and informs the outsider trio that it is for their own safety that they are not admitted to the club as he points to a sign that reads, "We cannot allow non-Brothers because of the danger involved with extensions."[11] Ever persistent, Jan sees an Irish police officer walking down the street and enlists his help to get into the club by suggesting that the doorman is discriminating against them and not allowing them entrance based on their race. After earnest attempts to keep the group out, the doorman finally succumbs to the advances of the group and police officer.

In the club, Probe begins to fall into a trance as he plays his rare saxophone for the audience. His instrument is one of "only three afro-horns in the world," which "were forged from a rare metal found only in Africa and South America" (89). The music is characterized as Black at its core as "Inside the center of gyrations is an atom stripped of time, black. . . . They are building back the wall, crumbling under the disturbance" (90). The music and, more specifically, the sounds emanating from Probe's horn knock the three white patrons into an unconscious state and ultimately kill them. The members of the audience learn, "It's true then. It's true" (91). Apparently, the belief that the sound could be fatal to "non-Brothers" was confirmed by the death of the white patrons.

Dumas's story attests to the tremendous power of Black music in urban settings. The story also highlights the view that there are indeed insiders and outsiders, this time indicating that music affects Black and white people in dissimilar ways. The nightclub represents a specific space where Black people can enjoy themselves without influences and pressures from a white world. For the Black people inside the club, the gathering and music provide them with freedom from Eurocentric standards that limit their historical and social awareness of Black culture. Probe and others in attendance see the club as a liberating physical and cultural space that is exclusively for Black patrons.

Moreover, they do not have to accommodate white people. The club is an important, exclusive space where Black music and people thrive.

The all-Black jazz setting highlights cultural differences that cannot be interrupted or comprehended by outsiders, in this case non-Black people. The main white character, Jan, cannot understand "why the cats would want to bury themselves in Harlem and close the doors to the outside world" (656). As a jazz critic, Jan thinks Probe and other Harlem musicians should welcome the exposure offered by majority white audiences. But no, they are unwanted.

Echoing Fisher and Baldwin, Dumas makes music central in his story. According to Lorenzo Thomas, Dumas's story is set during a time in the 1960s when "avant-garde jazz musicians were talking about 'separating' from white America," and he explains how Dumas uses "jazz as a discourse able to visit retribution for the wrongs this society has perpetrated upon Black people."[12] The all-Black setting becomes even more important as a physical space outside the purview of the white world. The impressions the music makes upon the audience can only be understood and experienced along racial lines. Dumas uses a jazz club as the main setting and "as a metaphor for an unblemished and inviolable essence," Linda Dittmar has explained.[13] For the white characters in the story, the consequences of integrating this club are deadly.

Dumas's story also responds to the prevalence of white critics' misinterpreting and misrepresenting jazz music during the 1960s. In his essay "Jazz and the White Critic," Amiri Baraka notes that "Most jazz critics have been white Americans, but most important jazz musicians have not been."[14] He explains, "The major flaw in this approach to Negro music is that it strips the music too ingenuously of its social and cultural intent" and "seeks to define jazz as an art (or a folk art) that has come out of no intelligent body of sociocultural philosophy" (139). Dumas utilizes the short story form to critique white jazz critics and white jazz listeners. At the same time, his story advances cultural nationalism by indicating that Black music contains messages for Black ears only. The story advances the notion that a distinct cultural space is important for the development of Black consciousness.

In his essay "The Changing Same (R&B and New Black Music)," Baraka suggests that Dumas's story most likely influenced his own story "The Screamers" (1967).[15] Baraka's story takes place in his hometown of Newark, New Jersey, and highlights the idea of Black music as transfixing and revolutionary, notably in an urban environment. The story opens as the unnamed protagonist sits in a jazz club waiting on famed musician Lynn Hope to perform.[16] After being moved by the spirit and impulse of the music, Hope's band members leave the stage and take off marching in the streets as "Five or six hundred hopped up woogies tumbled out into Belmont Avenue."[17]

Initially, the narrator is experiencing an internal conflict that puts him at odds with his immediate environment, making him an outsider. By falling in line with the other people at the club, the power of music leads him to find a home within the group. The narrator begins to feel a sense of belonging and starts to feel a familiarity with his environment akin to that of a homegrown character. The experiences at the club, particularly the music, prompt the narrator to break free of invisible class barriers that restrict his identity as a Black man. While the music in Dumas's story leads to the deaths of white patrons, the music in Baraka's story inspires Black jazz club patrons to pursue revolutionary action.[18] The protagonist of "The Screamers," energized by the performance and defiance, "then fell in line behind the last wild horn man, strutting like the rest of them" since "the thing they wanted was right there and easily accessible" (176). The "thing" the protagonist refers to is freedom from Eurocentric values along with the joy of being Black together. The actions of the protagonist and others in the audience represent a cultural awakening in which the music gives them the courage to defy Eurocentric expectations of decorum and express themselves through screams and chants. Moreover, after the protagonist transforms from an outsider to a homegrown character, the story also confirms that Black music has the ability to break down social barriers. The musical setting creates an opportunity for the protagonist to forge deeper and more meaningful bonds with his Black peers.

The club setting of "The Screamers" becomes even more significant as we consider spaces where Black music can blossom. Music has a transformative effect on the characters and makes them move and come out of hidden or private spaces. The narrator describes jazz as a vehicle for liberation. He explains, "the sound itself became a basis for thought, and the innovators searched for uglier modes" as it "spread like fire thru the cabarets and joints of the black cities" (174). He describes his experiences in the club as so galvanizing and rousing that "We screamed and screamed at the clear image of ourselves as we should always be. Ecstatic, completed, involved in a secret communal expression" (176). Hope's performance signals a return to the fuller self for the audience members and disregard for rigid middle-class American values. As Hope and his band nurture the souls of the crowd through music, soon this club setting cannot contain the spirit and energy of the people.

In this space, music becomes a vehicle to awaken the consciousness of the homegrown narrator and club patrons. Patrick Burke contends that Baraka's story "highlights both the sense of power and release that audiences can find in screaming" and the "fights for control of urban public space that often occur in response."[19] Once the club patrons spill out into the street, the narrator of the story says that "The paddy wagons and cruisers pulled in from both sides, and sticks and billies started flying, heavy streams of water splattering the marchers up and down the street" (176). Within the physical space of the club, the music and the patrons were contained and did not mix with the outside world. Once in the street, however, they posed a threat, at least from the perspective of law enforcement.

The presentation of music in short fiction by Fisher, Dumas, and Baldwin highlights the interplay between space and culture.[20] Music serves as a connector to racial and regional expressions.[21] Consequently, these types of settings attest to a writer's creative possibilities in using music, especially in adding sensory details to the story. Writers typically use dialogue in their stories; but, with these musical settings, they also describe the sounds of instruments and visions of patrons. The writers position their protagonists within settings where large groups of people are gathered to socialize with one another while listening to popular Black music.

In short stories, settings are usually contained to only the main characters. Rarely do writers emphasize the background characters in a pronounced manner. These stories by Baldwin, Fisher, Dumas, and Baraka, however, focus their attention on the main characters as well as the musical performers. The writers produce split scenes of sorts by focusing on the main plot unfolding with the story's protagonist and also offering details about actions taking place in the background, which happen to be on the main stage. The presentation of nightclub scenes allows writers to show an alternative environment that displays insider and outsider characters in the same setting.

NEW YORK CITY AND BLACK GIRL PROTAGONISTS

Like Baldwin though more than a decade younger, Bambara is another short fiction author who became one of the most widely anthologized "new" Black writers. Bambara began publishing in the 1950s while in college; however, during the 1960s, her writings began to gain wider notice. In 1964, her story "Mississippi Ham Rider" appeared in the *Massachusetts Review*, and in 1966, her story "The Hammer Man" appeared in *Negro Digest*. "Since that time," said Bambara, "the publishing has been fairly steady"; "I've gotten a lot of stories in school readers, put out by major publishing houses, and the books have been taken very quickly."[22] Her publishing activities during this period definitely became more pronounced. She served as the book reviewer for the *Liberator*, a New York City-based magazine, from 1966 until 1972; edited two anthologies, *The Black Woman* and *Tales and Stories for Black Folks* (1971); and released two collections of short stories, *Gorilla, My Love* (1972) and *War of the Walls* (1976). The opportunities she secured in the 1970s as a rising literary artist raised her visibility. Bambara's high visibility among Black women writers heightened the chances that her work would come to the attention of editors preparing anthologies.

Three of her most popular stories—"Raymond's Run," "The Lesson," and "Gorilla, My Love"—come from her 1972 collection, *Gorilla, My Love*, and feature homegrown Black girl characters as the protagonists. Her stories do not include dramatic acts of violence like stories by Hurston, Wright, and Ellison. There are also no intense scenes of interracial or intraracial conflict. Instead, Bambara's stories place smart and confident children at the center of unfolding events in New York City. Her narratives focus on knowledge-building events, while demonstrating the developing social consciousness of Black child characters.

"Raymond's Run," a popular story by Bambara, first appeared in *Tales and Short Stories for Black Folks* in 1971. The story is about a young girl named Hazel Elizabeth Deborah Parker, known as Squeaky, a native of Harlem. Squeaky's life is defined by her two major tasks: caring for her autistic and slightly older brother, Raymond, and being the fastest runner in her age group. Squeaky attends a May Day race determined to keep her title as the fastest runner. In running the race, Squeaky notices Raymond ran alongside her with a very polished form and technique, leading her to think: "I've got a roomful of ribbons and medals and awards. But what has Raymond got to call his own?"[23] After the announcer proclaims Squeaky the winner, she smiles sincerely at her rival Gretchen, because when it came to running, Squeaky thinks, "she's good no doubt about it" and "maybe she'd like to help me coach Raymond" (43). Bambara's story offers a moment of insight from the perspective of a Black child protagonist.

Squeaky's capacity to navigate her Harlem neighborhood makes geographic markers such as landmarks and cross streets an essential feature of this story. Squeaky's ability to travel throughout her neighborhood alone contributes to her independence. In all the top anthologized short stories by African American writers, Squeaky is the only Black girl who displays so much physical mobility. Bambara in fact presents one of the few Black girls in frequently republished short stories by major writers. Squeaky notes the specific routes she takes throughout the story as well as her comfort level, remarking how she strolled "down Broadway toward the ice man on 145th with not a care in the world," and she mentions her "high-prance down

34th Street" (37, 34). Her movements around the busy neighborhood and streets are notable given that she is a third grader.

"Raymond's Run" also creates an important opportunity to consider the uncommon occurrence, at least in short fiction, of a Black girl exuding the confidence and ability to navigate city streets alone and to care for her autistic brother. Squeaky explains, "I'm standing on the corner admiring the weather and about to take a stroll down Broadway" (33). At the same time, she is attentive to her brother. She has "Raymond walking on the inside close to the buildings" just in case he starts thinking "he's a circus performer" and that "the curb is a tightrope." Aware of his "fits of fantasy," Squeaky is preemptive and keeps Raymond safe while freely navigating her Harlem neighborhood. As a caregiver to Raymond, Squeaky has a familiarity with her environment that is evidenced in her homegrown nature and attests to her maturity.

With Squeaky, Bambara creates an extraordinary, confident-talking, homegrown Black city girl who boasts about her athletic abilities. At several points in the story, she makes clear that "I'm serious about my running," "I'm the fastest thing on two feet," and "I always win cause I'm the best" (36). Squeaky is a competitor who really believes in her skills. As a result, her language is bold and somewhat cocky, and her demeanor leads to clashes with her peers. Bambara illustrates how the socialization of young urban girls sometimes places them at odds with each other because of their tough or overly confident demeanor. Oftentimes overlooked, Black girls' coming of age experiences appear in very few stories that circulate in anthologies on a regular basis. Bambara, taking on the persona of a Black girl, offers an alternative to frequently anthologized stories that typically feature adults. Squeaky's inner musings shed light on how impressions of her urban home environment shape her interactions with other girl characters.

Through Squeaky, Bambara offers social commentary about conflicts among women and how those conflicts begin as young girls. When other girls in the story challenge Squeaky's ability as a runner, she becomes competitive. She takes time to offer reasons about the tension between girls, noting that "Girls never really smile at each other because they don't know how and don't want to know how and there's probably no one to teach us how cause grown-up girls don't know either" (36). Squeaky is introspective and observant about her environment, evidenced by how her dialogue is reflective about interactions with characters in the story.

Another Bambara story, "Gorilla, My Love," also focuses on a homegrown Harlem native, this one named Hazel. The girl is riding in a car coming back from an unidentified location in the South after "pecan haulin" with her Grandfather Vale, her younger brother, Baby Jason, and her uncle, Hunca

Bubba.[24] In the car, Hunca Bubba shows off a picture of his girlfriend, and Hazel becomes upset when she realizes she is not the most important female in her uncle's life. She calls Hunca Bubba "a lying dawg" and reminds him that he once told her that he would marry her when she got older (30). Hazel begins to cry, prompting her little brother to also cry. The story ends with Hazel thinking she and her little brother "must stick together or be forever lost" since "grownups playin change-up and turnin you round every which way so bad. And don't even say they sorry."

"Gorilla, My Love" operates as a story within a story to show how physical mobility of a young Black girl contributes to her geographic awareness and social competency. Bambara incorporates a flashback to a time Hazel traveled to a neighborhood theater with her brothers to see a film, *Gorilla, My Love*, without adult supervision. In this movie setting, Bambara shows how Hazel came to be so distrustful of adults after a different film, *King of Kings*, about the life of Jesus, plays instead (24). All of the children began to "go wild" and begin "Yellin, booin, stompin and carryin on" (23). Hazel confronts a manager and demands a refund because she is "really furious cause I get so tired of grownups messin over kids just cause they little and can't take em to court" (26). After the manager disregards her, she sets fire to the candy stand, which leads to the theater being closed for a week. She says that "even gangsters in the movies say 'My word is my bond,'" which leads her parents to assume the theater was wrong for misleading the patrons (27). Bambara portrays Hazel as being wise and assertive, demonstrating how growing up in an urban environment reinforces her confident disposition.

Hazel's awareness of her surroundings contributes to her status as a homegrown character in New York City. Before traveling to the theater, Hazel runs down a list of theaters that come to mind. She explains that they did not go to "the Dorset" because it did not have any new movies they had not seen (23). They cannot go to the "RKO Hamilton" since it was closed while "readying up for the Easter Pageant that night." She mentions the "Regun" and "Sunset," but says they cannot go there since those theaters are "too far" and the children didn't "have any grownups with us." Hazel's familiarity with the movie theaters suggests her in-depth knowledge as a city dweller. Finally, Hazel says, "we walk up Amsterdam Avenue to the Washington and *Gorilla, My Love* playin.'"

Beyond displaying information about the preferred movie theater, Hazel gains a larger perspective riding in the car coming home from picking pecans. In the car, she sits in the front seat with her grandfather, while her brother and uncle are in the back. Her grandfather calls anyone sitting in the front passenger seat "Scout" since he or she has to help navigate. In the front seat, Hazel has to look at "the roads and signs," so when her grandfather says, "Which way, Scout," she could "say take the next exit or take a left or whatever it is" (22). She is also responsible for reading the map to guide her grandfather, thus highlighting her navigational expertise. It is common to speak of literacy and the practice of reading books in African American literature. Bambara instills her character Hazel, though, with a keen sense of geographic literacy.

In "Gorilla, My Love" and "Raymond's Run," Bambara focuses on young people in environments with which they are familiar, but in "The Lesson," the children characters travel outside of their home environments. Miss Moore, a retired schoolteacher living in the neighborhood, attempts to educate the protagonist Sylvia and her group of friends on socioeconomic and political ideas by visiting the famous toy store FAO Schwarz at 767 5th Avenue in New York City. Observing the upper-class people on Fifth Avenue walking around in fur coats in the summer, Sylvia thinks, "White folks crazy."[25] In the toy store, the children notice a boat that costs $1,000, and Sylvia thinks to herself, "Who are these people that spend that much. . . . What kinda work they do and how they live and how come we ain't in on it?" (103). This setting, an upscale toy store, prompts engaging, thoughtful questions from Black children.

When Miss Moore looks directly at Sylvia and asks, "Anybody else learn anything today?," Sylvia does not respond and walks away. She is resistant to the teachings of Miss Moore; however, the trip to the toy store sparked her thinking. By the story's end, Sylvia realizes she has a lot to consider based on visiting a wealthy location on Fifth Avenue as she lags behind her friends in order to "think this day through" (105). Sylvia had participated in a notable educational experience in which a visit to a toy store served as the basis for building consciousness about wealth disparities.

In Harlem, Sylvia is quite familiar with her environment and is self-assured, but a trip to FAO Schwarz, an unfamiliar place in the city, disrupts her views. In a wealthy setting, she feels like an outsider. In this instance, being connected to a given environment goes beyond an awareness of the physical landscape and social customs. Sylvia is not acquainted with Fifth Avenue and the income disparities that exist in the city. Bambara accentuates these issues by showcasing the limited knowledge of her homegrown character. Some things are simply beyond her reach.

This story directly connects issues of economic prosperity and disparity in urban spaces. More so than the frequently anthologized stories set in New York City by other Black writers, Bambara's "The Lesson" deals with wealth disparities in an overt manner. No other story by Big 7 writers incorporates so many words directly related to money. Collectively, terms such as "money," "cents," "price," "dollars," "store," "buy," "costs," and "spend" appear more than forty times in "The Lesson."[26] The preponderance of terminology related to capital demonstrates Bambara's concern with costs and commodities in New York City. Short story writers have focused on characters' navigating the physical terrains of given settings; but Bambara extends this practice by showing how wealth can give rise to a high-end toy store, which is an oddity for Sylvia and her peers. Becoming aware of FAO Schwarz prompts Sylvia to think about the limits of her knowledge and experience. The trip exposes Sylvia to new ideas related to economics and shows her how spaces are embedded with class politics. Undoubtedly, these factors influence characters' actions from one setting to another.

Miss Moore in "The Lesson" is a rare homegrown figure in well-known African American short stories. Miss Moore works to raise consciousness about wealth inequality with a group of children in a Harlem neighborhood. She takes her pupils to a toy store in the city to make them aware of the disparities between Black and white people and, just as important, between low-income and wealthy people. Southern fiction usually affirms that white characters command power, but rarely do writers offer a sense of the specifics such as people in this story who can afford $300 microscopes, $480 paperweights, and $1,195 toy sailboats (99). Miss Moore facilitates these discoveries among her young neighbors and in the process seeks to extend their worldview. She makes the children aware of the costs associated with different parts of New York by connecting them to physical terrains outside of their working-class neighborhoods.

The scholarly discourse on African American literature regularly highlights the involvement of men characters in formal political conversations and activities.[27] Bambara, however, presents an unlikely figure to highlight political economy. In "The Lesson," a retired Black woman, Miss Moore, serves as the impetus for considerations of wealth disparity and the vast gulf between rich white people and low-income Black children. Furthermore, Bambara's story illustrates the significance of intergenerational relationships—showing how an elder homegrown figure introduces knowledge to youth, who are native to a city but unaware about aspects of its environments. Therefore, on the one hand, "The Lesson" highlights wealth inequality in a major city, while at the same time the story shows the possibility of an urbanite passing knowledge on to Black youth in her community.

New York City, one of the financial capitals of the world, proved to be an ideal setting for bestowing vital lessons on Black children. Their field trip to a place that seemed a world away from their familiar neighborhood was nonetheless in their home city. The children began learning about disparities between Harlem streets and Fifth Avenue. They discovered that a toy store could also serve as a classroom. Miss Moore, a nonconventional teacher, showed the importance of introducing young African American pupils to a political education in FAO Schwarz, of all places.

The countless fascinating locales in New York City provide writers with invaluable geographic elements to produce compelling short fiction. Considerations of drug use, peer and sibling rivalries, musical influences, and economic disparities across different neighborhoods in the city allow Bambara and Baldwin to enhance the complexity and narrative tension in their stories. They situate their compositions in a variety of settings, including street corners, public parks, taxi cabs, movie theaters, apartment homes, and a toy store. Taken together, the diversity of settings in Bambara's and Baldwin's northern short fiction outnumbers the locales presented in southern stories by Chesnutt, Hurston, Wright, Ellison, and Walker. New York City apparently gave these Black writers abundant sites, routes, and smaller environments within the larger cityscape to explore.

Homegrown city dwellers serve as critical vehicles for traversing the metropolis in short fiction by Bambara and Baldwin. The protagonists navigate streets with confidence and describe locations in their immediate environment with ease. The sense of place and knowledge of physical environments possessed by the characters are integral to the quality and quantity of geotagging that takes place in the stories. The widespread circulation of Baldwin's "Sonny's Blues" and Bambara's "The Lesson" contribute to the important presence of urbanites in African American literature. In those stories, New York City is the central locale. The most extensive treatments of Black city dwellers in short fiction, however, appear in works by a writer whose stories are set in Washington, DC, to be explored in the next chapter.

Chapter 5

UP SOUTH

Geo-Tagging DC and Edward P. Jones's Homegrown Characters

Cultural geo-tagging occurs naturally for Edward P. Jones. In June 2016, Jones had barely taken his seat for dinner, and he was describing his movements across the city. He, Maryemma Graham, and I were at the Old Ebbitt Grill in Washington, DC, and in casual conversation he was charting out routes the way he has done so thoroughly in his short stories. He spoke of traveling to the restaurant, of standing at 13th and G Streets, of walking along 15th Street to his destination. He pointed out that the building we were in had once been a theater long before becoming a restaurant. He described memories from his childhood and explained how he visited this location to see a movie. As he looked up and down at the tall ceilings, it was evident that he was thinking about the transformation of the space. If this is what Jones is like during his down time, it's no small wonder that his cultural cartography is so pronounced when he is at work producing short stories.[1]

Poet Sterling Brown (a DC native), Paul Laurence Dunbar, Alice Dunbar-Nelson, Langston Hughes, Zora Neale Hurston, Georgia Douglass Johnson, and Ta-Nehisi Coates are among the most well-known Black writers who lived in the nation's capital at some point in their lives. Still, New York City and the South are discussed far more. Thus, Jones's short stories create new opportunities for thinking about literary representations of DC. More important, he offers possibilities for considering extensive representation of a single city through the production of twenty-eight short stories.

Jones, who covers neighborhoods that are largely occupied by Black people in the nation's capital, charts Washington, DC's cultural geography. Jones preserves and extends the tradition of African American short stories. On the one hand, his stories demonstrate a connection to his literary predecessors, as he presents homegrown characters, southern migrations, intraracial violence, and AAVE dialogues. At the same time, he breaks new ground, offering original contributions to the realm of African American short stories. There are few, if any, series of compositions by a single short story writer that present such a meticulous map and treatment of where and how Black residents live in a city. In his stories, Jones incorporates references to more than 250 landmarks and residences. He documents streets and travel routes as numerous pedestrian characters navigate the city. The abundance of place references in his stories is quite extraordinary.

Geographic descriptions are integral to Jones's portrayals of homegrown characters. Where his characters live, travel, and spend leisure time is linked to their depictions. The varied settings inform the story's plot as Jones shows characters interacting with the physical terrain of the District. Whether a person walks, takes a taxi or train, or drives a car, Jones is especially attuned to navigation, demonstrating how the movements of characters in environments facilitate their experiences. Jones's identifying several DC-specific settings in a single story signals his interest in the geographies of his city.

The first section of this chapter surveys the place referencing in his collections, *Lost in the City* and *All Aunt Hagar's Children*. A consideration of the residences, neighborhoods, and varied locations in Jones's stories reveals the significant geo-tagging he enacts in his work. The second section illuminates how Jones presents various DC natives to explore cultural and historical dimensions of Black people in the city. The presentation of a large, diverse cast of homegrown characters is a defining feature of Jones's work. The third section highlights the centrality of DC as a setting by analyzing two of his interconnected stories, "Young Lions" and "Old Boys, Old Girls."

READING SHORT STORIES WITH A MAP

In a review of *All Aunt Hagar's Children*, John Harrison takes note of the centrality of geography in the stories. "Jones's heavy reference to the street plan of D.C.," he writes, "leads me to recommend having a map of the area handy. Each story traces a journey—planned or unplanned, taken or failed—and an obvious root/route symbolism runs throughout the collection."[2] Jones shows his familiarity with the layout and design of the city in his stories. Washington is administratively divided into four quadrants of unequal size (Northwest, Northeast, Southwest, and Southeast) with the US Capitol building at the center of the four dividing lines. Streets run east and west, north and south, as well as diagonally. Lettered streets run east-west, numbered streets run north-south, and diagonal streets have state names.[3] In addition to reading Jones's stories with a map, what can be really rewarding is to cover his short fiction with an awareness of locales and settings in the city. With that awareness, it becomes clear just how Jones meticulously geo-tags Black sectors of DC in his body of work. The cumulative place-based details in his stories reflect the richness and multidimensionality of Jones's capabilities as a writer-storyteller.

Jones became motivated to compose narratives about Washington, DC, based on what he viewed as a lack of knowledge about the city. In an interview with Dan Rivas, Jones explained, "I was in college and was shocked at the ignorance of my fellow students about life in D.C. They knew only that it was the seat of government." Commenting on his first collection of short stories, *Lost in the City*, Jones continued, "The stories, over two decades, came with my effort to set the record straight. D.C. is a place of neighbors where people do good and bad things to each other, just as they do in Dubuque and Seattle and Worcester." Jones was interested in presenting stories about a world that was racially segregated from others: "We lived in a black world and had little to do with white people in the rest of D.C."[4]

Not surprisingly, given his interests, Jones geo-tags numerous streets and landmarks in order to present views of the District beyond governmental and national politics. Taken together, his stories constitute one of the most outstanding, data-rich treatments of places and spaces in the history of African American literature.

The Northwest quadrant is a primary focus for Jones. He makes nearly two hundred place-based references to locales in this area of the city, contributing to the enormous cultural geo-tagging within the stories. He presents characters either living in or passing through Shaw, Franklin Square, and Mount Vernon Square—all places situated in this one quadrant. Northwest is the largest of the four quadrants and includes many notable DC landmarks such as the National Mall and Smithsonian Museums as well as institutions of higher learning such as Howard and Georgetown universities. The quadrant includes Fifth to Eighth Streets, and New Jersey and New York Avenues, and M Street and North Capitol. By mentioning so many well-known and specific places, Jones acts as a cartographer of sorts in his literary mapping of DC. He utilizes these locations and populates them with African American characters not by happenstance. Instead, he composes narratives to deliberately highlight places where African Americans live and interact with each other in the city.

He presents characters navigating the city using cars, taking public transportation, and walking. Consider "The Night Rhonda Ferguson Was Killed," in which Jones covers considerable ground by describing characters navigating the city from the perspective of a car ride. The protagonist, Cassandra, agrees to take Gladys Harper to her father's house in Anacostia, while Melanie and another friend, Anita Hughes, ride along. As they are riding in the car, the narrator references multiple streets and navigational directions: "The birds in their trees continued to make a racket as they turned off 11th onto P Street. Just before 9th, they passed a group moving boxes and furniture into an apartment building across from Shiloh Baptist."[5] Later on, "by the time they reached 8th and H streets Northeast, and after they had crossed East Capitol Street, Cassandra pulled over to ask directions to Anacostia of a young man." The narrator identifies every turn Cassandra takes while also commenting on the sights they see from the car window, such as Cardozo High School, the gas station, and an apartment building.

In "An Orange Line Train to Ballston," the story's protagonist, Marvella Watkins, takes the Metrorail system with her three children, and we witness her directional awareness: "It did not matter if they took the orange line, which ended at Ballston, or the blue line, which ended at National Airport, because both lines, traveling over the same tracks, went past their McPherson Square stop."[6] The narrator references specific stops, adding a level of detail attesting to Marvella's familiarity with her surroundings. Marvella is not just passively taking the train, but instead is quite conscious of her routes.

Jones is especially attuned to geographic details when presenting characters walking. He indicates streets characters walk past, landmarks they see, and local businesses and social venues they encounter. In "The First Day," a young girl narrator describes the excitement of her mother taking her to her first day of school. "We cross New York Avenue, we cross Pierce Street, and we cross L and K," notes the unnamed protagonist. "At I Street, between New Jersey Avenue and Third Street, we enter Seaton Elementary School, a timeworn, sad-faced building across the street from my mother's church, Mt. Carmel Baptist."[7] When the girl's mother arrives and tells the secretary they live at 1227 New Jersey Avenue, she is informed that they "are at the wrong school, that we should be at Walker-Jones," a different school. The knowledge of and references to streets, schools, routes, and landmarks reveal the inclinations of a writer invested in charting the geographies of a city through short fiction.

Pedestrians are crucial to Jones's ability to chart various locations in his stories. In "A New Man," Woodrow L. Cunningham searches for his daughter, Elaine, after she runs away from home after the two have an awful fight. Coming home from work early one afternoon, Woodrow finds Elaine cutting school with friends and smoking cigarettes. Woodrow loses his temper and slaps his daughter. After Elaine runs away, Woodrow and his wife, Rita, canvas the neighborhood on foot, first making a report at the police station on 16th and V Streets, before searching by themselves on U and 10th Streets and Lincoln Park and then returning to their apartment on R Street. They continue their search over several months, taking the train to Petworth and Anacostia to look for her in other neighborhoods around DC.[8] In "Blindsided," after Roxanne Stapleton suddenly loses her sight while riding a city bus, she depends on a stranger to navigate her home safely to her apartment at 1708 10th Street. Without eyesight, Roxanne still "knew the area well" and recalls her surroundings, remembering a liquor store at the corner of Florida Avenue next to her landlord's office, as well as a restaurant at the corner of 14th and S called Swann where she went on a date with her boyfriend.[9] The plentiful references to streets and movements along various routes are dependent on the presence of so many pedestrians in the stories.

For Jones, pedestrians are narrative vehicles, the means of transportation to homes, neighborhoods, stores, downtown streets, and corners. The various descriptions of routes that Jones presents explain how characters directly interact with the physical landscape of the city. In "A Butterfly on F Street," the narrator describes the protagonist's movements, explaining that "Mildred had crossed to the island from Morton's, going to Woolworth's, her eyes fixed upon a golden-yellow butterfly that fluttered about the median."[10] In "Bad Neighbors," a character notices a neighbor "walking alone down 11th Street," and decides to separate from her friends and walk home with him.[11] In "All Aunt Hagar's Children," the unnamed narrator imagines himself coming into a large sum of money after a gold hunting expedition: "I saw myself walking down M Street, strutting about New York Avenue, my pockets bulging with nuggets, big pockets, big as some boy's pockets fat with candy."[12] Perhaps no African American short story writer has been as committed to pedestrians as Jones, as his stories are filled with characters walking and encountering different types of people on the city streets.

Jones does not drive a car and instead walks and takes public transportation. When asked once why he did not own a car, he responded, "I don't want to own anything I can't fold up and bring into my apartment every night."[13] He draws his inspiration and knowledge from living a pedestrian lifestyle in the city. Discussing the sources of his ideas for stories, Jones said, "You don't go to the library and walk along and pick out a topic," but instead, "You are riding the bus, or shopping at Safeway, and all of a sudden the idea comes to you."[14] His personal experiences moving around and closely observing the city influence his artistic outlook. His identity as a DC pedestrian is central to his stories.

For many people, Washington, DC, prompts ideas about the White House, historical monuments, and elected officials. Jones's DC, as Nichole

Rustin-Paschal observed, is "unapologetically a black world with its norms rooted in black culture."[15] Therefore, he includes references to locales and landmarks that carry special significance for Black people, such as Howard University, DC General, Dupont Circle, and Dunbar High School. The uses of recurring sites suggest that the characters and narratives are elements of a larger interconnected production. In this way, each story is like an episode of an overall show or program. The links between individual stories also reveal the artistry of Jones's storytelling. Cultural geo-tagging is one method that he effectively and artfully utilizes common locations to unite his varied stories.

In "The Girl Who Raised Pigeons," "All Aunt Hagar's Children," "The Store," and "Blindsided," for instance, Jones uses the Howard Theatre as a recurring setting. According to NPR's Tim Cooper, the theatre, constructed in 1910, "was the country's first large music venue for black audiences," was then known as "Black Broadway," and hosted entertainers such as "Duke Ellington, Ella Fitzgerald and some of Motown's biggest acts."[16] Characters in Jones's stories walk past the venue, attend concerts, and go on romantic dates there. Incorporating the theatre into stories reflects the practice of including historical landmarks in fiction. But Jones also uses the site as a cultural reference that solidifies the importance of the venue in the day-to-day lives of DC citizens. Jones references the Howard Theatre casually to demonstrate how interconnected to DC this specific site is for Black people living there.

Jones refers to Anacostia, a historic African American neighborhood, in "Common Law," "Lost in the City," "The Sunday Following Mother's Day," and "All Aunt Hagar's Children." In "The Night Rhonda Ferguson Is Killed," as characters are driving through Anacostia, Jones identifies Curtis Brothers' Furniture Store. The store is home of "the Big Chair"—a nineteen-and-a-half-foot replica of a Duncan Phyfe-style chair located at the intersection of Martin Luther King Avenue and V Street, SE. John Muller describes the Anacostia landmark as "a homegrown landmark, out of sight of the monumental core."[17] In "The Store," the unnamed protagonist mentions being a student at Dunbar High School—the nation's first Black public high school.[18] By geo-tagging these and many other landmarks and locales, Jones confirms his interest in documenting the city through literary art.

The stories also identify many residences. In "Young Lions," the narrator notes "Sherman's two-bedroom apartment on 16th Street, a few blocks up from Malcolm X Park."[19] In "All Aunt Hagar's Children," the protagonist mentions his mother moved to a new home, "half a block past North Capitol Street, her first venture into Northeast" (261). In "Bad Neighbors," the Benningtons move in at 1406 Eighth Street, NW, an upwardly mobile African American neighborhood. Their neighbors on the same street are identified by their home addresses as the Staggs living at 1406, the Forsythe family living at 1408, the Palmers living at 1409, and the Thorntons living at 1414. Whereas canonical Black writers like Hurston, Wright, and Baldwin rarely mention specific addresses, Jones is just the opposite. He pinpoints numerous home addresses, and in the process, he displays an attentiveness to where Black people live. Jones's focus on so many exact locations is perhaps unmatched in American and African American literature.

Jones also uses the same residential location in different stories, demonstrating multiple uses for a single setting. Claridge Towers is a recurring setting in "Gospel," "Dark Night," and "Marie" from *Lost in the City* and in "A Rich Man" from *All Aunt Hagar's Children*. In "Gospel," a quartet of women known as the Gospelteers travels around DC to perform at local churches, and the oldest member, "Maude Townsend, a blind woman ... lived at Claridge Towers on M Street Northwest, an apartment house for old people and the disabled."[20] Claridge Towers is the residence of retired senior characters in all of Jones's stories. In "A Rich Man," the narrator points out that, since 1977, the two elder characters "lived most unhappily together for more than twelve years in Apartment 230 at Claridge Towers, a building for senior citizens at 1221 M Street, N.W."[21] The recurring mentions of Claridge Towers and other residences and landmarks give us some sense of locales that are integral to the mapping that Jones does in his stories.

The abundance of homes that appear in Jones's overall body of work is noteworthy. Residential areas comprise the majority of the locations mentioned in his stories. Jones includes eighty-one residential settings across twenty-eight stories. The many mentions show his interest in documenting Black home life in the city and his desire to depict different types of Black neighborhoods and domestic spaces. The varied representations of home life attest to Jones's tendency to focus primarily on diverse and often private locales occupied by African Americans. The high number and assortment of residential settings reflect an effort by Jones to shed new light on the experiences and environments of Black people.

Just as Jones covers an expansive area, he sometimes narrows his coverage to explore a concentrated space. *Lost in the City* begins with "The Girl Who Raised Pigeons," a story that focuses on a young girl named Betsy Ann Morgan and her father, Robert, who attempts to raise her on his own after the girl's mother, Clara, dies giving birth. The events in the story are largely confined to close-knit neighborhoods within walking distance of Betsy Ann's Myrtle Street, NE, apartment. By presenting a confined setting, Jones can offer details about the Myrtle Street community and focus on the concerns and issues that shape the interests of a select group of characters.

Hardly concerned at all with the politics of DC, the children in this story are primarily interested in a neighborhood rumor that "the railroad people were planning to take all the land around Myrtle Street."[22] When the neighborhood children began to argue among themselves, one retorted, "It's a true fact, they called my daddy at his work and told him we could stay, but yall gotta go. Yall gotta" (33). According to Jeremy Dean, "Even as blacks became the majority in Washington, D.C. in the late 1950s, it was African American neighborhoods that were often appropriated for redevelopment and transportation improvement by mid-century urban planners."[23] Similarly, over the course of the story, the Myrtle Street residents are slowly displaced for an urban renewal project. Consequently, as Dean explains, "Myrtle Street cannot be found on a contemporary map of the District. Today, a complex of city and federal buildings occupy the block where Myrtle Street once stood." Jones does more than offer a view of a Black neighborhood. He instead charts important ways that an area evolved or was diminished based on larger, powerful forces.

Flashbacks in "The Girl Who Raised Pigeons" show how aspects of the city have shifted over time as Jones geo-tags notable historical locales. He uses locations as landmarks to contrast the present day with the past. In one instance, the narrator recalls a scene when Robert and his future wife, Clara, were still dating: "Miss Jenny came upon Clara and Robert one rainy Saturday in the library park at Mt. Vernon Square" after having "come out of Hahn's shoe store" and crossed New York Avenue . . . going up 7th Street" (13). Many years later, Betsy is caught stealing at Peoples Drug Store, the very same place on the corner of 7th and Massachusetts, and at that time, "the farthest she had ever been without her father or Miss Jenny or some other adult" (38). Even years after that, Mt. Vernon Park becomes her favorite place—"the same park where Miss Jenny had first seen Robert and Clara together, across the street from the Peoples where Betsy Ann had been caught stealing" (47). That location and businesses to describe the positioning of characters or explain how specific places are located in close proximity to one another serve as recurring landmarks over the course of several years. Familiar locales are integral to people's lives and Jones's stories.

He presents some small businesses as a way of remembering or historicizing places that have since left or changed. Jones incorporates Peoples Drug Store and Hahn's Shoes in other stories, including "The Store," "All Aunt Hagar's Children," and "Spanish in the Morning." Hahn's Shoes was founded in Washington, DC, in 1876 by William Hahn, who opened many stores in the region, including the one on 7th Street. He eventually expanded to sixty-six stores in thirteen states, though in 1995 Hahn's Shoes liquidated its assets after filing for bankruptcy.[24] The mentions of the now-defunct 7th Street location of Hahn's remind some and make others aware that this store was a place where DC residents met and interacted with each other. Jones takes a similar approach by mentioning Peoples Drug, a chain of drugstores that operated for several decades before being bought by CVS Pharmacy in 1994.[25] By referencing Hahn's, Peoples Drug, the DC Armory, Curtis Brothers Furniture Store, Woolworth's Department Store, and other places in DC in his stories, Jones enacts the role of neighborhood preservationist.

The short story writer as neighborhood preservationist means that Jones incorporates an extensive inventory of businesses, parks, subway stops, notable intersections, social venues, and hospitals in the process of composing stories. His catalogue is remarkably reliable since he mentions stores, schools, monuments, and parks that exist or existed. The abundance of establishments that he mentions charts the evolution of DC's geography. For Jones, storytelling presents opportunities for geo-tagging a Washington, DC, that likely did not appear in official tourist guides and maps. Jones is giving recognition to those settings that he is most familiar with, which are also inhabited by large numbers of Black people.

HOMEGROWN DC CHARACTERS

Jones presents an expansive variety of characters in his works. Across twenty-eight stories, he introduces a total of 524 Black characters in his two collections.[26] In some individual stories, Jones presents more than twenty characters. Those are outstanding numbers. The most-anthologized short story writers in this study rarely present more than ten characters in their stories. Jones, by contrast, chooses to populate some of his stories with large numbers of characters.

Dan Rivas argues that Jones is "one of the most brilliant writers living in America today," due in large part to his representation of an "intricate web of characters" and the fact that, at some point, those characters meet "everyone else eventually on the D.C. grid."[27] In the stories, 465 (89 percent) of the total 524 characters are African American. Jones depicts diverse Black characters contending with an assortment of challenges. The quantity and kinds of characters he presents reflect and facilitate his interest in geo-tagging the multiplicity of Black experience in DC.

In Jones's body of work, we encounter Methuselah Harrington, a forty-seven-year-old teacher at the New Day Arising Christian School. There are also the siblings Adam and Elsa Robinson, who live with their grandparents,

Noah and Maggie Robinson, on Independence Avenue in Southeast. Amy Witherspoon, Carlos Newman, Ethel Brown, Billie Montcrief, Betsy Ann Morgan, Ralph Holley, Marvin Watkins, Alvis Watkins, and Marcus Watkins are some of the dozens of children who appear in the stories "Common Law," "The Girl Who Raised Pigeons," and "An Orange Line Train to Ballston." Lydia Walsh is the main character of the title story of Jones's first collection, "Lost in the City." The unnamed veteran depicted in the title story of Jones's second collection, "All Aunt Hagar's Children," works downtown on F Street. There is also Vernelle Wise, a receptionist at the Social Security office at 21st and M Streets, NW. Multrey Wilson and Tony Cathedral are first-degree murderers, serving life sentences in a DC area prison.

Collectively, Jones's short stories constitute one of the most extensive fictional renderings of Black characters living in the nation's capital and arguably any other place. Jones populates his numerous settings with homegrown characters to reveal the range of attitudes among Black people in DC. William Jelani Cobb observed that Jones's stories provide a "wide-angle vision of the African-American citizens" who come from all walks of life and neighborhoods throughout the District.[28] Jones presents characters beyond the narrowly defined world of DC politics by focusing on intraracial conflicts related to love and betrayal, family and children, and even prison and murder. Jones's devotion to homegrown characters enables him to explore areas of his hometown that are outside the purview of most popular portrayals of DC.

He provides the backstories of major and minor characters in order to offer complex or multilayered depictions. Jones has explained that "even if you have one page about a person eating his lunch you should have a history [of that character] in your head."[29] He continues, "Even though you will never ever use it, you should have a history of, well, what he ate for breakfast and what he did the night before, in order to be able to write about him eating lunch." For Jones, a backstory shows how past events contribute to a character's current disposition. Even minor characters, Jones suggests, need backstories or histories. Those backstories will inevitably strengthen the presentation of those characters.

Beyond the quantity of characters, what's remarkable is Jones's ability to present such a diverse array of personalities: children, middle-aged adults, senior citizens, males and females, convicts, attorneys, social workers, busboys, veterans, and teachers. "When you read one story and went on to another one, you wouldn't come across any character you had seen in the previous story," says Jones.[30] He explains that "Every major character, and even most of the minor characters, would be different, so that each story would be distinct from the others. I didn't want someone to come along and be able to say that the stories are taken out of the same bag." From highly educated characters to common criminals, Jones incorporates a range of personalities in his stories and keenly illustrates that diversity of Black people in a central locale.

In "Common Law," Jones chronicles the abuse the protagonist, Miss Georgia, suffers at the hands of her common-law husband, Kenyon, a chauffeur with a drinking problem. The entire neighborhood bands together to protect Miss Georgia. According to Cobb, "The final paragraph is otherworldly, revealing Miss Georgia's fate throughout the rest of her life, giving enormous meaning to the collective act—the common law—of the neighborhood."[31] Jones focuses on several households—children and their parents included—to show the interconnectedness of a single neighborhood. The composition of a story in which neighbors come together to support one of their own facilitates a fairly large number of Black characters interacting.

A defining feature of Jones's short fiction has been his tendency to connect characters across collections. He presents at least one character from the first story in *Lost in the City* again in the first story in *All Aunt Hagar's Children*, and he does so with the second story in the collections, the third, and all the additional stories. In "Lost in the City," the eighth story in the collection, a secondary character, Georgia, reprises her role in "Common Law," which is the eighth story in *All Aunt Hagar's Children*. In "The Store," the fifth story in *Lost in the City*, Penelope "Penny" Jenkins appears in a larger role than in "Aunt Hagar's Children."

One character, Anita Hughes, appears in three of Jones's stories: "The Night Rhonda Ferguson Was Killed" and "The Gospel" in *Lost in the City* and "Resurrecting Methuselah" in *All Aunt Hagar's Children*. Anita is a teenager and secondary character in *Lost in the City*, and she is an adult protagonist when she appears in Jones's second collection. By returning to common characters, he reveals a commitment to them over extended periods of time. Furthermore, the characters represent a kind of continuity between his collections.

Women characters play consequential roles in Jones's stories and are twenty-one of the protagonists of his twenty-eight stories. Jones depicts women characters across a broad age spectrum from young, middle-aged, to elderly. "The Girl Who Raised Pigeons," "The First Day," and "Spanish in the Morning" make young girls the central focus. In "Common Law," "His Mother's House," and "A Butterfly on F Street," the women characters are middle-aged. And, in "Marie," "A Dark Night," and "Gospel," the women are senior citizens. Jones's inclination to represent women characters at different stages in life allows him to further accentuate the diversity of representations in his stories.

In an interview with poet E. Ethelbert Miller, Jones speaks of the influence of his mother and how "a certain cadence . . . a certain poetry" in her language shapes the voices in his short stories.[32] The presence of so many girl and women protagonists in stories by a Black man writer is unusual. By and large, Black women short story writers showcase female characters, while Black men short story writers cast male protagonists. Jones does more than experiment by occasionally presenting a lead woman character. Indeed, women protagonists are the norm in his works.

Girls and women are frequent protagonists in the stories, but Jones relies heavily on males as supporting characters. In Jones's two collections, 270 of his characters are male. He presents a drug dealer, a retired mechanic, a bus driver, a homeless man, a moneylender, a drug addict, a taxi driver, and more. Jones is committed to exploring public spaces in DC. Consequently, he shows men occupying street corners, traveling to and from different neighborhoods, working in downtown and other parts of town, and riding in cars. Men characters are also more likely to be involved in troublesome activities.

In "His Mother's House," even though Joyce Moses is the protagonist, men have more speaking parts. Joyce's son, Santiago Moses, moves his mother from a Northeast neighborhood home into an upper-middle class house in Northwest. Joyce is confined primarily to the Northwest home throughout the story, while the men characters roam throughout the city and are rarely at home. The men are highly mobile and participate more actively in decisive actions. Joyce's son is a drug dealer and supports his mother from the profits of his illegal business. He enlists Rickey Madison, Joyce's common-law husband of six years, to help in this criminal operation.

In this story, Jones dramatizes the tensions between Santiago and Rickey by inserting scenes in which the two men go back and forth verbally. Santiago is unnerved by the relationship between his mother and Rickey. As a result, he uses intimidation tactics to keep Rickey in check. Santiago is constantly chastising his mother's husband, shouting, "Rickey, you can't tell nobody shit!" and "Just do what I tell you and keep your mouth shut."[33] Santiago and Rickey have several disagreements, contributing to the uneven increased dialogue between men and women in the story. Further, the men characters contribute to dramatic action and tension, though the story is about Joyce.

In "Bad Neighbors," Sharon Palmer is the story's protagonist, yet men characters dominate in terms of speaking roles. Women characters contribute to 31 percent of the overall dialogue, while men characters provide

69 percent.[34] In the story, the Benningtons move to Eighth Street, NW, an upwardly mobile African American neighborhood, and immediately, the neighbors "along both sides of the 1400 block of Eighth Street N.W., could see the Benningtons for what they really were" (581). Their new neighbors immediately ostracize them and comment disapprovingly on how they are moving at least twelve people into a three-bedroom home. Over the course of the story, Sharon observes the interactions among her neighbors as conflicts ensue between the Benningtons and primarily the men characters of Eighth Street.

Sharon is the focal point of the story, and the men characters vie for her attention. The narrator explains, "Sharon had, in the eleventh grade, become aware of her effect on boys—almost all of them" (584). Therefore, the actions of the men characters are most pronounced, and they speak more than women in dialogues. Sharon's boyfriend, Terence Staggs, a fellow Eighth Street resident, is a medical student at Howard University and a character foil to Derek Bennington, "a man in his early twenties, a well-built and too often shirtless loudmouth" (583). The two men get into a physical altercation during a crucial scene in which Derek "took but one hit to the lower part of the jaw to send Terence to the ground" (604). The conflict between the two men evidences Jones's proclivity to depict men characters involved in troublesome situations. The extended argument between the two characters leading up to the altercation reveals why male dialogue is so pervasive in the story.

Jones further exemplifies his commitment to portraying a range of characters by incorporating children. Three of his stories, "The Girl Who Raised Pigeons," "The First Day," and "Spanish in the Morning," feature children as the protagonists. In "The First Day" and "Spanish in the Morning" in particular, the children are intently focused on the adults and rarely describe their personal feelings. However, throughout other stories in his collections, children play consequential roles as background characters. In "Adam Robinson Acquires Grandparents and a Sister," Noah and Maggie Robinson take their grandchildren in after their son falls victim to drug addiction. Although the story focuses on Noah's perspective, Adam and his younger sister, Elsa, are also a central focus as their grandparents raise them. In these stories, age plays a role in where a character can travel throughout DC by contrasting children and adult characters. Children are largely confined to the neighborhood, interacting with their peers who live on the same street or in close proximity. Adults tend to accompany children as they are traveling outside of their neighborhoods by walking on foot, taking public transportation, or riding in cars.

Jones adds variation to the speakers in his stories to diversify his character portrayals. According to Aaron Thier, "Upwardly mobile characters in *Lost in the City* and later in *All Aunt Hagar's Children* are keen to speak 'white man's English' and carefully pronounce the g's at the ends of their '-ing' words."[35] By contrast, Jones presents working-class and low-income characters who use vernacular speech. In "Lost in the City," Lydia, an Ivy League-trained attorney, speaks differently from her cab driver, thereby suggesting a social distance between them. While Lydia's pronunciation is in line with Standard English, the cab driver speaks a form of AAVE, stating at different points: "where you goin?," "I ain't allowed to get lost," and "I'm tryin'."[36] These two characters represent different classes of people, but they are both homegrown characters in Jones's work.

Lydia and the cab driver in "Lost in the City" are homegrown and knowledgeable about the various communities within DC. Many of Jones's characters display their intimate knowledge about DC by showing a familiarity with neighborhoods, landmarks, and travel routes. Lydia is so acquainted with her environment that she must deliberately disorient herself. When she calls a cab to take her to the hospital to say her final goodbyes to her mother, she tells the driver, "Just keep on driving and get us lost in the city" (264). The driver "passed the federal buildings along 7th, then the mall and its museums," and "At New York Avenue, he turned right, then left on 5th Street" (265). The driver thinks that he is showing her places she has never seen, but in fact, she grew up all over the city and recognizes all the places the driver shows her. Her high geographic IQ of DC means that she simply cannot get lost.

For Jones, homegrown characters are a crucial mode of transportation for an author looking to move across a single setting and depict its diverse nature. These and several other instances of detailed travel routes attest to how well Lydia and other homegrown characters know the layout of their neighborhoods and city. Most of Jones's characters are native to DC, but some of them occasionally appear detached from their home environment. Lydia wants to momentarily relinquish her connection to DC. With this character, Jones shows a woman outgrowing or seeking to move beyond her home environment.

In the story "All Aunt Hagar's Children," Jones narrates from the perspective of an unnamed twenty-four-year-old narrator who is recently back from the Korean War. This homegrown character becomes restless and desires to leave on a gold-hunting expedition in Alaska. In his mind, going to Alaska will present him with an opportunity to increase his finances and sense of self-worth and to take a much-needed break from DC. At one point, the narrator states, "I was a veteran of Washington, D.C., and there was nothing else for me to discover" (180). He comments on routes he takes as he easily navigates the city and mentions places such as Dunbar High School, Kann's Department Store, and Shiloh Baptist Church. Traveling to the same old places increasingly bores and frustrates him.

In this story, Jones also introduces characters from outside of DC to diversify his representations of types of people living there. The unnamed narrator is tasked by his family—his mother, Bertha; his aunt, Penny Jenkins; and close family friend Miss Agatha—with investigating the murder of a family friend. The three women had migrated to DC from Alabama. One day, when coming back from school in Alabama, a white man tried to take a younger Miss Agatha into the woods and rape her. Her two friends came to her rescue and "picked up rocks and beat the man down to the ground until he was no more than an unconscious lump" (181). Fearful that he will report them to law enforcement once he regained consciousness, the three young women had left Alabama and resettled in DC. In this instance, Jones's backstories explain motivations for characters to make migrations.

The three women in the story are southern natives, and their speech is represented in AAVE. Miss Agatha greets the narrator, telling him that he looks well, so "workin downtown mongst white folks grees with you" (179). She continues explaining how she wants him to help solve the case of her murdered son since "Near bout two years gone by, and they ain't done any more than the day it happened" (180). Jones uses various alternative spellings to represent the speaking patterns of the characters—including abbreviations of words such as "bout" (about) and "wanna" (want to). He also incorporates presumably southern sayings such as "Worries the heart so much," "God knows I don't ask for much," and "It's a shame before God, the way they do all Aunt Hagar's children" (180–81). While his examples are not as extensive as those by Chesnutt, Hurston, or Wright, Jones uses a slight variation of Standard English to emphasize the distinctions of southern speech.

Southern migrants like these three women are often important figures in Jones's stories. In "Blindsided," the protagonist, Roxanne Stapleton, observes a woman on the bus with "a southern accent so thick it insulted Roxanne's ears."[37] Roxanne had moved to DC from Louisiana as a young adult, but the woman sitting next to her on the bus "was much older" and "would probably never speak any other way, as Roxanne had succeeded in doing." In "Adam Robinson Acquires Grandparents and a Little Sister," Noah Robinson "still had the gentlemanly quality of the countrified South about him," despite having moved to DC from South Carolina with his family when he was only seven.[38] Highlighting the southern sensibilities of characters allows Jones to further extend his practice of showing the diversity of his homegrown characters.

THE SAGA OF A CITY-DWELLING BLACK MALE

Lost in the City and *All Aunt Hagar's Children* cover a large number and variety of characters. However, "Young Lions" and "Old Boys, Old Girls," which focus on one protagonist, Caesar Matthews, are particularly important for understanding the remarkable work that Jones does in geo-tagging and tracing the movements of a homegrown Black male character in two stories published over a decade apart. Together, the stories represent one of the most extended and detailed accounts of an African American male in short fiction.

"Young Lions" and "Old Boys, Old Girls" follow Caesar, a native of DC, as he falls into a life of crime and eventually prison. In "Young Lions," Caesar is twenty-four years old and carries a Berretta handgun everywhere he goes, wanting the respect of others even if he must take it by force. Throughout this story, Caesar seems to become increasingly enthralled by committing violent crimes. In "Old Boys, Old Girls," Caesar is on trial ten years later for murder. This story takes place over eight years, with the majority of the action set in the DC area's Lorton Prison and focused on Caesar as he navigates prison life. After his release from prison, Caesar lives a low-key and reclusive life—a significant contrast with his younger self.

A seemingly bad character often gives an author the opportunity to uncover hidden possibilities.[39] In an interview with Maryemma Graham, Jones said, "You look at Caesar Matthews and you think what is there good about a guy like that?"; yet "despite the depravity of every human being, there is something, some kernel or something there can be saved," so "I try to show how there is something meaningful to his existence, no matter who he is."[40] In "Young Lions," Caesar as a young man does not fully understand the gravity and consequences of burglarizing homes and robbing people. In "Old Boys, Old Girls," he has matured and served a prison sentence and begun to consider making amends for the harm he once caused. By remaining with a single character for so long and charting so many of his experiences, Jones works through the processes of a young man first becoming a criminal and then moving toward rehabilitation.

Geographic explorations of the city are important in "Young Lions" and "Old Boys, Old Girls." The stories cover more than thirty locales. The writer-cartographer Jones mentions parks, homes, a bar, a courtroom, a restaurant, a prison, a transitional house, and more in the process of narrating Caesar's life experiences. Caesar is rooted to specific locales across DC, but he represents a varying perspective in comparison to other characters in Jones's stories. Caesar presents the opportunity to consider settings and character types of DC that are underexplored or unexplored.

In "Young Lions," Caesar roams freely around the city. He rarely likes being at home and is always "anxious to be out in the streets" since "there was nothing like an empty apartment to bring down the soul" (101). The narrator describes the movements and frequented locales of a young Caesar. He grew up on French Street, NW, and went to Cardozo High at 1200 Clifton Street. After getting kicked out of his home, he moves in with a friend, Sherman, on 16th Street, NW. He associates with other Black males at Manny's Haven at "Georgia Avenue and Ingraham Street," where he works as a bartender. Then, Caesar robs a man at gun point at "New Hampshire Avenue near the Silver Spring line" (105). As always, the presentation of homegrown characters—that is, characters intimately connected to the local environment—makes it possible for Jones to show figures traversing many places in the story. Characters familiar with the DC environment end up covering a wide range of landmarks, streets, and other locales.

Jones also sheds light on the limits of Caesar's mobility in this story. Caesar "had never come down to the world below Constitution Avenue, except for those times when relatives came from out of town" (144). The narrator continues, noting that Caesar's "mother and father would bring everyone down to see the Washington they put on postcards and in the pages of expensive coffee-table books." Furthermore, "He knew that his father worked in one of the government buildings, but he didn't know which one." Caesar is disinterested in and, in some cases, restricted from visiting all sectors of the nation's capital. He inhabits a DC that is predominantly Black, devoid of national politics, and not pictured in postcards. As a result, with Caesar, Jones is charting terrains that are apparently off the map.

Caesar travels to several places, but the main plot of the story is contained in a central area. After his burglary partner gives up a life of crime and Caesar is in desperate need of money, he concocts a plan to rob a mentally challenged woman with the help of his girlfriend, Carol. For two months prior to the robbery, Caesar follows the woman from a group home where she stays with six other mentally challenged people, as she gets off the bus at K Street to walk to her job at "a French restaurant on Connecticut Avenue near Lafayette Park" (114). He learns that each Friday, after work, she "walked up Connecticut Avenue to Dupont Circle" and "deposited her paycheck at American Security" (115). He moves along Connecticut Avenue, remaining inconspicuous and not drawing attention to himself. As with many of Jones's homegrown characters, Caesar is comfortable moving along DC streets and by public transportation.

Caesar develops a plan to have Carol play upon the sympathy of the mentally challenged woman and tell her a made-up story about her sick son needing $5,000 for an operation. She convinces the woman to empty her savings, and then she steals the money. Afterwards, Carol regrets her involvement with manipulating the woman and begins to cry and withhold the stolen money from Caesar. In response, Caesar attacks Carol and puts a gun to her face, and all of the money spills out of her bag. Carol intends to return the money to the woman as she exits the park, walking away slowly with tears in her eyes. Caesar does not prevent her from doing so, realizing that the bond between them is broken. At the close of "Young Lions," Caesar is uncertain about his future: "There was something in the air, but he could not make out what it was" (137). Jones leaves the story open-ended, not offering a clear indication of what will happen to Caesar.

Jones alternates between the past and the present in the story to provide multifaceted takes on Caesar's experiences. Father figures and older role models play an important role in the main character's development. These older male characters influence the decisions that Caesar makes. When he was sixteen, his father declared, "I gave you more chances than you deserved," before kicking him out of the house (123). This conflict haunts Caesar throughout "Young Lions" and "Old Boys, Old Girls"—a timespan of nearly twenty years. Caesar is hurt and never able to recover emotionally from the conflict with his father. By dramatizing this father-son conflict, Jones suggests one possibility for a young man turning to crime or harboring troubling thoughts.

In "Young Lions," Jones also introduces other characters that served as influences and helped shepherd Caesar into a life of crime. After Caesar's mother died, his cousin, Angelo Billings, stole flowers from an "I Street florist" and took them to the funeral, but Caesar interpreted Angelo's actions as proof that his cousin "loved Caesar's mother as much as he loved anyone" (120). Another figure, Sherman Wheeler, burglarizes homes and eventually enlists Caesar to join him in the crimes. When they first begin working together, Sherman does not like Caesar carrying a gun, and "in their first months together he pulled rank and told him to leave the guns at home when they weren't needed" (105–6). Caesar also occasionally works as a bartender for a widely known criminal, Manny Soto, who runs a fencing business out of his bar. Manny seems to unnerve Caesar and make him uncomfortable. However, Caesar still admires Manny's money and contemplates robbing him. Interacting with various felonious men accelerates Caesar's involvement in a life of crime.

When "Old Boys, Old Girls" begins, Caesar is on trial for the murder of Antwoine Stoddard. However, Caesar cannot even remember whom he killed after he had gotten away with the murder of Percy "Golden Boy" Weymouth. Over the years, Caesar has become an even more troubling criminal. As Jones writes, "The world had done things to Caesar since he'd left his father's house for good at sixteen, nearly fourteen years ago, but he had done far more to himself."[41] The courtroom is a rare setting in African American short fiction. This opening scene serves as a point of reckoning for Caesar where he must come face-to-face with at least some of the harm he has caused and take responsibility for his actions. Up until this point, Caesar "was not insane, but he was three doors from it," as he disassociates himself from all of the crimes he has committed as he has lost a firm grip on reality (132). It is only after the judge sentences him to seven years in prison that he regains a sense of clarity and starts to consciously process how he is being punished directly for the death of Antwoine Stoddard and indirectly for the several other violent crimes he committed that had gone unnoticed.

The majority of "Old Boys, Old Girls" takes place in DC's now-closed Lorton Reformatory, a prison located in nearby Lorton, Virginia. The prison gave Jones an opportunity to present a place occupied by thousands of Black men at any given moment. Prison is another unusual setting in African American short stories. The lives of prisoners typically fall out of the purview of most short story writers, despite the high incarceration rates of Black people in the US.[42] Jones's focus on Black characters in this setting reveals his interest in showing places where Black people really reside. The presentation of a prison constitutes one more instance of Jones showing a side of DC that does not appear on postcards or in coffee-table books. The depiction of multiple prisoners in "Old Boys, Old Girls" expands the range of Black characters who appear in short stories. Jones introduces figures who primarily live their lives behind bars.

In the story, at Lorton, Multrey Wilson and Tony Cathedral take Caesar under their wing. They are acquaintances from Caesar's "Northwest and Northeast days" and are both in prison for first-degree murder, "destined to die there" (133). They encourage Caesar to be violent and assert his dominance over others in order to maintain power and respect in Lorton. Cathedral reminds Caesar, "you can't let nobody fuck with your humanity." He advises Caesar to intimidate his roommate: "Listen, man, even if you like the top bunk, you fuck him up for the bottom just cause you gotta let him know who rules. You let him know that you will stab him through his motherfuckin heart and then turn around and eat your supper, cludin the dessert" (134–35). Caesar obeys and violently attacks his cellmate.

Jones introduces several types of characters in Lorton. Caesar's first cellmate, Pancho, is a recovering drug addict, and his second roommate, Watson Rainey, is a three-time rapist of elderly women. Caesar encounters one of Multrey's prison wives, who is a father outside of prison but inside is a submissive partner, referred to with female pronouns. There is "a part-time deacon who had killed a Southwest bartender for calling the deacon's wife 'a woman without one fuckin brain cell,'" who received the name "the Righteous Desulter" (142). A dead man, or so Cathedral thinks, also makes appearances, to haunt the one who had murdered him. There is a convicted armed robber who becomes an amateur tattoo artist in the prison. The setting of Lorton gives Jones a special opportunity to showcase his knack for introducing a wide variety of Black characters from DC.

African American short fiction rarely focuses on imprisoned criminals. For one reason or another, writers have avoided depicting the lives of incarcerated Black people. Crimes and even murders take place in short stories by Black writers, but the consequences of such acts with respect to the judicial system and incarceration are not presented. Jones covers unfamiliar ground, at least in the context of short stories, by demonstrating the range of personalities that converge in a single prison setting. By portraying interactions among different types of imprisoned men, Jones illustrates the various dimensions of prison and highlights how incarcerated people operate by strict codes of conduct. The writer exercises a degree of freedom by apparently not worrying about whether he will present Black people in a negative light by showing them as such ruthless criminals.

In "Old Boys, Old Girls," when Caesar is released from prison after eight years, he believes "men and women were now speaking a new language, and that he would never learn it" (153). His time in prison was disorienting. Caesar had grown accustomed to solitude and confined spaces at Lorton. Thus, upon his release, he restricts his movements in the city and keeps busy at his job. "He worked as many hours as they would allow him at the restaurant, Chowing Down," and spent the remainder of his time at the movies until the shows closed, and "then sat in Franklin Park, at 14th and K, in good weather and bad" (152).

After his release, Caesar takes up residence in a boardinghouse "in the middle of the 900 block of N Street, Northwest" (151). By happenstance, he encounters a former lover, Yvonne Miller, but she does not seem to recognize or even remember Caesar in part because of her drug addiction. One evening coming home after work, Caesar finds Yvonne dead in her home. The cause is not confirmed, but finally, "he knew that the victim and the perpetrator were one and the same" (167). Presumably, Yvonne died of an overdose. As a final act of kindness, Caesar meticulously cleans her room, brushes her hair, and makes her presentable for whoever might find her body. At that moment, Caesar realizes he "was not a young man anymore" and begins to contemplate his next moves (170).

As he walks outside, the identification of locations and street names increases. To his left "was 9th Street and all the rest of N Street, Immaculate Conception Catholic Church at 8th, the bank at the corner of 7th," while to his right "was 10th Street, and down 10th were stores and the house where Abraham Lincoln had died and all the white people's precious monuments" (172). The two streets available to Caesar offer multiple possibilities. To decide, he flips a quarter, allowing chance to determine his impending journey.

The narrator makes references to Caesar's surroundings as they reconnect to memories of his boyhood home on French Street, convenience stores he remembers on 11th and Q Streets, and general remarks about 9th and N Streets. As he is busy observing people going about the area, Caesar suddenly has an epiphany, and "it came to him, as it might to a man who had been momentarily knocked senseless after a punch to the face, that he was of that world" (172). Caesar realizes that he is "of that world" despite his being reserved and generally antisocial. He recalls an earlier conversation when his younger brother told Caesar "the one giant truth" in this world was that "Daddy loves you. . . . I think he loves you more than us because he never knew what happened to you" (173). Similar to the close of "Young Lions," Jones leaves the story open-ended. This time, however, Caesar's disposition seems more optimistic and hopeful.

Jones uses minor characters to populate his settings and complement the unfolding of events in a given space. In "Young Lions," there are thirty-one characters, and at least twenty of them are minor characters. Sitting in Lafayette Park, Caesar mentions seeing a woman "eating orange pieces from a small plastic bag" and a Black family crossing Pennsylvania Avenue to take pictures at the White House (117–18). In "Old Boys, Old Girls," there are thirty-four characters, and eighteen are minor. The story mentions prison guards, different types of prisoners, and even a mother and son who are residents at the boardinghouse he lives in after prison. Jones rarely expands upon these characters or incorporates the minor roles into significant portions of the story. The minor characters are part of the background and integral to the settings that Jones presents.

A relatively small number of women characters appear in "Young Lions" and "Old Boys, Old Girls." The image of Caesar's mother lingers most prominently in the background. She is never mentioned by name, but her memory is carried through both stories, even in the prison scenes. While in jail, in

"Old Boys, Old Girls," Caesar remembers his mother's birthday and decides to get a tattoo commemorating her memory. He decides to have "the words 'Mother Forever' tattooed on his left bicep" (144). At first, he considers briefly getting Carol's or Yvonne's name tattooed on his arm, but finally decides against it. The abundance of criminal activities in the stories might explain why there are few women. Most of the law-breaking and violent behavior is enacted by Black male characters.

The women who do appear in the stories endure terrible abuse. In "Young Lions," Carol recognizes the coldness in Caesar's heart. When Caesar unleashes a violent attack upon Carol, she is unfazed: "if he beat her with the pistol . . . shot her in the face . . . or through the heart . . . she would not have been surprised" (137). Carol had grown accustomed to Caesar's increasingly violent nature, thus anticipating his further decent into wrongdoing. In "Old Boys, Old Girls," Caesar is not physically abusive to Yvonne. Even still, Yvonne has led a painful life thinking "happiness was the greatest trick God had invented" (133). Caesar's interactions with Carol contrast with those with Yvonne. The portrayals of the two women demonstrate Jones's creative dexterity and ability to create two dissimilar characters at distinct points in Caesar's life. These two characters thus complement Caesar's life transitions over more than twenty years.

In a 2006 NPR interview, Jones described his fascination with exploring the lives of Black characters. He said that many writers begin by focusing on a political or social idea and then creating characters to illuminate those beliefs. His stories, however, "for the most part will be about people, not an idea." He explained that no person was ever born bad and it's up to the writer to "find the moment or moments when that person turned off the good road and went on the bad road." He is interested in telling the stories of people without portraying the group in overly simplistic and troubling ways. As he noted, "When you can find those moments and tell them as detailed as possible, then maybe, maybe you can avoid the stereotype."[43]

Jones's stories about DC counteract stereotypes by presenting dozens and dozens of Black people inhabiting and navigating the nation's capital. The journeys of those homegrown city dwellers depicted in *Lost in the City* and *All Aunt Hagar's Children* expand the maps of African American literary art.

CONCLUSION

On March 12, 2020, I was in Washington, DC, retracing the steps of characters from Edward P. Jones's short fiction. I wanted to take photographs of key settings to complement my discussions of the stories when I returned to my students at the University of Texas at Arlington. There's no doubt that I could have found the locations on Google Earth or other GPS online programs. But navigating those DC streets in person would supply me with much better experiences to share with my students. Plus, I wanted to create a time-lapse video that highlights the shifting landscape of various neighborhoods across the District.

I started on U Street and walked around, like Woodrow L. Cunningham does in "A New Man." I made my way up to Howard University, which is mentioned in "Bad Neighbors," and walked past the Howard University Hospital and Howard University Medical School, where the protagonist Terence Stagg was a student. I passed the Howard Theatre, near the Shaw-Howard Metro station as mentioned in "Blindsided," and walked about half a mile to Logan Circle. I decided to walk over to Claridge Towers, a retirement residence that was home to several characters in stories like "Marie," "A Rich Man," and "The Gospel." From Claridge Towers, I walked about a mile to Dupont Circle, where I ended my day by sitting and watching people pass by, just as Caesar Matthews did in "Young Lions."

Many of the places in DC that Jones describes in *Lost in the City* (1992) and *All Aunt Hagar's Children* (2006) have changed or are no longer there. The Peoples Drug Store, once located at 7th and Massachusetts, as well as Hahn's Shoes at 816 7th Street, both of which appear in several of Jones's stories, have been replaced, and the area is now a complex of city and federal buildings as well as high-rise, luxury apartments, clothing stores, and restaurants. Dunbar High School, mentioned in "The Store" and "Lost in the City," has been demolished and rebuilt twice, first in 1977 and again in 2013, at the same First Street location between N and O Streets, NW. The Woolworths department store on the corner of Park Road and 14th Street,

NW, mentioned in "Butterfly on F Street," has now been transformed into a modern shopping building that houses stores such as Target, Marshalls, Best Buy, and Bed, Bath & Beyond. Despite the many changes, Jones had provided me with wonderful maps and travel routes.

During my travels that day in March, I encountered a variety of people. Some were homegrown city dwellers with extensive knowledge of DC. They were quite familiar with its people and cultures. Others were outsiders—recent transplants from states like North Carolina and Tennessee, cities like St. Louis and Houston, and countries like Nigeria. Still others I interacted with were homegrown outsiders, who had lived in DC, moved away, and then returned after many years to find a city that was not fully the city they remembered.

In this experience, I gained a new perspective on DC and an immense appreciation for Jones's attention to details. Interacting with several DC natives, over a period time, I found that many had intimate connections to the environment. Natives of Anacostia reference the Big Chair, at the corner of Martin Luther King Avenue and V Street, as a symbol of pride for the Southeast community currently undergoing urban redevelopment. In Southwest, the Maine Avenue Fish Market is a cultural landmark and popular destination, where many of my friends regularly go on pleasant days to enjoy crabs at the Wharf. Ben's Chili Bowl is a historic restaurant and tourist destination, but many residents speak admiringly about it as a community gathering spot since opening in 1958. These various locations and landmarks around DC have a rich history and cultural resonance beyond dots on a map. In many ways, I realized, my engagements with African American short stories were now influencing the ways that I read a city and its citizens. Or perhaps my new approaches to navigating DC were giving me insight about how writers construct their short, place-based compositions.

TEACHING BLACK SHORT FICTION WITH DATA

At the University of Texas at Arlington, I've taught undergraduate and graduate courses on Black short fiction. In these courses, data collection and analysis have been central to our engagements with various texts. In the process, I became aware of how digital methodologies affect pedagogical practices. In class experiences, using digital tools to interpret literature facilitates the development of computational skills, data analytics, and visual design that reshape and remodel humanistic knowledge. "While research and teaching are complementary functions, they do not necessarily share the same social or intellectual space," explains Maryemma Graham, in pointing out the importance of restoring a connection between research and teaching.[1]

In my studies of literary art, I discovered that digital approaches and tools opened new possibilities. Close examinations reveal that short stories—individually and collectively—contain an extensive body of quantifiable information or, simply put, data. Maybe it's worthwhile to identify and manage some of that data. For a graduate seminar in fall 2016, my students and I read all of Jones's twenty-eight stories in order to create a dataset that identifies all locations mentioned, character demographics, and the number of times each character speaks. We produced a magnificent, multifaceted spreadsheet that gave us opportunities to chart the totality of Jones's numerous references. We created an expansive dataset encompassing all of Jones's stories, which made it possible for us to quantify his geo-tagging and trace the dialogue of more than five hundred characters. We were exercising a data-driven approach to reading short stories.

Many of my students were unfamiliar with DC, but even so, we were able to visualize Jones's renderings of the city using the dataset and mapping software. All of the locations mentioned in the stories were reference points that we used to find locations on a map and trace character movements. Martyn Jessop has pointed out how what we see stimulates us and prompts us to raise questions that may not have otherwise arisen: "there exists an instinctive deep understanding that one can enhance one's thought processes by finding ways of linking external perception with internal mental processes," he explains.[2] Visualizing the movements of Jones's characters by pinpointing locations on a map offers engagements that are not possible through conventional readings. In addition, taking account of the locations mentioned in Jones's stories highlights the shifting urban landscape of DC.

Kukhyoung Kim and I created two interactive maps about racial population shifts across DC from the 1970s to 2017. These two visual guides acted as supplementary materials that we used as we read Jones's short fiction. The maps of DC enhanced the ability of students to consider the actual inhabited spaces that Jones describes. In an online project for the class, Michael Dennis and Misty Falkenstein noted that using maps of Jones's stories led them to interpret current gentrification efforts in DC differently.[3] They described the current urban renewal efforts as "interrupting and rerouting a complex communal/geographical system, which involves real people with real stories." My students explained the maps gave them chances to consider neighborhood demographic changes, and the stories by Jones encouraged them to consider the kinds of people who once lived there.

The dataset on Jones extends far past geographic markers since we also collected information related to hundreds of characters that appear in his twenty-eight stories. Data librarian Peace Ossom-Williamson guided us as we created interactive charts that focused on Jones's characters. The charts display the percentage, by story, of the total dialogue spoken by each character. They also list the number of words spoken by men and women characters based on their roles—the protagonist and the primary, secondary, and tertiary characters—in the story. These visualizations allowed us to account for the entirety of Jones's character presentations. Our data work facilitated a comprehensive view of casting and dialogue in his twenty-eight stories.

The character visualizations encouraged us to think about gendered representations. Jones includes more men characters overall, but he privileges women speakers, especially in *All Aunt Hagar's Children*. There are 162 male characters and 130 female characters in Jones's second collection. However, the female characters play a more pronounced role in terms of dialogue—especially in *Lost in the City*. In his first collection, all the female characters utter a total of 11,582 words in dialogue compared to 6,590 words by male characters. In the second collection, dialogue is more even, with female characters uttering 10,818 words compared to 10,410 words by males. My students acknowledged initially focusing more on the number of male characters present. The dataset, however, shifted their attention to consider speaking roles. For their online class project, Hira Chaudhary and Angela Zitting explained, "once we consider the prominent role of women as both primary characters and primary speakers, we realize that these male characters are often taking a backseat to the daughters, sisters, and mothers that take the wheel in many of the stories."[4] Our charts showcasing characters and dialogue made it possible to consider, through visually stimulating means, the expansive body of data comprising Jones's stories.

After teaching my course on Jones, I decided to create a dataset that identifies geographic locales, character demographics, and structural features of stories by Charles Chesnutt, Zora Neale Hurston, Richard Wright, Ralph Ellison, James Baldwin, Toni Cade Bambara, and Alice Walker. That is, I took a data approach to considering the Big 7. Those writers do not offer as much specific geographical detail as does Jones. Nevertheless, there are dozens of data points related to settings and character demographics. The dataset on Jones amasses information on multiple compositions by a single writer, but the subsequent dataset concentrates on twenty-six stories by seven writers.

When I taught a course on short stories in the fall of 2019, I utilized this "Big 7 Short Story Dataset" to identify interrelated features of works. By its very definition, the parameters of a short story are elusive and vary from writer to writer. But my dataset on twenty-six short stories quantifies settings, characters, location and landmark references, narrative mode, violent interactions, and death, among other categories. Our examination of quantitative data related to select stories by the Big 7 guided our assessments of individual stories. Also, we were able to interpret how their works compared to each other. Of the twenty-six stories, only one is set in the Midwest. Six are set in the urban North, and nineteen are set in the Deep South. The abundance of stories set in the South made students realize how prominent the region is in literary history. However, the fact that fourteen of those southern stories were published prior to 1950 led students to wonder whether a focus on the South had changed over time.

The data and variance among compositions inclined us to question what is meant by the phrase "short story." Edgar Allan Poe defined a short story as anything that could be read in a single sitting.[5] This definition, however, does not account for the varying length of stories. A look at word counts reveals that some short stories are shorter than others. The shortest story in the dataset is Hurston's "Spunk" at 2,249 words, and the longest is Baldwin's "Sonny's Blues" at 13,722 words. Apparently, there are shorter short stories and longer short stories. This focus on length and genre definition also caused us to discuss novellas, novelettes, and flash fiction. Twenty of the stories contain between two thousand and seven thousand words. Based on this finding, we concluded that most canonical short stories by Black writers are under seven thousand words and focus on a single incident and a few central characters. This led us to consider how stories by Wright and Baldwin might be considered novelettes or novellas since these works contain several scenes and multiple characters and exceed ten thousand words. Conversely, we pointed out how shorter stories by Hurston and Walker were far more likely to be read in a single sitting or even, for some, right before class.

We considered how characters constitute a basis for organizing short fiction around key themes. The twenty-six stories by seven writers in the dataset have a total of 197 characters. Those stories by the Big 7 feature 127 men characters and sixty-four women characters. The information enhanced our discussions about the representation of male and female characters. My students were fascinated to learn, from my Jones dataset, that he cast more than twice as many characters in his stories as appeared in stories by the Big 7. The somewhat limited settings the Big 7 writers present in their stories diminish the likelihood that protagonists would encounter several characters. Unlike Jones, the protagonists in stories by the Big 7 do not usually encounter random people while walking down the street or riding a city bus. The settings of their stories offer relatively few minor characters.

Despite discussions about alterations to the canon, the circulation of a set number of Black short story writers has remained relatively stable. Stories by writers who did not appear in more than five anthologies prior to 1975 were not regularly chosen by their editors. My anthology dataset revealed that even though there are 297 total writers in the dataset, 181 have only one story across one hundred anthologies. My students were surprised to learn that the twenty-six stories in the anthology dataset represented only a small fraction—less than 4 percent—of the total stories that have appeared in one hundred anthologies. In most cases, anthologies expose readers to only a select few writers. The confines of space prevent us from experiencing the vast range of Black writers in a single collection.

While the use of datasets offers some advantages, it does not eliminate the need for well-established reading practices. Conventional literary analyses and domain knowledge are crucial. Pre-existing scholarship on African American literature was imperative to the kinds of datasets I developed with my students. Still, datasets created special opportunities for students to use spreadsheets and sort through data points related to dozens of the most widely anthologized short fiction. My students were empowered to consider implications of the production of literary art using data, and they now seek out narratives that emerge from quantitative data.

DATA WORK AND BLACK SHORT STORIES

The use of a "smart data" approach can assist us in engaging with the expansive information that appears in Black short fiction. Smart data concerns how "sources (including Big Data) are brought together, correlated, analyzed, etc., to be able to feed decision-making and action processes."[6] Focused information related to geography and character types present in the works of the Big 7 and Edward P. Jones, for instance, offers opportunities to incorporate "smart data" principles into investigations of short stories. We can expand our studies of African American literary art by compiling small and exact bodies of information related to characters and place settings. In other words, we have much to gain by pursing data work.

This book also demonstrates that we should take the notion of cultural geo-tagging seriously when analyzing short stories by Black writers. My work on Charles Chesnutt, Zora Neale Hurston, Richard Wright, Ralph Ellison, James Baldwin, Toni Cade Bambara, Alice Walker, and Edward P. Jones contributes to ongoing critical conversations related to their artistic compositions. Since the 1970s, there has been an extraordinary amount of scholarship produced that examines how Black writers make geography integral to their fictional narratives.[7] That scholarship often addresses novels. But short stories deserve critical attention too. We can enrich our engagements with literature by studying relatively short narrative compositions.

Chesnutt, Hurston, and Wright are the most famous and republished short story writers who depict the South. Chesnutt was interested in revising Black stereotypes at the turn of the twentieth century. Hurston was interested in presenting the vibrant lives of predominantly African American communities to illustrate how Black people exist independent of white people and culture. Wright showcased the value of exposing the intensity of southern racial conflicts. Taken together, these three writers indicate that stories about southern homegrown characters can deal with interrelated and distinct themes or points of cultural data.

Ellison and Walker, in their stories, further enhanced depictions of characters in the South. By presenting first-person narratives about southern homegrown outsiders, they highlighted the tensions that emerge when supposed insiders become displaced from their home environments. Further, Ellison and Walker crucially used flashbacks to expand the realm of spaces where they presented their protagonists. Ellison presented scenes from character memories to intensify the haunting drama of the past, while Walker incorporated protagonist recollections to show characters during previous, presumably consequential moments. More than just manipulating the flow of time in a story, flashbacks also expand the very "zone of action" presented in short fiction.[8]

While canonical southern African American stories are set in multiple locales across the region, the most well-known northern short fiction is concentrated in a single place: New York City. The metropolis is integral to Baldwin's and Bambara's storytelling. Baldwin's "Sonny's Blues" attests to the expansiveness of New York City by showing his unnamed protagonist traversing multiple settings, including a school courtyard, a busy sidewalk, a Harlem neighborhood, a jazz club, an apartment residence on an upper floor high above the ground, and the urban landscape available to someone riding a taxi along Lenox Avenue. The children in Bambara's stories navigate Harlem streets, sidewalks, movie theaters, a toy store, a park, and a convenience store in the city. Baldwin and Bambara set their stories in New York City and then draw on the seemingly limitless scenic and sensory possibilities available in a vibrant, multifaceted cityscape.

The body of work that Jones has produced lends itself to considerations of geography, homegrown characters, and exciting data work. Jones's knowledge of Washington, DC, presented him with the opportunity to incorporate many settings from his childhood and adult life in the District. Characters drive the action of the stories as the plots unfold on street corners, parks, sidewalks, and other public as well as domestic settings. The characters that Jones depicts are familiar with numerous places, and they collectively become the means through which he presents multiple underexplored aspects of the city. His stories operate like intricate graphs of data that highlight numerous locales and landmarks of a distinct area.

The large number of characters who populate Jones's stories demonstrates his devotion to chronicling the lives of homegrown Black citizens of DC. Physicians, lawyers, gospel singers, taxi drivers, prisoners, ex-cons, high school students, and neighborhood children make appearances in *Lost in the City* and *All Aunt Hagar's Children*. They are hopeful, depressed, antagonistic, caring, determined, apathetic, loving, and hateful. They represent a rich diversity of Black people, dissimilar in all kinds of ways, yet linked to a common location—Washington, DC. The presentation of so many homegrown characters allows Jones to explore DC locations that otherwise go unnoticed in fiction and to do so from an insider perspective. The experiences of Jones's characters are intertwined with the physical landscape of the District. Their points of view are associated with landmarks, and they navigate the city as a way of coming to terms with their circumstances.

Cultural geo-tagging reveals the interplay among space, characters, and historical settings. Geography in short fiction, however, consists of more than just descriptions of physical landscapes. Gathering and interpreting data about stories clarify how writers populate settings with a variety of character types. Charting how characters interact with their immediate surroundings, navigate various settings, and intermingle with other people reveals the cultural components of geography and how writers envision spaces that people inhabit. By documenting the number and variety of geographical references, including regional settings, landmarks, street names, neighborhoods, and regional dialects, we begin to understand how Black writers mark and plot cultural spaces and position characters within specific settings. These data-driven observations create views of stories that highlight the interrelated approaches writers employ when representing common locations.

Identifying homegrown, outsider, and homegrown outsider protagonists brings attention to how authors position central characters in stories to enhance views of locales. The orientation of characters to their settings highlights how history and social customs have a bearing on geographic renderings. In his stories, Wright offers inside perspectives on the dangers that emerge when racial boundaries are crossed. Ellison shows how unsettling a lynching can be to a white outsider unfamiliar with violent, racist traditions.

And Walker depicts homegrown outsiders who grow distant from family based on travel and educational pursuits. Attention to homegrown, outsider, or homegrown outsider characters places emphasis on the positioning of the figures within a given context.

Pursuing and sharing data work on the publishing histories of short stories mean integrating digital tools and methods more readily into literary research. We live in an era of increasing automation, and expansive, complex datasets can reveal patterns, trends, and associations, as shown in this book about Black short fiction. Given the recent advancements in data collection capabilities, it's important for us to develop research practices and pedagogical approaches that seek to account for the large body of compositions produced by Black writers. With more than eight hundred short stories by Black writers reprinted in anthologies, we have an abundance of materials to consider. We cannot reasonably assign all those stories in a single semester, but data work makes it possible for us to survey a wide body of materials in order to track the types of settings and characters that writers use to create narratives.

Talented storytellers captivate us with fanciful tales. They make geography integral to their portrayals of characters. They also depict a range of locales—front porches, local stores, open fields, lakes, city streets. In the process, the writers leave a trail of data about characters and settings. They deliberately or inadvertently situate their works within distinct cultural contexts. Geo-tagging offers one possibility for reading short stories, not to mention other compositions, with attention to how writers use geographic markers and distinct character types to drive the action of the place-based imperatives that shape narratives. Like following in the footsteps of a writer who referenced hundreds of locales across DC, the practice of geo-tagging gives us chances to explore the geographies of short fiction.

ACKNOWLEDGMENTS

I now understand that writing a book is no easy task. Throughout this process, I was fortunate enough to have an unwavering support system that made me truly understand the saying "If I have seen further, it is by standing on the shoulders of Giants." I am humbled and deeply grateful.

To my parents, my first and best teachers, thank you for making me believe in the value of education. I'm so grateful for your teachings and constantly reminding me education is the key to freedom. To answer a question you ask me often: Yes, education is worth it. I owe so much to my older siblings, Phillis h. Rambsy and Howard Rambsy II, and Howard's wife, Psyche Southwell. I'm fortunate to be the younger sibling and get to watch you all live (and move through the world) with such style and grace.

Drs. William J. Harris, Tony Bolden, Randal Jelks, and Mary Jo Reiff each played a distinct role in helping me to develop my scholarly voice. Dr. Maryemma Graham greatly influenced my pursuits into *literary archeology* and helped deepen my appreciation for Black verbal art.

Several colleagues and professional mentors have played a pivotal role in mentoring me and consulting with me on various topics related to the professoriate and this book project in particular. I owe an incredible amount of gratitude to Drs. Jerry W. Ward Jr., Dana Williams, and Amy Earhart, who played consequential roles in helping me to complete this project.

At the University of Texas at Arlington (UTA), Dr. Elisabeth Cawthon, Dean of the College of Liberal Arts, and Dr. Kevin Porter, English Department Chair, encouraged and supported my pursuits to secure funding sources to complete this book. My UTA colleagues Peace Ossom-Williamson and Amy Berhand as well as Drs. Estee Beck, Erin Murrah-Mandril, and Sonja Watson provided me with invaluable advice and continued support while wrestling with ideas and writing. I was also fortunate to have the support of scholars including Drs. Adam Banks, Kalenda Eaton, Kim Gallon, Candice Love-Jackson, Angel David Nieves, Nikki Taylor, and Doretha K. Williams who invited me to give talks on my work in progress. Drs. DaMaris Hill,

Sanderia Faye Smith, Jacinta Saffold, Crystal Donkor, Crystal Webster, and Nneke Dennie were invaluable and consistent writing partners during this time when we were all working on scholarly publications. I am grateful for the feedback and motivation from so many different support groups.

I am especially appreciative of the generosity of the Institute for Citizens & Scholars (formerly known as the Woodrow Wilson National Fellowship Foundation) and the University of Texas at Arlington's Endowment for Faculty Research. As a recipient of these awards, I was able to devote deliberate amounts of interrupted time to research and writing. The financial support afforded by these awards enabled me to spend a lot of time with this book. I am also grateful to the Mellon-Mays Undergraduate Research Fellowship Program (Dr. Cynthia Neale Spence, Donna Akiba Sullivan Harper, and Ms. Ada Jackson), the Social Science Research Council (Dr. Cally Waite), and the Dallas Institute for the Humanities (Dr. J. Larry Allums). The support from these institutions came at a crucial time while writing this book.

My friends, my greatest support system, played a major role in pushing and pulling me along through this process. Constant phone calls, text messages, and even visits gave me purpose while working on this project. Dr. David Hill, Carolyn Johnson, and Tiara Beard, three of my oldest friends, took a genuine interest in my professional interests and encouraged me to keep believing in the power of Black art. And Desmond Handon Sr.—my personal, homegrown tour guide to Washington, DC—exposed me to several worlds within the nation's capital. Thanks for the extra motivation and bestowing me with my "legendary status" as an honorary resident of "Chocolate City."

I'm thankful for the tremendous amount of support I've received. I am overwhelmed with gratitude.

NOTES

INTRODUCTION

1. In the *Concise Oxford Companion to African American Literature*, Cheryl Wall describes the publication history of Hurston's "Spunk."

2. Nagel, *Contemporary American Short-Story Cycle*, 14.

3. Henry Louis Gates Jr.'s *The Signifying Monkey* (1988), Deborah E. McDowell's *"The Changing Same": Black Women's Literature, Criticism, and Theory* (1994), Barbara Christian's *Black Women Novelists: The Development of a Tradition, 1892–1976* (1980), and Robert Stepto's *From Behind the Veil: A Study of Afro-American Literature* (1979) are landmark works that offer critical insight into the history of African American literature. These works, however, focus primarily on novels in their discussions and rarely deal with poetry and short stories.

4. Funded by a 2017 UTA iLASR (Liberal Arts + Smart Revolution) Grant, "The Black Short Story Dataset—Vol. 1" contains information related to over six hundred African American short stories that appeared in one hundred African American and American anthologies published between 1925 and 2017. This dataset was produced by Dr. Kenton Rambsy with Jade Harrison and Rebecca Newsom serving as research assistants. This dataset can be used to track the circulation histories of Black short fiction across one hundred anthologies. Ultimately, this dataset emphasizes how editorial decisions shaped the formation of African American publishing histories involving short fiction.

5. Csicsila, *Canons by Consensus*, 180.

6. Dickson-Carr, *Columbia Guide to Contemporary African American Fiction*, 72.

7. Gates, "The Master's Pieces: On Canon Formation and the Afro-American Tradition," 29.

8. Gates, "Preface to the Second Edition, *The Norton Anthology of African American Literature*, with Nellie Y. McKay," 184.

9. Fox, "Shaping an African American Literary Canon."

10. Graham and Ward, *Cambridge History of African American Literature*, 1.

11. Knowles, *Race and Social Analysis*, 80.

12. Neely and Samura, "Social Geographies of Race: Connecting Race and Space," 1946.

13. Davis, *Southscapes*, 2.

14. Paul Laurence Dunbar's "The Lynching of Jube Benson," William Faulkner's "That Evening Sun," Tennessee Williams's "Desire and the Black Masseur," Flannery O'Connor's "Revelation," and Gayl Jones's "White Rat" suggest the diverse ways that writers characterize those troubling, physical conflicts in their short fiction.

15. Harris, *Scary Mason-Dixon Line*, 1.

16. Hakutani and Butler, *City in African-American Literature*, 11.

17. Jones [Baraka], "City of Harlem," 108.

18. Hakutani and Butler, *City in African-American Literature*, 11.

19. Cataliotti, *Music in African American Fiction*, 89.

20. Burroway's *Writing Fiction: A Guide to Narrative Craft* (2019), Card's *Elements of Fiction Writing: Characters & Viewpoint* (2011), Corbett's *The Art of Character: Creating Memorable Characters for Fiction, Film, and TV* (2013), and Maass's "Creating Your Story's Time & Place" (2011) all discuss strategies creative writers employ to create memorable and effective characters.

21. Corbett, *Art of Character*, xxv.

22. Card, *Elements of Fiction Writing*, 96.

23. Maass, "Creating Your Story's Time & Place," 268.

CHAPTER 1: LOCATING THE BIG 7: ONE HUNDRED ANTHOLOGIES AND THE MOST FREQUENTLY ANTHOLOGIZED BLACK SHORT STORIES

1. Abrams, *Glossary of Literary Terms*, 38.

2. Kinnamon notes that almost all anthologies focused on Black writers were published after 1920. He writes, "Several anthologies appeared in the 1920s, few in the 1930s and 1940s, almost none in the 1950s. Beginning in the 1960s, the production of anthologies accelerated, and the brisk pace continues to the present" (461). He also notes that "most anthologies of fiction are confined to short stories and excerpts from novels" (474).

3. Even though Ernest Gaines's "The Sky Is Gray" (republished fifteen times) and Paule Marshall's "To Da-duh, in Memoriam" (republished eleven times) are among the most frequently republished stories, these two writers do not circulate with the same degree of frequency in a wide range of anthology types.

4. In the introduction to *Multiethnic Literature and Canon Debates*, editors Mary Jo Bona and Irma Maini explain, "In addition, one of the major publishing events that further helped to propel this appetite for multiethnic works was the first edition of the *Heath Anthology of American Literature* in 1989. The first anthology to include a multiplicity of voices and genres, the *Heath* played a pivotal role in canon expansion and transformation" (10).

5. Davis and Redding, *Cavalcade*, 122.

6. In *Down Home: Origins of the Afro-American Short Story*, Robert Bone points to journalist Joel Chandler Harris and his transcribing and publishing of *Uncle Remus: His Song and His Sayings* to explain how the rise of the short story form in popular media during the time has direct connections to American oral traditions. While Bone points out that Harris was a "an active propagandist in the cause of white supremacy . . . full of

neurotic conflicts and self-deceiving ways," he acknowledges Harris's transcription and publication of the Uncle Remus stories as "saving them from possible oblivion" (19). The folktales of Brer Rabbit for African Americans "represent the first attempt of black Americans to define themselves through the art of storytelling," but for many white Americans represented an innovation in storytelling techniques with the use of dialect, folklore, and race-related content. Bone proposes that the Brer Rabbit tales were "a heroic effort on the part of chattel slaves to transmute the raw materials of their experience into forms of fiction" (22). These oral stories represent a distinct African American perspective on social relations and an intervention into the developing American short story form.

7. Martin, "The Two-Faced New South," 21.

8. Nagel, *Anthology of the American Short Story*, 747.

9. Wallach, *Richard Wright: From Black Boy to World Citizen*, 77.

10. Richard Wright does not ever identify where any of his stories are set. He uses several context clues to alert readers that his stories are set in the rural Jim Crow South. I assume that the stories are set in Mississippi because of his essay "The Ethics of Living Jim Crow." In this essay, included in the 1940 rereleased edition of *Uncle Tom's Children*, Wright describes his boyhood experiences with racism in Mississippi.

11. Lucy, "'Flying Home': Ralph Ellison, Richard Wright, and the Black Folk during World War II," 258.

12. Mitgang, "'Invisible Man,' as Vivid Today as in 1952," 13.

13. The prepublication circulation of Ellison's story raised anticipation for his debut novel. Arnold Rampersad notes that those printings gave Ellison's work "a far bigger American readership" than from its initial appearance in the British periodical *Horizon* and adds that, in fact, the publication of "Battle Royal" in '48 "appeared to overshadow an essay by Albert Einstein and poems by Stephen Spender" (217).

14. Based on my dataset, between 1925 and 1989, the numbers for the top five writers were: Chesnutt, thirty-one; Wright, twenty-six; Hughes, twenty-four; Ellison, nineteen; and Fisher, fourteen.

15. Bambara, *Black Woman*, 3–4.

16. Washington, *Black-Eyed Susans/Midnight Birds*, 4.

17. Carby, "Politics of Fiction, Anthropology, and the Folk: Zora Neale Hurston," 24.

18. This short story would be the basis for her play *Mule Bone* that she cowrote with Langston Hughes.

19. Gates, "A Tragedy of Negro Life," 5.

20. Gates and Lemke, "Introduction," *Complete Stories*, x.

21. Smith in Smith and Jones, *Prentice Hall Anthology*, 301.

22. Across one hundred anthologies, ten stories by Toni Cade Bambara have been republished: "The Organizer's Wife," "Raymond's Run," "The Toad and the Donkey," "Mama Hazel Takes Her Bed," "My Man Bovanne," "Gorilla, My Love," "The Lesson," "A Girl's Story," "A Tender Man," and "Medley."

23. Bambara, *Conversations with Toni Cade Bambara*, 28.

24. Davis and Redding, *Cavalcade*, xvii.

25. Thomas Brock notes in "Young Adults and Higher Education: Barriers and Breakthroughs to Success" how the mid- to late 1960s marked a turning point in higher

education for African Americans (111). That period also marked a turning point in the production of African American literature. With the momentum of the civil rights and Black Power movements, changes in federal policy, most notably the Higher Education Act of 1965, and the formation of Black Studies programs across the country, the late 1960s and early 1970s witnessed the increased publication of anthologies solely dedicated to Black writers.

26. Mason, "African-American Anthology," 186.

27. Gustafson, "Prologue: What's in a Date?"

28. In *Rereading the Harlem Renaissance*, Sharon L. Jones writes, "The Great Depression reduced the number of publishing companies and magazines that served as outlets for literary works" (10). She continues, "Publishing companies had less capital for manufacturing books and fewer consumers with monetary resources to buy them, and so they contracted few books."

29. Marrs and Hager, "Introduction," *Timelines of American Literature*, 1.

30. Harold Bloom's *Richard Wright: Bloom's Modern Critical Views* (1985), William J. Maxwell's *New Negro, Old Left* (1999), and Mark Christian Thompson's *Black Fascisms: African American Literature and Culture Between the Wars* (2007) note the disagreement between Zora Neale Hurston and Richard Wright over artistic differences during the 1930s. Specifically, these writers point to Wright's review, "Between Laughter and Tears" (1937), of Hurston's novel, along with Hurston's critique, "Stories of Conflict" (1938), of Wright's *Uncle Tom's Children* as the culmination of their artistic differences.

31. McDowell and Spillers, "Introduction to Realism, Naturalism, Modernism: 1940–1960," *Norton Anthology of African American Literature*, 94.

32. Lawrence Jackson's *The Indignant Generation: A Narrative History of African American Writers and Critics, 1934–1960* documents the neglected literary period immediately following the Harlem Renaissance that spans up until the civil rights movement. Jackson pays attention to the political and social climate that facilitated the rise and circulation of works by writers such as Wright, Gwendolyn Brooks, Baldwin, Lorraine Hansberry, and Ellison. In addition, Jackson pays attention to those artistic movements occurring in New York, Chicago, and Washington and details how African American literary criticism began to grow during this period as well.

33. McDowell and Spillers, "Introduction to Realism, Naturalism, Modernism: 1940–1960," *Norton Anthology of African American Literature*, 101.

34. Ward, "Introduction," *Trouble the Water*, xxi.

35. Marrs and Hager, "Introduction," *Timelines of American Literature*, 1.

36. Jarrett, *Wiley Blackwell Anthology of African American Literature*, Volume 2, xvii.

37. Ward and Butler, "Almos' a Man," *Richard Wright Encyclopedia*.

38. Boyd and Allen, "Introduction," *Brotherman*, xxi.

39. Penzler, "Excerpt: 'Black Noir.'" This excerpt from Penzler's introduction to the collection *Black Noir* was published on NPR's website. The collection was published by Pegasus in 2009.

40. Thomas, *Dark Matter*, 7.

41. On Black population shifts from 1900 to the 1970s, see James N. Gregory's *The Southern Diaspora*.

NOTES

CHAPTER 2: WRITING THE SOUTH: CHARLES CHESNUTT, ZORA NEALE HURSTON, AND RICHARD WRIGHT

1. The following scholarly essays, newspaper articles, books, and encyclopedia/reference guides mention the feud between Zora Neale Hurston and Richard Wright: "Why Richard Wright Hated Zora Neale Hurston" by Henry Louis Gates Jr.; "A Society of One: Zora Neale Hurston, American Contrarian" by Claudia Roth Pierpont; "James Baldwin Denounced Richard Wright's 'Native Son' as a 'Protest Novel'; Was He Right?" by Ayana Mathis and Pankaj Mishra; *100 Amazing Facts about the Negro with Complete Proof: A Short Cut to the World History of the Negro* by J. A. Rogers; *Encyclopedia of the Harlem Renaissance* by Cary D. Wintz and Paul Finkelman; *Keepin' It Real: Essays on Race in Contemporary America* by Elwood David Watson; and *Constructing the Literary Self: Race and Gender in Twentieth-Century Literature* by Patsy J. Daniels.

2. Wright, "Between Laughter and Tears."

3. Hurston, "Uncle Tom's Children."

4. Baker, *Long Black Song*, 20.

5. In "Focalization as Education," Geordie Hamilton explains, "Chesnutt self-identified as seven-eighths white, may have felt 'intellectually and racially' estranged from both blacks and whites, and once claimed never to have written 'as a Negro.' Photographs prove that one could probably not distinguish Chesnutt as having African-American ancestry without being told so" (50).

6. In *An American Crusade: The Life of Charles Waddell Chesnutt*, Keller notes that Chesnutt's work was so well received that editors at *The Atlantic Monthly* contacted him to submit another short story to publish as a follow-up to "The Goophered Grapevine" (100, 118).

7. Baker, *Blues Aesthetic and the Making of American Identity in the Literature of the South*, 35–36.

8. Jarrett, "Dialect of New Negro Literature," 170.

9. Chesnutt, "The Goophered Grapevine," 12. Subsequent citations to this story appear in the text.

10. According to Donald M. Shaffer Jr. in "African American Folklore as Racial Project in Charles W. Chesnutt's *The Conjure Woman*," Chesnutt effectively writes against the grain of that popular fiction by appropriating African American folklore as a counterhegemonic racial narrative (325).

11. Julius sets out to protect his home on the vineyard and his economic interests at all costs and, in the process, uses John and Annie for his personal gain. According to Trudier Harris's "The Trickster in African American Literature," in "Po' Sandy" Chesnutt offers "subtle commentary on the harshness of slavery and suggests the need for current-day democratic fairness even as he entertains his audience with the Aesop's fable quality of the tales."

12. Shaffer, "African American Folklore," 326.

13. Tunc, "De(con)struction of Black/White Binaries," 679.

14. Chesnutt, "The Wife of His Youth," 1. Subsequent citations to this story appear in the text.

15. Duncan, *Northern Stories of Charles W. Chesnutt*, 4.

16. Chesnutt, "The Sheriff's Children," 65. Subsequent citations to this story appear in the text.

17. Deborah Plant, *Zora Neale Hurston: A Biography of the Spirit*, 34.

18. Plant also explains how Charles Johnson facilitated Hurston's interactions with financially prosperous and influential aristocrats, publishers, and donors, who would play vital roles in getting Hurston published in significant venues. These invitations to parties and other social functions typically go undocumented in anthology biographical sketches.

19. Gates and Lemke, "Introduction," *Complete Stories*, xi.

20. In all of Hurston's stories, she includes a geographic signifier that alerts the reader that the setting is somewhere in Florida. She references nearby towns or distinct Florida landmarks to create these impressions.

21. Hurston, "Gilded Six-Bits," 1043. Subsequent citations to this story appear in the text.

22. Harris, *Scary Mason-Dixon Line*, 2.

23. Chinn and Dunn, "'The Ring of Singing Metal on Wood,'" 789. They continue, "The character development of Joe and Missie May Banks is anything but simple. Nor is the story of their relationship a straightforward tale of love, betrayal, and reconciliation."

24. Hurston, "Sweat," 1038. Subsequent citations to this story appear in the text.

25. Patterson, *Zora Neale Hurston and a History of Southern Life*, 43.

26. Similar to Hurston, Alice Walker's *The Color Purple* (1982) and Ernest Gaines's *A Gathering of Old Men* (1983) make front porch scenes central to their stories. These settings are important for gathering places for Black characters in rural and towns across the South.

27. I used Voyant-Tools to data mine "Sweat." This story contains 4,768 total words and 1,395 unique words. Unique words or word types refer to nouns, adjectives, verbs, and adverbs in a document. "Stop words" refers to common words such as "the," "a," "at," and "is" that may be filtered out of searches for key words in a text. The word density or ratio for this story is 29 percent. The ratio of unique words or word types to total words or tokens (unique words/total words), expressed as a percentage—higher numbers generally mean greater vocabulary diversity.

28. Joseph, "The Verdict from the Porch: Zora Neale Hurston and Reparative Justice," 475.

29. Hurston, "Spunk," 31. Subsequent citations to this story appear in the text.

30. Jones, *Critical Companion to Zora Neale Hurston*, 166.

31. In "Rootedness: The Ancestor as Foundation," Toni Morrison explains: "I could blend the acceptance of the supernatural and a profound rootedness in the real world at the same time with neither taking precedence over the other. It is indicative of the cosmology, the way in which Black people looked at the world. We are a very practical people, very down to earth, even shrewd people. But within that practicality we also accepted what I suppose could be called superstition and magic, which is another way of knowing things. But to blend those two worlds together at the same time was enhancing, not limiting. And some of those things were 'discredited knowledge' that Black people had; discredited only because Black people were discredited and therefore what they knew was 'discredited'" (342). This same concept applies to Hurston's characters and how they interpret Spunk's death. They also believed in a certain cosmology that was a form of ultimate justice.

32. Storm, "Alice Dunbar-Nelson, Zora Neale Hurston, and the Creation of 'Authentic Voices' in the Black Women's Literary Tradition," 143–44.

33. Roosevelt, "My Day."

34. Wallach, *Richard Wright*, 69

35. Gussow, "Fingering the Jagged Grain: Ellison's Wright and the Southern Blues Violences," 142.

36. David P. Demarest Jr.'s "Richard Wright: The Meaning of Violence" (1974), Robert James Butler's "The Function of Violence in Richard Wright's *Native Son*" (1986), Rodwell Makombe's "Apartheid, Crime, and Interracial Violence in 'Black Boy'" (2013), and Patrick Wilmot's "The Role of Violence in the Works of Wright and Fanon" (2014) discuss Wright's illustrations of violence, especially interracial violence. Each critic notes that violent, racist interactions were a through line connecting his fiction, nonfiction, and sometimes poetry.

37. Wright, "Big Boy Leaves Home," 65. Subsequent citations to this story appear in the text.

38. Ellison, "Richard Wright's Blues," 490.

39. Ryan, "Dangerous Refuge: Richard Wright and the Swimming Hole," 28.

40. In "Dangerous Refuge," Ryan writes: "It's interesting that the trigger for the killings in 'Big Boy'—the particular form of trespass that sets the cycle of violence in motion—involves laying claim to a swimming hole. This story is in a sense as much about swimming as it is about lynching; as an oblique echo of the drowning that instigated a riot (which itself both reenacts and anticipates an ongoing assault on black bodies in lakes and pools and rivers), 'Big Boy' raises fundamental questions about access to nature, or how one can interact with or make use of nature. Swimming is play, a resistance to the imperative of labor that governs black lives in the Jim Crow South and, for that matter, in the would-be promised land of the North. In Richard Wright's world, swimming pools both South and North, both natural and built, are marked 'No Trespassing'" (28).

41. Joyce Ann Joyce ("Richard Wright's 'Long Black Song': A Moral Dilemma") and Matthew Teusch ("When the Roll Is Called Up Yonder in Richard Wright's 'Long Black Song'") have both speculated about whether the character was raped or not.

42. Harris, "Peace in the War of Desire: Richard Wright's 'Long Black Song.'"

43. Harris, "Peace in the War of Desire," 201.

44. Wright, "Long Black Song," 252.

45. Wright, "Bright and Morning Star," 395. Subsequent citations to this story appear in the text.

46. In Wright's memoir *Black Boy (American Hunger): A Record of Childhood and Youth*, he details several instances of interracial violence. He writes, "A dread of white people now came to live permanently in my feelings and imagination. As the war drew to a close, racial conflict flared over the entire South, and though I did not witness any of it, I could not have been more thoroughly affected by it if I had participated directly in every clash" (130). He suggests that white people are perverse and demented in the South and take their anger out on Black people out of frustration and for grisly entertainment.

47. Jackson, "Richard Wright in a Moment of Truth," 3.

48. Wright, *Black Boy*, 73.

49. Williams, "Papa Dick and Sister Woman: Reflections on Women in the Fiction of Richard Wright," 67.

50. The story became popular in the last thirty years, beginning to be republished the most between 1990 and 2010. The story has two spellings across anthologies: before 1990, the story is most likely to be titled "The Man Who Was Almost a Man"; after 1990, editors use the title "Almos' a Man."

51. Wright, "The Man Who Was Almost a Man," 3.

52. Hurston, "Uncle Tom's Children."

53. Davis, *Southscapes*, 4–5.

CHAPTER 3: THE PARADOX OF HOMEGROWN OUTSIDERS: RALPH ELLISON, JAMES BALDWIN, AND ALICE WALKER

1. Davis, "Expanding the Limits: The Intersection of Race and Region," 5.

2. In *The New Encyclopedia of Southern Culture, Volume 3: History*, editor Charles Reagan Wilson writes, "Memoirs, histories, journalistic accounts, travel accounts, fiction, poetry, paintings, and music are among some of the cultural forms that black writers have used to explore their complex love-hate relationship with the American South" (34).

3. O'Meally, "The Rules of Magic: Hemingway as Ellison's 'Ancestor,'" 150.

4. Callahan, "Introduction," *Trading Twelves: The Selected Letters of Ralph Ellison and Albert Murray*, xxii.

5. In this book, Parrish posits that Ralph Ellison's political and cultural achievements have not been fully recognized. He argues that Ellison contributed far more to American arts and letters beyond his breakout novel, *Invisible Man*.

6. Watts, *Heroism and the Black Intellectual*, 86.

7. Ellison, "Battle Royal," 273. Subsequent citations to this story appear in the text.

8. Tewarie, "Southern Elements in Ellison's *Invisible Man*," 191.

9. Ellison, "Flying Home," 215. Subsequent citations to this story appear in the text.

10. In *Integration of the Armed Forces, 1940–1965*, Morris J. MacGregor discusses the evolution of the services' racial policies and practices between World War II and 1965. Even though African Americans participated in every American conflict, formal discrimination persisted until President Harry S. Truman's Executive Order 9981 in 1948.

11. Lucy, "'Flying Home': Ralph Ellison, Richard Wright, and the Black Folk during World War II," 260.

12. Wilkerson, *Warmth of Other Suns*, 25–26.

13. Ellison, "King of the Bingo Game," 173.

14. Chaffee, "Slippery Ground: Ralph Ellison's Bingo Player," 23.

15. Harris, *Scary Mason-Dixon Line*, 1.

16. Davis, *Southscapes*, 16.

17. Ore, *Lynching: Violence, Rhetoric, and American Identity*, 8.

18. Baldwin, "Going to Meet the Man," 351. Subsequent citations to this story appear in the text.

19. Jones, "Style, Form, and Content in the Short Fiction of James Baldwin," 145.

20. Birmingham, "No Name in the South: James Baldwin and the Monuments of Identity," 230.

21. Mazurek, "Writer on the Left: Class and Race in Ellison's Early Fiction," 119. Mazurek estimates that "A Party Down at the Square" was written sometime in the 1930s or 1940s.

22. Ellison, "A Party Down at the Square," 54. Subsequent citations to this story appear in the text.

23. Mazurek, "Writer on the Left," 120.

24. Lieberman, "Ralph Ellison's Technological Humanism," 13.

25. In "The Southern Rite of Human Sacrifice: Lynching in the American South," Mathews explains, "The silence about the religious penumbra of lynching is strange because of the common knowledge that crucifixion, an act of violence, is at the very core of the Christian paradigm that was so essential a part of Southern culture. African Americans understood this; they understood that Christ, too, had been lynched" (31).

26. Taylor, "Denigration, Dependence, and Deviation: Black and White Masculinities in James Baldwin's *Going to Meet the Man*," 46.

27. Anderton, "Fire and Water: Opposites and Pairings in 'A Party Down at the Square,'" 104.

28. Richard Wright's "Between the World and Me" (1935) and Colson Whitehead's *The Underground Railroad* (2016) contain lynching scenes. James Allen's *Without Sanctuary: Lynching Photography in America* (2000) chronicles the practice through pictures.

29. Walker was involved in civil rights campaigns from 1965 until 1968. In "Alice Walker's Life and Works: The Essays," Maria Lauret writes, "She canvasses for voter-registration in her native Georgia, and is employed by [the] Student Non-violent Co-ordinating Committee" (80).

30. Davis, *Southscapes*, 41–42.

31. Walker, "Everyday Use," 1192. Subsequent citations to this story appear in the text.

32. Farrell, "Fight vs. Flight," 180.

33. Farrell, "Fight vs. Flight," 181.

34. Mullins, "Antagonized by the Text, Or, It Takes Two to Read Alice Walker's 'Everyday Use,'" 43.

35. Walker, "To Hell with Dying," 156. Subsequent citations to this story appear in the text.

36. Hollister, "Tradition in Alice Walker's 'To Hell with Dying,'" 93.

37. Walker, "I Know What the Earth Says," 12.

38. Walker, "Advancing Luna and Ida B. Wells," 121. Subsequent citations to this story appear in the text.

39. According to Maria V. Johnson in "Voices of Struggle," "Walker's story 'Nineteen Fifty-Five' and unnamed song signify even more clearly on the story of Willie Mae 'Big Mama' Thornton and Elvis Presley and 'their' song, 'Hound Dog'—perhaps the most famous 'cover' story" (223).

40. Walker, "Nineteen Fifty-Five," 13. Subsequent citations to this story appear in the text.

41. Johnson, "Voices of Struggle," 235.

CHAPTER 4: NEW YORK CITYSCAPES: JAMES BALDWIN AND TONI CADE BAMBARA

1. Lopate, *Writing New York*, xvii.
2. Albert, "Jazz-Blues Motif in James Baldwin's 'Sonny's Blues,'" 178.
3. Tackach, "Biblical Foundation of James Baldwin's 'Sonny's Blues,'" 71.
4. Baldwin, "Sonny's Blues," 427. Subsequent citations to this story appear in the text.
5. Claborn, "Who Set You Feelin'?," 91–92.
6. Baldwin, "Harlem Ghetto," 57.
7. Sherard, "Sonny's Bebop," 691.
8. Amiri Baraka believes that Black music has revolutionary implications and that liberation is not solely physical. In "The Changing Same," he writes, "But evolution is not merely physical: yet if you can understand what the physical alludes to, is reflexive of, then it will be understood that each process in 'life' is duplicated at all levels" (189).
9. Fisher, "Miss Cynthie," 105. Subsequent citations to this story appear in the text.
10. Fisher, "City of Refuge," 1239, 1248. Subsequent citations to this story appear in the text.
11. Dumas, "Will the Circle Be Unbroken," 88. Subsequent citations to this story appear in the text.
12. Thomas, "'Communicating by Horns,'" 295.
13. Dittmar, "Will the Circle Be Unbroken?: The Politics of Form in *The Bluest Eye*," 138.
14. Baraka, "Jazz and the White Critic," 179.
15. In the essay, Baraka references Dumas's "Will the Circle Be Unbroken" and explains how the story leaves readers understanding how Black music is "an autonomous judge of civilizations" (212).
16. Baraka has a long-standing interest in Black music and its larger connections to the psyche of Black people. In "Changing Same," he explains that the blues' "song quality is, it seems, the deepest expression of memory. Experience re/feeling. It is the racial memory. It is the 'abstract' design of racial character that is evident, would be evident, in creation carrying the force of that racial memory" (189).
17. Baraka, "The Screamers," 176. Subsequent citations to this story appear in the text.
18. In "The Development of the Black Revolutionary Artist," James Stewart highlights how the Black artists sought to create "our own conventions, a convention of procedural elements, a kind of stylization, a sort of insistency which leads inevitably to a certain kind of methodology—a methodology informed by the spirit" (6). Certainly, Black Arts writers Dumas and Baraka built their work on predecessors such as Fisher and Baldwin and sought to present more layered considerations of race.
19. Burke, "The Screamers," 12.
20. Houston A. Baker Jr.'s *Blues, Ideology, and Afro-American Literature: A Vernacular Theory*, Tony Bolden's *Afro-Blue: Improvisations in African American Poetry and Culture*, Craig Werner's *A Change Is Gonna Come: Music, Race & the Soul of America*, and Guthrie Ramsey's *Race Music: Black Cultures from Bebop to Hip-Hop* all deal with the overlaps between literature and music. More specifically, these scholars think about music and literature as falling under the purview of Black artistic expression and reveal overlaps in compositions of musicians and writers.

21. In "Changing Same," Baraka explains his belief that Black music has revolutionary implications and that liberation is not solely physical. He writes, "But evolution is not merely physical: yet if you can understand what the physical alludes to, is reflexive of, then it will be understood that each process in 'life' is duplicated at all levels" (189).

22. Bambara, *Conversations with Toni Cade Bambara*, 56.

23. Bambara, "Raymond's Run," 42. Subsequent citations to this story appear in the text.

24. Bambara, "Gorilla, My Love," 27. Subsequent citations to this story appear in the text.

25. Bambara, "The Lesson," 97. Subsequent citations to this story appear in the text.

26. I used Voyant Tools to text mine Bambara's "The Lesson." I found words such as "money," "cents," "price," "dollars," "store," "buy," "costs," and "spend" appear more than forty times. I compared these findings to data analysis of words in short stories by Chesnutt, Hurston, Wright, Baldwin, and Ellison discussed earlier in this book. What I found was that Bambara stands out in relation to her peers because of her direct references to economic terms. In comparison to her Big 7 peers, she is unmatched in her use of these types of words.

27. Black writers oftentimes have used Marxist philosophies in their fiction as a way to construct story plots, characterizations, and settings. For instance, Wright's *Native Son*, Ellison's *Invisible Man*, and Baraka's expansive collection of poetry and short stories employed Marxist ideologies as a means of critiquing white power structures as well as Black activist groups.

CHAPTER 5: UP SOUTH: GEO-TAGGING DC AND EDWARD P. JONES'S HOMEGROWN CHARACTERS

1. I had dinner with Jones and Maryemma Graham on June 24, 2016 (see Rambsy, "Meeting Edward P. Jones at Old Ebbitt Grill").

2. Harrison, "*All Aunt Hagar's Children* by Edward P. Jones."

3. "Driving in DC: A Crash Course on the Grid System."

4. Rivas, "10 Questions with Edward P. Jones."

5. Jones, "The Night Rhonda Ferguson Was Killed," 73.

6. Jones, "An Orange Line Train to Ballston," 197.

7. Jones, "The First Day," 73.

8. Jones, "A New Man," 373.

9. Jones, "Blindsided," 501.

10. Jones, "A Butterfly on F Street," 315.

11. Jones, "Bad Neighbors," 585. Subsequent citations to this story appear in the text.

12. Jones, "All Aunt Hagar's Children," 184. Subsequent citations to this story appear in the text.

13. Nance, "Edward P. Jones on Receiving the Harold Washington Literary Award."

14. Goldenberg, "Suzanne Goldenberg Meets Pulitzer Prize Winner Edward P. Jones."

15. Rustin-Paschal, "A Rich Man: Celebrating Edward P. Jones During National Short Story Month."

16. NPR Staff, "In D.C., a Bastion of Black Entertainment Returns."

17. Muller, "Anacostia's Larger-Than-Life Big Chair Is Full of Neighborhood History."

18. In *First Class: The Legacy of Dunbar, America's First Black Public High School*, Alison Stewart describes how in 1870 Washington, DC, residents opened the Preparatory High School for Colored Youth, the first Black public high school in the United States. It would later be renamed Dunbar High.

19. Jones, "Young Lions," 147. Subsequent citations to this story appear in the text.

20. Jones, "Gospel," 334.

21. Jones, "A Rich Man," 435.

22. Jones, "The Girl Who Raised Pigeons," 32. Subsequent citations to this story appear in the text.

23. Dean, "Repairing Urban Renewal in Story: Edward P. Jones's Imaginary Remapping of Washington, D.C. in *Lost in the City*."

24. Jackie Spinner and Margaret Webb Pressley, "Hahn Shoes Chain for Sale After 119 Years in District."

25. John DeFerrari, "The Once-Ubiquitous Peoples Drug Stores."

26. *Lost in the City* contains 216 characters. There are 110 male characters and 106 female characters. The characters' roles range from primary characters to extras: there are thirty-six primary characters, twenty-five secondary characters, forty-one tertiary characters, and 114 extras. His second collection, *All Aunt Hagar's Children*, contains 307 characters. There are 174 male characters and 133 female characters. There are thirty-nine primary characters, sixty-five secondary characters, fifty tertiary characters, and 153 extras.

27. Rivas, "10 Questions with Edward P. Jones."

28. Cobb, "*All Aunt Hagar's Children* by Edward P. Jones."

29. Leyshon, "A Writer in His Own Mind."

30. Jackson, "An Interview with Edward P. Jones," 97.

31. Cobb, "*All Aunt Hagar's Children* by Edward P. Jones."

32. Miller, "Edward P. Jones Talks about 'The Known World' and His Washington, D.C., Short Stories."

33. Jones, "His Mother's House," 272.

34. The dataset shows how many words each character speaks in the story. To calculate the percentage, I compared the number of times women spoke to the number for men.

35. Thier, "Motives and Apprehensions: On Edward P. Jones."

36. Jones, "Lost in the City," 263, 264, 265. Subsequent citations to this story appear in the text.

37. Jones, "Blindsided," 494.

38. Jones, "Adam Robinson Acquires Grandparents and a Little Sister," 402.

39. In *Bad Men: Creative Touchstones of Black Writers*, Howard Rambsy II describes how bad Black male figures serve as creative muses for a wide range of writers and musicians including Elizabeth Alexander, Amiri Baraka, Paul Beatty, Ta-Nehisi Coates, Tyehimba Jess, Trymaine Lee, Adrian Matejka, Aaron McGruder, Evie Shockley, and Kevin Young.

40. Graham, "An Interview with Edward P. Jones," 433.

41. Jones, "Old Boys, Old Girls," 131–32. Subsequent citations to this story appear in the text.

42. In *Why Are So Many Black Men in Prison?*, Demico Boothe outlines how mass incarnation disproportionally affects African Americans in the US. He writes, "African-American males are being imprisoned at an alarming and unprecedented rate. Out of the more than 11 million black adult males in the U.S. population, nearly 1.5 million are in prisons and jails with another 3.5 million more on probation or parole or who have previously been on probation or parole" (59).

43. Elliott, "Edward P. Jones's Tales of 'Aunt Hagar's Children.'"

CONCLUSION

1. Graham, "Black Is Gold: African American Literature, Critical Literacy, and Twenty-First-Century Pedagogies," 84.

2. Jessop, "Digital Visualization as a Scholarly Activity," 281.

3. Dennis and Falkenstein, "Project Conclusion," *Lost in the City: An Exploration of Edward P. Jones's Short Fiction*.

4. Chaudhary and Zitting, "Section 2: Character Demographics of *All Aunt Hagar's Children*," *Lost in the City: An Exploration of Edward P. Jones's Short Fiction*.

5. Students were quick to note that "a single sitting" had drastically changed given the many distractions such as television, social media, and even part-time vs. full-time employment.

6. Iafrate, *From Big Data to Smart Data*, 13.

7. All the following explore geographic representations in African American fiction: *Ride Out the Wilderness: Geography and Identity in Afro-American Literature* (1987) by Melvin Dixon; *Looking for Harlem: Urban Aesthetics in African-American Literature* (2000) by Maria Balshaw; *Violence, the Body, and "The South"* (2001) edited by Houston A. Baker Jr. and Dana D. Nelson; *Black Masculinity and the U.S. South: From Uncle Tom to Gangsta* (2007) edited by Riché Richardson; *South of Tradition: Essays on African American Literature* (2010) by Trudier Harris; and *Black Atlas: Geography and Flow in Nineteenth-Century African American Literature* (2015) by Judith Madera.

8. The phrase "zone of action" is one of five categories identified by Barbara Piatti in "Mapping Literature" that describe the several settings that are combined to make a single city or region (185).

SELECTED BIBLIOGRAPHY

Abrams, M. H. *A Glossary of Literary Terms*. 7th ed., Harcourt Brace, 1999.
Albert, Richard N. "The Jazz-Blues Motif in James Baldwin's 'Sonny's Blues.'" *College Literature*, vol. 11, no. 2, 1984, pp. 178–85. *JSTOR*, www.jstor.org/stable/25111592.
Anderton, May. "Fire and Water: Opposites and Pairings in 'A Party Down at the Square.'" *The Explicator*, vol. 70, no. 2, Apr. 2012, pp. 104–7.
Andrews, William L., et al., editors. *The Literature of the American South: A Norton Anthology*. W. W. Norton, 1998.
Baker, Houston A., Jr. *The Blues Aesthetic and the Making of American Identity in the Literature of the South*. Peter Lang, 2003.
Baker, Houston A., Jr. *Blues, Ideology, and Afro-American Literature: A Vernacular Theory*. U Chicago P, 1987.
Baker, Houston A., Jr. *Long Black Song: Essays in Black American Literature and Culture*. UP of Virginia, 1972.
Baker, Houston A., Jr. *Turning South Again: Re-Thinking Modernism/Re-Reading Booker T*. Duke UP, 2001.
Baker, Houston A., Jr., and Dana D. Nelson, editors. *Violence, the Body, and "The South."* Duke UP, 2001.
Baldwin, James. "Going to Meet the Man." *Going to Meet the Man*, Vintage International, 1993, pp. 318–51.
Baldwin, James. "The Harlem Ghetto." *Notes of a Native Son*, Beacon Press, 2012, pp. 77–92.
Baldwin, James. "Sonny's Blues." *The Norton Anthology of African American Literature*, edited by Henry Louis Gates Jr. and Valerie Smith, 3rd ed., vol. 2, W. W. Norton, 2014, pp. 413–35.
Balshaw, Maria. *Looking for Harlem: Urban Aesthetics in African-American Literature*. Pluto Press, 2001.
Bambara, Toni Cade, editor. *The Black Woman: An Anthology*. Washington Square Press, 1970.
Bambara, Toni Cade. *Conversations with Toni Cade Bambara*, edited by Thabiti Lewis, UP of Mississippi, 2012.
Bambara, Toni Cade. "Gorilla, My Love." *Gorilla, My Love*, Vintage Books, 1992, pp. 21–30.
Bambara, Toni Cade. "The Lesson." *Gorilla, My Love*, Vintage Books, 1992, pp. 93–104.

Bambara, Toni Cade. "Raymond's Run." *Gorilla, My Love*, Vintage Books, 1992, pp. 31–43.
Baraka, Amiri. "The Changing Same." *Black Music: Essays*, Akashic, 2010, pp. 175–205.
Baraka, Amiri. "Jazz and the White Critic." *The LeRoi Jones/Amiri Baraka Reader*, edited by William J. Harris, Thunder's Mouth, 1991, pp. 179–85.
Baraka, Amiri. "The Screamers." *The LeRoi Jones/Amiri Baraka Reader*, edited by William J. Harris, Basic Books, 2009, pp. 171–76.
Bausch, Richard, and Ronald V. Cassill, editors. *The Norton Anthology of Short Fiction*. Norton, 2006.
Bell, Bernard W., et al., editors. *Call & Response: The Riverside Anthology of the African American Literary Tradition*. Houghton Mifflin, 1998.
Birmingham, Kevin. "No Name in the South: James Baldwin and the Monuments of Identity." *African American Review*, vol. 44, no. 1/2, 2011, pp. 221–34. *JSTOR*, www.jstor.org/stable/41328716.
Bolden, Tony. *Afro-Blue: Improvisations in African American Poetry and Culture*. U of Illinois P, 2004.
Bona, Mary Jo, and Irma Maini. "Introduction: Multiethnic Literature in the Millennium." *Multiethnic Literature and Canon Debates*, State U of New York P, 2006, pp. 1–20.
Bone, Robert. *Down Home: Origins of the Afro-American Short Story*. Columbia UP, 1988.
Boothe, Demico. *Why Are So Many Black Men in Prison?* Full Surface, 2007.
Boyd, Herb, and Robert L. Allen. "Introduction." *Brotherman: The Odyssey of Black Men in America*, One World, 1996, pp. xxi–xxxiv.
Brock, Thomas. "Young Adults and Higher Education: Barriers and Breakthroughs to Success." *The Future of Children*, vol. 20, no. 1, 2010, pp. 109–32. *JSTOR*, www.jstor.org/stable/27795062.
Burke, Patrick. "The Screamers." *Daedalus*, vol. 142, no. 4, 2013, pp. 11–23. *JSTOR*, www.jstor.org/stable/43297994.
Burroway, Janet, et al. *Writing Fiction: A Guide to Narrative Craft*. U of Chicago P, 2019.
Butler, Robert James. "The Function of Violence in Richard Wright's *Native Son*." *Black American Literature Forum*, vol. 20, no. 1/2, 1986, pp. 9–25. *JSTOR*, www.jstor.org/stable/2904549.
Callahan, John. "Introduction." *Trading Twelves: The Selected Letters of Ralph Ellison and Albert Murray*, Vintage, 2000.
Carby, Hazel V. "The Politics of Fiction, Anthropology, and the Folk: Zora Neale Hurston." *Zora Neale Hurston's Their Eyes Were Watching God: A Casebook*, edited by Cheryl A. Wall, Oxford UP, 2000.
Card, Orson Scott. *Elements of Fiction Writing: Characters & Viewpoint*. Writer's Digest Books, 2010.
Cataliotti, Robert H. *The Music in African American Fiction: Representing Music in African American Fiction*. Routledge, 2019.
Chaffee, Patricia. "Slippery Ground: Ralph Ellison's Bingo Player." *Negro American Literature Forum*, vol. 10, no. 1, 1976, pp. 23–24. *JSTOR*, www.jstor.org/stable/3041276.
Chaudhary, Hira, and Angela Zitting. "Section 2: Character Demographics of 'All Aunt Hagar's Children.'" *Lost in the City: An Exploration of Edward P. Jones's Short Fiction*, edited by Kenton Rambsy and Peace Ossom-Williamson, Afro-PWW, 2019.

Chesnutt, Charles. "The Goophered Grapevine." *The Conjure Woman*, Houghton, Mifflin and Company, 1899. *Documenting the American South*, 1997, University of North Carolina at Chapel Hill, pp. 1–35, https://docsouth.unc.edu/southlit/chesnuttconjure/conjure.html.

Chesnutt, Charles. "Po' Sandy." *The Conjure Woman*, Houghton, Mifflin and Company, 1899. *Documenting the American South*, 1997, University of North Carolina at Chapel Hill, pp. 36–63, https://docsouth.unc.edu/southlit/chesnuttconjure/conjure.html.

Chesnutt, Charles. "The Sheriff's Children." *The Wife of His Youth and Other Stories of the Color Line*, Houghton, Mifflin and Company, 1901. *Documenting the American South*, 1997, University of North Carolina at Chapel Hill, pp. 60–93, https://docsouth.unc.edu/southlit/chesnuttwife/cheswife.html.

Chesnutt, Charles. "The Wife of His Youth." *The Wife of His Youth and Other Stories of the Color Line*, Houghton, Mifflin and Company, 1901. *Documenting the American South*, 1997, University of North Carolina at Chapel Hill, pp. 1–24, https://docsouth.unc.edu/southlit/chesnuttwife/cheswife.html.

Chinn, Nancy, and Elizabeth E. Dunn. "'The Ring of Singing Metal on Wood': Zora Neale Hurston's Artistry in 'The Gilded Six-Bits.'" *Mississippi Quarterly: The Journal of Southern Cultures*, vol. 49, no. 4, 1996, pp. 775–90. *EBSCOhost*, search.ebscohost.com/login.aspx?direct=true&db=mzh&AN=1997061932&site=ehost-live.

Christian, Barbara. *Black Women Novelists: The Development of a Tradition, 1892–1976*. Greenwood Press, 1980.

Claborn, John. "Who Set You Feelin'? Harlem, Communal Affect, and the Great Migration Narrative in James Baldwin's 'Sonny's Blues.'" *English Language Notes*, vol. 48, no. 1, 2010, pp. 89–100.

Cobb, William J. "*All Aunt Hagar's Children* by Edward P. Jones." *Houston Chronicle*, 12 Aug. 2011, www.chron.com/life/books/article/All-Aunt-Hagar-s-Children-by-Edward-P-Jones-1894766.php.

Corbett, David. *The Art of Character: Creating Memorable Characters for Fiction, Film, and TV*. Penguin Books, 2013.

Csicsila, Joseph Thomas. *Canons by Consensus: Critical Trends and American Literature Anthologies*. U of Alabama P, 2011.

Davis, Arthur Paul, and J. Saunders Redding, editors. *Cavalcade: Negro American Writing from 1760 to the Present*. Houghton Mifflin, 1971.

Davis, Thadious M. "Expanding the Limits: The Intersection of Race and Region." *The Southern Literary Journal*, vol. 20, no. 2, Spring 1988, pp. 3–11. *JSTOR*, http://www.jstor.org/stable/20077924.

Davis, Thadious M. *Southscapes: Geographies of Race, Region, and Literature*. U of North Carolina P, 2011.

Dean, Jeremy. "Repairing Urban Renewal in Story: Edward P. Jones's Imaginary Remapping of Washington, D.C. in *Lost in the City*." American Studies Association Convention, 22 Oct. 2011, Hilton Baltimore, Baltimore, MD. Conference Presentation.

DeFerrari, John. "The Once-Ubiquitous Peoples Drug Stores." *Streets of Washington*, 5 Dec. 2011, www.streetsofwashington.com/2011/11/once-ubiquitous-peoples-drug-stores.html.

Demarest, David P. "Richard Wright: The Meaning of Violence." *Negro American Literature Forum*, vol. 8, no. 3, 1974, pp. 236–39. *JSTOR*, www.jstor.org/stable/3041464.

Dennis, Michael, and Misty Falkenstein. "Project Conclusion." *Lost in the City: An Exploration of Edward P. Jones's Short Fiction*, edited by Kenton Rambsy and Peace Ossom-Williamson, Afro-PWW, 2019.

Dickson-Carr, Darryl. *The Columbia Guide to Contemporary African American Fiction*. Columbia UP, 2005.

Dittmar, Linda. "Will the Circle Be Unbroken? The Politics of Form in *The Bluest Eye*." *NOVEL: A Forum on Fiction*, vol. 23, no. 2, 1990, pp. 137–55. *JSTOR*, www.jstor.org/stable/1345735.

Dixon, Melvin. *Ride Out the Wilderness: Geography and Identity in Afro-American Literature*. U of Illinois P, 1987.

"Driving in DC: A Crash Course on the Grid System." *Washingtonian*, 22 Feb. 2008, www.washingtonian.com/2008/02/22/driving-in-dc-a-crash-course-on-the-grid-system/.

Dumas, Henry. "Will the Circle Be Unbroken." *The Norton Anthology of African American Literature*, edited by Henry Louis Gates Jr. and Valerie Smith, 3rd ed., vol. 1, W. W. Norton, 2014, pp. 655–59.

Duncan, Charles Waddell. *The Northern Stories of Charles W. Chesnutt*. Ohio UP, 2004.

Elliott, Debbie. "Edward P. Jones's Tales of 'Aunt Hagar's Children.'" *NPR*, 27 Aug. 2006, www.npr.org/templates/story/story.php?storyId=5711385.

Ellison, Ralph. "Battle Royal." *The Norton Anthology of African American Literature*, edited by Henry Louis Gates Jr. and Valerie Smith, 3rd ed., vol. 2, W. W. Norton, 2014, pp. 264–74.

Ellison, Ralph. "Flying Home." *Flying Home and Other Stories*, edited by John F. Callahan, Vintage International, 2012, pp. 198–225.

Ellison, Ralph. *Invisible Man*. Vintage International, 1995.

Ellison, Ralph. "King of the Bingo Game." *Flying Home and Other Stories*, edited by John F. Callahan, Vintage International, 2012, pp. 173–87.

Ellison, Ralph. "A Party Down at the Square." *Flying Home and Other Stories*, edited by John F. Callahan, Vintage International, 2012, pp. 46–55.

Ellison, Ralph. "Richard Wright's Blues." *The Antioch Review*, vol. 74, no. 3, 2016, pp. 490–503. *JSTOR*, www.jstor.org/stable/10.7723/antiochreview.74.3.0490.

Farrell, Susan. "Fight vs. Flight: A Re-Evaluation of Dee in Alice Walker's 'Everyday Use.'" *Studies in Short Fiction*, vol. 35, no. 2, 1998, pp. 179–86.

Fisher, Rudolph. "The City of Refuge." *The Norton Anthology of African American Literature*, edited by Henry Louis Gates Jr. and Valerie Smith, 3rd ed., vol. 1, W. W. Norton, 2014, pp. 1237–49.

Fisher, Rudolph. "Miss Cynthie." *The City of Refuge: The Collected Stories of Rudolph Fisher*, edited by John McCluskey, U of Missouri P, 2008, pp. 97–110.

Fox, Robert Elliot. "Shaping an African American Literary Canon." *Postmodern Culture*, vol. 9, no. 1, 1998. *Project MUSE*, doi:10.1353/pmc.1998.0035.

Gates, Henry Louis, Jr. "The Master's Pieces: On Canon Formation and the Afro-American Tradition." *The Bounds of Race: Perspectives on Hegemony and Resistance*, edited by Dominick LaCapra, Cornell UP, 1991, pp. 17–38.

Gates, Henry Louis, Jr. "Preface to the Second Edition, *The Norton Anthology of African American Literature*, with Nellie Y. McKay." *The Henry Louis Gates, Jr. Reader*, edited by Abby Wolf, Basic Civitas Books, 2012.

Gates, Henry Louis, Jr. *The Signifying Monkey: A Theory of African-American Literary Criticism*. Oxford UP, 1988.

Gates, Henry Louis, Jr. "A Tragedy of Negro Life." *Mule Bone: A Comedy of Negro Life*, by Zora Neale Hurston and Langston Hughes, edited by Henry Louis Gates Jr. and George Bass, Perennial, 1991, pp. 5–24.

Gates, Henry Louis, Jr., and Sieglinde Lemke. "Introduction." *Complete Stories*, by Zora Neale Hurston, HarperCollins Publishers, 2008, pp. ix–xxiii.

Goldenberg, Suzanne. "Suzanne Goldenberg Meets Pulitzer Prize Winner Edward P. Jones." *The Guardian*, Guardian News and Media, 14 July 2004, www.theguardian.com/books/2004/jul/14/fiction.usa.

Graham, Maryemma. "Black Is Gold: African American Literature, Critical Literacy, and Twenty-First-Century Pedagogies." *Contemporary African American Literature: The Living Canon*, edited by Lovalerie King and Shirley Moody-Turner, Indiana UP, 2013, pp. 55–90.

Graham, Maryemma, and Edward P. Jones. "An Interview with Edward P. Jones." *African American Review*, vol. 42, no. 3–4, 2008, pp. 421–38. *JSTOR*, http://www.jstor.org/stable/40301244.

Graham, Maryemma, and Jerry W. Ward, editors. *The Cambridge History of African American Literature*, Cambridge UP, 2015.

Gregory, James N. *The Southern Diaspora: How the Great Migrations of Black and White Southerners Transformed America*. U of North Carolina P, 2007.

Gussow, Adam. "Fingering the Jagged Grain: Ellison's Wright and the Southern Blues Violences." *boundary 2*, vol. 30, no. 2, 2003, pp. 137–55. *Project MUSE*, muse.jhu.edu/article/44475.

Gustafson, Sandra. "Prologue: What's in a Date?" *Timelines of American Literature*, edited by Cody Marrs and Christopher Hager, Johns Hopkins UP, 2019, pp. 11–20.

Hakutani, Yoshinobu, and Robert Butler. *The City in African-American Literature*. Fairleigh Dickinson UP, 1996.

Hamilton, Geordie. "Focalization as Education: The Race Relation of the Narrator of Charles Chesnutt's *The Marrow of Tradition* (1901)." *Style*, vol. 42, no. 1, 2008, pp. 49–72. MLA International Bibliography, EBSCO, accessed 6 Apr. 2020.

Harris, Trudier. "Peace in the War of Desire: Richard Wright's 'Long Black Song.'" *CLA Journal*, vol. 56, no. 3, 2013, pp. 188–208. *JSTOR*, www.jstor.org/stable/44329585.

Harris, Trudier. *The Scary Mason-Dixon Line: African American Writers and the South*. Louisiana State UP, 2013.

Harris, Trudier. *South of Tradition: Essays on African American Literature*. U of Georgia P, 2002.

Harris, Trudier. "The Trickster in African American Literature." Freedom's Story, TeacherServe, National Humanities Center, 6 Apr. 2020, http://nationalhumanitiescenter.org/tserve/freedom/1865-1917/essays/trickster.htm.

Harrison, John. "'All Aunt Hagar's Children' by Edward P. Jones." *The Quarterly Conversation*, 2006.

Hollister, Michael. "Tradition in Alice Walker's 'To Hell with Dying.'" *Studies in Short Fiction*, vol. 26, no. 1, 1989, pp. 90–94. *EBSCOhost*, search.ebscohost.com/login.aspx?direct=true&db=mzh&AN=1989060578&site=ehost-live.

Hurston, Zora Neale. "The Gilded Six-Bits." *The Norton Anthology of African American Literature*, edited by Henry Louis Gates Jr. and Valerie Smith, 3rd ed., vol. 1, W. W. Norton, 2014, pp. 1043–50.

Hurston, Zora Neale. "The Man Who Was Almost a Man." *Eight Men: Short Stories*, Harper Perennial Modern Classics, 2008, pp. 3–18.

Hurston, Zora Neale. "Spunk." *Complete Stories*, edited by Henry Louis Gates and Sieglinde Lemke, HarperCollins Publishers, 2008, pp. 26–32.

Hurston, Zora Neale. "Sweat." *The Norton Anthology of African American Literature*, edited by Henry Louis Gates Jr. and Valerie Smith, 3rd ed., vol. 1, W. W. Norton, 2014, pp. 1032–40.

Hurston, Zora Neale. "Uncle Tom's Children." *Richard Wright: Critical Perspectives Past and Present*, edited by Henry Louis Gates Jr. and K. A. Appiah, Amistad Press, 1993.

Iafrate, Fernando. *From Big Data to Smart Data*. Wiley-ISTE, 2015.

Jackson, Blyden. "Richard Wright in a Moment of Truth." *The Southern Literary Journal*, vol. 3, no. 2, 1971, pp. 3+. *Gale Academic OneFile*, accessed 5 May 2020.

Jackson, Lawrence Patrick. *The Indignant Generation: A Narrative History of African American Writers and Critics, 1934–1960*. Princeton UP, 2011.

Jackson, Lawrence P., and Edward P. Jones. "An Interview with Edward P. Jones." *African American Review*, vol. 34, no. 1, 2000, pp. 95–103. *JSTOR*, www.jstor.org/stable/2901186.

Jarrett, Gene Andrew. "The Dialect of New Negro Literature." *A Companion to African American Literature*, edited by Gene Andrew Jarrett, Wiley Blackwell, 2013.

Jarrett, Gene Andrew, editor. *The Wiley Blackwell Anthology of African American Literature*. Wiley Blackwell, 2014.

Jessop, Martyn. "Digital Visualization as a Scholarly Activity." *Literary and Linguistic Computing*, vol. 23, no. 3, Sept. 2008, pp. 281–93, doi:10.1093/llc/fqn016.

Johnson, Maria V. "Voices of Struggle: An Exploration of the Relationship Between African American Women's Music and Literature." Diss. U of California, Berkeley, 1992.

Jones, Edward P. "Adam Robinson Acquires Grandparents and a Little Sister." *All Aunt Hagar's Children*, HarperCollins e-Books, 2006, pp. 398–451.

Jones, Edward P. "All Aunt Hagar's Children." *All Aunt Hagar's Children*, HarperCollins e-Books, 2006, pp. 175–227.

Jones, Edward P. "Bad Neighbors." *All Aunt Hagar's Children*, HarperCollins e-Books, 2006, pp. 580–625.

Jones, Edward P. "Blindsided." *All Aunt Hagar's Children*, HarperCollins e-Books, 2006, pp. 491–540.

Jones, Edward P. "A Butterfly on F Street." *Lost in the City: Stories*, HarperCollins e-Books, 2003, pp. 314–22.

Jones, Edward P. "The First Day." *Lost in the City: Stories*, HarperCollins e-Books, 2003, pp. 49–58.

Jones, Edward P. "The Girl Who Raised Pigeons." *Lost in the City: Stories*, HarperCollins e-Books, 2003, pp. 7–48.

Jones, Edward P. "Gospel." *Lost in the City: Stories*, HarperCollins e-Books, 2003, pp. 323–57.

Jones, Edward P. "His Mother's House." *Lost in the City: Stories*, HarperCollins e-Books, 2003, pp. 269–313.

Jones, Edward P. "Lost in the City." *Lost in the City: Stories*, HarperCollins e-Books, 2003, pp. 251–68.

Jones, Edward P. "A New Man." *Lost in the City: Stories*, HarperCollins e-Books, 2003, pp. 358–82.

Jones, Edward P. "The Night Rhonda Ferguson Was Killed." *Lost in the City: Stories*, HarperCollins e-Books, 2003, pp. 59–98.

Jones, Edward P. "Old Boys, Old Girls." *All Aunt Hagar's Children*, HarperCollins e-Books, 2006, pp. 130–74.

Jones, Edward P. "An Orange Line Train to Ballston." *Lost in the City: Stories*, HarperCollins e-Books, 2003, pp. 188–207.

Jones, Edward P. "A Rich Man." *All Aunt Hagar's Children*, HarperCollins e-Books, 2006, pp. 541–79.

Jones, Edward P. "Young Lions." *Lost in the City: Stories*, HarperCollins e-Books, 2003, 99–138.

Jones, Harry L. "Style, Form, and Content in the Short Fiction of James Baldwin." *James Baldwin: A Critical Evaluation*, edited by Therman B. O'Daniel, Howard UP, 1981, pp. 144–50.

Jones, LeRoi [Amiri Baraka]. "City of Harlem." *Home: Social Issues*, Akashic, 2009, pp. 107–14.

Jones, Sharon L. *Critical Companion to Zora Neale Hurston: A Literary Reference to Her Life and Work*. Facts On File, 2009.

Jones, Sharon L. *Rereading the Harlem Renaissance: Race, Class, and Gender in the Fiction of Jessie Fauset, Zora Neale Hurston, and Dorothy West*. Greenwood Press, 2002.

Joseph, Philip. "The Verdict from the Porch: Zora Neale Hurston and Reparative Justice." *American Literature*, vol. 74, no. 3, 2002, pp. 455–83. Project MUSE, muse.jhu.edu/article/1844.

Keller, Frances Richardson. *An American Crusade: The Life of Charles Waddell Chesnutt*. Brigham Young UP, 1978.

Kinnamon, Kenneth. "Anthologies of African-American Literature from 1845 to 1994." *Callaloo*, vol. 20, no. 2, 1997.

Knowles, Caroline. *Race and Social Analysis*. Sage, 2003.

Lauret, Maria. "Alice Walker's Life and Works: The Essays." *Alice Walker*, edited by Harold Bloom, Infobase Pub., 2007, pp. 75–102.

Leyshon, Cressida. "A Writer in His Own Mind: An Interview with Edward P. Jones." *The New Yorker*, 25 Apr. 2004, www.newyorker.com/magazine/2004/05/03/a-writer-in-his-own-mind.

Lieberman, Jennifer L. "Ralph Ellison's Technological Humanism." *MELUS: Multi-Ethnic Literature of the U.S.*, vol. 40, no. 4, 2015, pp. 8–27. Project MUSE, muse.jhu.edu/article/610032.

Lopate, Phillip. *Writing New York: A Literary Anthology*. Library of America, 2008.

Lucy, Robin. "'Flying Home': Ralph Ellison, Richard Wright, and the Black Folk during World War II." *The Journal of American Folklore*, vol. 120, no. 477, 2007, pp. 257–83. *JSTOR*, www.jstor.org/stable/20487555.

Maass, Donald. "Creating Your Story's Time & Place." *Crafting Novels & Short Stories: The Complete Guide to Writing Great Fiction*. Writer's Digest Books, 2011.

MacGregor, Morris J. *Integration of the Armed Forces, 1940–1965*. Center of Military History, U.S. Army, 1981.

Makombe, Rodwell. "Apartheid, Crime, and Interracial Violence in 'Black Boy.'" *Journal of Black Studies*, vol. 44, no. 3, 2013, pp. 290–313. *JSTOR*, www.jstor.org/stable/23414672.

Marrs, Cody, and Christopher Hager. "Introduction." *Timelines of American Literature*, Johns Hopkins UP, 2019.

Martin, Matthew R. "The Two-Faced New South: The Plantation Tales of Thomas Nelson Page and Charles W. Chesnutt." *The Southern Literary Journal*, vol. 30, no. 2, 1998, pp. 17–36. *JSTOR*, www.jstor.org/stable/20078206.

Mason, Theodore O. "The African-American Anthology: Mapping the Territory, Taking the National Census, Building the Museum." *American Literary History*, vol. 10, no. 1, 1998, pp. 185–98. *JSTOR*, www.jstor.org/stable/490266.

Mathews, Donald G. "The Southern Rite of Human Sacrifice: Lynching in the American South." *Mississippi Quarterly: The Journal of Southern Cultures*, vol. 61, no. 1–2, 2008, pp. 27–70. *EBSCOhost*, search.ebscohost.com/login.aspx?direct=true&db=mzh&AN=2009640853&site=ehost-live.

Matthews, Kadeshia L. "Black Boy No More?: Violence and the Flight from Blackness in Richard Wright's *Native Son*." *MFS Modern Fiction Studies*, vol. 60, no. 2, 2014, pp. 276–97. *Project MUSE*, doi:10.1353/mfs.2014.0016.

Mazurek, Raymond A. "Writer on the Left: Class and Race in Ellison's Early Fiction." *College Literature*, vol. 29, no. 4, 2002, pp. 109–35. *JSTOR*, www.jstor.org/stable/25112680.

McDowell, Deborah E. *"The Changing Same": Black Women's Literature, Criticism, and Theory*. Indiana UP, 1995.

McDowell, Deborah E., and Hortense Spillers. "Introduction to Realism, Naturalism, Modernism: 1940–1960." *The Norton Anthology of African American Literature*, edited by Henry Louis Gates Jr. and Valerie Smith, 3rd ed., vol. 2, W. W. Norton, 2014, pp. 93–107.

Miller, E. Ethelbert. "Edward P. Jones Talks about 'The Known World' and His Washington, D.C., Short Stories." *YouTube*, uploaded by Howard County Poetry and Literature Society, 9 Mar. 2012, https://www.youtube.com/watch?v=W5sPWxFiVZI.

Mitgang, Herbert. "'Invisible Man,' as Vivid Today as in 1952." *The New York Times*, 1 Mar. 1982, p. 13.

Morrison, Toni. "Rootedness: The Ancestor as Foundation." *Black Women Writers (1950–1980)*, edited by Mari Evans, Anchor, 1984, pp. 339–45.

Mullen, Bill. *Revolutionary Tales: African American Women's Short Stories, from the First Story to the Present*. Laurel, 1995.

Muller, John. "Anacostia's Larger-Than-Life Big Chair Is Full of Neighborhood History." *Greater Greater Washington*, 27 Mar. 2015, ggwash.org/view/37647/anacostias-larger-than-life-big-chair-is-full-of-neighborhood-history.

Mullins, Matthew. "Antagonized by the Text, Or, It Takes Two to Read Alice Walker's 'Everyday Use.'" *Comparatist: Journal of the Southern Comparative Literature Association*, vol. 37, May 2013, pp. 37–53. *EBSCOhost*, search.ebscohost.com/login.aspx?direct=true&db=mzh&AN=2013392796&site=ehost-live.

Nagel, James, editor. *Anthology of the American Short Story*. Houghton Mifflin, 2008.

Nagel, James. *The Contemporary American Short-Story Cycle: The Ethnic Resonance of Genre*. Louisiana State UP, 2004.

Nance, Kevin. "Edward P. Jones on Receiving the Harold Washington Literary Award." *Chicago Tribune*, 28 May 2015, www.chicagotribune.com/entertainment/books/ct-prj-edward-jones-harold-washington-20150528-story.html.

Neely, Brooke, and Michelle Samura. "Social Geographies of Race: Connecting Race and Space." *Ethnic and Racial Studies*, vol. 34, no. 11, 2011, pp. 1933–52, doi:10.1080/01419870.2011.559262.

NPR Staff. "In D.C., A Bastion of Black Entertainment Returns." *NPR*, 8 Apr. 2012, www.npr.org/2012/04/08/150200240/in-d-c-a-bastion-of-black-entertainment-returns.

O'Meally, Robert. "The Rules of Magic: Hemingway as Ellison's 'Ancestor.'" *Ralph Ellison's Invisible Man: A Casebook*, edited by John F. Callahan, Oxford UP, 2004.

Ore, Ersula J. *Lynching: Violence, Rhetoric, and American Identity*. UP of Mississippi, 2019.

Parrish, Timothy. *Ralph Ellison and the Genius of America*. U of Massachusetts P, 2012.

Patterson, Tiffany Ruby. *Zora Neale Hurston and a History of Southern Life*. Temple UP, 2005.

Penzler, Otto. "Excerpt: 'Black Noir.'" *NPR*, 26 May 2009, www.npr.org/templates/story/story.php?storyId=104392785.

Piatti, Barbara. "Mapping Literature: Towards a Geography of Fiction." *Cartography and Art*, edited by William Cartwright et al., Springer, 2009, pp. 177–94.

Plant, Deborah G. *Zora Neale Hurston: A Biography of the Spirit*. Rowman & Littlefield, 2011.

Rambsy, Howard, II. *Bad Men: Creative Touchstones of Black Writers*. U of Virginia P, 2020.

Rambsy, Kenton. "Meeting Edward P. Jones at Old Ebbitt Grill." *Cultural Front*, 1 Jan. 1970, www.culturalfront.org/2016/10/meeting-edward-p-jones-at-old-ebbitt.html?m=1.

Rambsy, Kenton, et al. "The Black Short Story Dataset—Vol. 1." Data file and code book. University of Texas at Arlington, 2018, Texas Data Repository Dataverse, doi:10.18738/T8/5TBANV.

Rampersad, Arnold. *Ralph Ellison: A Biography*. Vintage Books, 2008.

Ramsey, Guthrie P. *Race Music: Black Cultures from Behop to Hip-Hop*. U of California P, 2004.

Richardson, Riché. *Black Masculinity and the U.S. South: From Uncle Tom to Gangsta*. U of Georgia P, 2007.

Rivas, Dan. "10 Questions with Edward P. Jones." *Politics and Prose Bookstore*, July 2004, www.politics-prose.com/book-notes/10-questions-edward-p-jones.

Roosevelt, Eleanor. "My Day, April 1, 1938." *The Eleanor Roosevelt Papers Digital Edition*, 2017, accessed 13 Feb. 2020, https://www2.gwu.edu/~erpapers/myday/displaydoc.cfm?_y=1938&_f=md054916.

Rustin-Paschal, Nicole. "A Rich Man: Celebrating Edward P. Jones During National Short Story Month." *The Pickaninny Papers*, 31 May 2011, thepickaninnypapers.com/arts

-culture/2011/5/31/a-rich-man-celebrating-edward-p-jones-during-nationalshort.html#targetText=Except%20for%20mid%2Dsummer%20in,story%2C%20"A%20Rich%20Man.&targetText=The%20story%20recounts%20the%20end,couldn't%20stand%20each%20other.

Ryan, Melissa. "Dangerous Refuge: Richard Wright and the Swimming Hole." *African American Review*, vol. 50, no. 1, 2017, pp. 27–40. *Project MUSE*, doi:10.1353/afa.2017.0002.

Saunders, Judith P. "Paternal Confidence in Hurston's 'The Gilded Six-Bits.'" *American Classics: Evolutionary Perspectives*, Academic Studies Press, 2018, pp. 226–45. *JSTOR*, www.jstor.org/stable/j.ctv4v3226.16.

Shaffer, Donald M., Jr. "African American Folklore as Racial Project in Charles W. Chesnutt's *The Conjure Woman*." *Western Journal of Black Studies*, vol. 36, no. 4, 2012, pp. 325–36. *EBSCOhost*, search.ebscohost.com/login.aspx?direct=true&db=mzh&AN=2013308551&site=ehost-live.

Sherard, Tracey. "Sonny's Bebop: Baldwin's 'Blues Text' as Intracultural Critique." *African American Review*, vol. 32, no. 4, 1998, pp. 691–705. *JSTOR*, www.jstor.org/stable/2901246.

Smith, Rochelle, and Sharon L. Jones, editors. *The Prentice Hall Anthology of African American Literature*. Prentice Hall, 2000.

Spinner, Jackie, and Margaret Webb Pressley. "Hahn Shoes Chain for Sale after 119 Years in District." *The Washington Post*, 23 June 1995.

Stepto, Robert B. *From Behind the Veil: A Study of Afro-American Narrative*. U of Illinois P, 1979.

Stewart, Alison. *First Class: The Legacy of Dunbar, America's First Black Public High School*. Chicago Review, 2015.

Stewart, James. "The Development of the Black Revolutionary Artist." *Black Fire: An Anthology of Afro-American Writing*, edited by Amiri Baraka and Larry Neal, Black Classic Press, 1968, pp. 3–10.

Storm, Anna. "Alice Dunbar-Nelson, Zora Neale Hurston, and the Creation of 'Authentic Voices' in the Black Women's Literary Tradition." Diss. University of Wisconsin-Milwaukee, 2016, https://dc.uwm.edu/etd/1419.

Tackach, James. "The Biblical Foundation of James Baldwin's 'Sonny's Blues.'" *Renascence: Essays on Values in Literature*, vol. 59, no. 2, 2007, pp. 109–18. *EBSCOhost*, search.ebscohost.com/login.aspx?direct=true&db=mzh&AN=2007300204&site=ehost-live.

Taylor, Sara. "Denigration, Dependence, and Deviation: Black and White Masculinities in James Baldwin's *Going to Meet the Man*." *Obsidian III: Literature in the African Diaspora*, vol. 9, no. 2, 2008, pp. 43–61. *EBSCOhost*, search.ebscohost.com/login.aspx?direct=true&db=mzh&AN=2011392456&site=ehost-live.

Tewarie, Bhoendradatt. "Southern Elements in Ellison's *Invisible Man*." *The Journal of General Education*, vol. 35, no. 3, 1983, pp. 189–200. *JSTOR*, www.jstor.org/stable/27796962.

Thier, Aaron. "Motives and Apprehensions: On Edward P. Jones." *The Nation*, 29 June 2015, www.thenation.com/article/archive/motives-and-apprehensions-edward-p-jones/.

Thomas, Lorenzo. "'Communicating by Horns': Jazz and Redemption in the Poetry of the Beats and the Black Arts Movement." *African American Review*, vol. 26, no. 2, 1992, pp. 291–98. *JSTOR*, www.jstor.org/stable/3041856.

Thomas, Sheree R. *Dark Matter: A Century of Speculative Fiction from the African Diaspora*. Warner, 2000.

Thorsteinson, Katherine. "From Escape to Ascension: The Effects of Aviation Technology on the Flying African Myth." *Criticism: A Quarterly for Literature and the Arts*, vol. 57, no. 2, 2015, pp. 259–81. *EBSCOhost*, search.ebscohost.com/login.aspx?direct=true&db=mzh&AN=2016390540&site=ehost-live.

Tunc, Tanfer Emin. "The De(con)struction of Black/White Binaries: Critiques of Passing in Charles Waddell Chesnutt's 'The Wife of His Youth' and Other Stories of the Color Line." *Callaloo*, vol. 37, no. 3, 2014, pp. 676–91. *Project MUSE*, doi:10.1353/cal.2014.0106.

Walker, Alice. "Advancing Luna and Ida B. Wells." *You Can't Keep a Good Woman Down: Stories*, Open Road Media, 2011, pp. 6–30.

Walker, Alice. "Everyday Use." *The Norton Anthology of African American Literature*, edited by Henry Louis Gates Jr. and Valerie Smith, 3rd ed., vol. 2, W. W. Norton, 2014, pp. 1188–94.

Walker, Alice. "I Know What the Earth Says." Interview by William Ferris. *Southern Cultures*, vol. 10, no. 1, Spring 2004, pp. 5–24.

Walker, Alice. "Nineteen Fifty-Five." *You Can't Keep a Good Woman Down: Stories*, Open Road Media, 2011.

Walker, Alice. "To Hell with Dying." *In Love & Trouble: Stories of Black Women*, Harcourt, 2004, pp. 156–67.

Wall, Cheryl A. "Zora Neale Hurston." *The Concise Oxford Companion to African American Literature*, edited by William Leake Andrews et al., Oxford UP, 2001, pp. 209–12.

Wallach, Jennifer Jensen. *Richard Wright: From Black Boy to World Citizen*. Ivan R. Dee, 2010.

Ward, Jerry W. "Introduction." *Trouble the Water: 250 Years of African-American Poetry*, Mentor, 1997, pp. xix–xxiii.

Ward, Jerry W., Jr., and Robert Butler. "Almos' a Man." *The Richard Wright Encyclopedia*, edited by Ward and Butler, Greenwood Press, 2008, pp. 17–18.

Washington, Mary Helen, editor. *Black-Eyed Susans/Midnight Birds: Stories by and about Black Women*. Anchor Books, 1990.

Watts, Jerry Gafio. *Heroism and the Black Intellectual: Ralph Ellison, Politics, and Afro-American Intellectual Life*. U of North Carolina P, 1994.

Werner, Craig. *A Change Is Gonna Come: Music, Race & the Soul of America*. U of Michigan P, 2006.

Wilkerson, Isabel. *The Warmth of Other Suns: The Epic Story of America's Great Migration*. Penguin Random House, 2016.

Williams, Sherley Anne. "Papa Dick and Sister-Woman: Reflections on Women in the Fiction of Richard Wright." *American Novelists Revisited: Essays in Feminist Criticism*, edited by Fritz Fleischmann, G. K. Hall, 1982.

Wilmot, Patrick. "The Role of Violence in the Works of Wright and Fanon." *The Black Scholar*, vol. 39, no. 1/2, 2009, pp. 17–22. *JSTOR*, www.jstor.org/stable/41069377.

Wilson, Charles Reagan. *The New Encyclopedia of Southern Culture, Volume 3: History*. U of North Carolina P, 2014.

Wright, Richard. "Between Laughter and Tears." *University of Virginia: Relations of Race*, 8 Feb. 2020, http://people.virginia.edu/~sfr/enam358/wrightrev.html.

Wright, Richard. "Big Boy Leaves Home." *Uncle Tom's Children*, HarperCollins, 1995, pp. 16–61.

Wright, Richard. *Black Boy (American Hunger): A Record of Childhood and Youth*. Perennial Classics, 1998.

Wright, Richard. "Bright and Morning Star." *Uncle Tom's Children*, HarperCollins, 1995, pp. 221–64.

Wright, Richard. "Long Black Song." *Uncle Tom's Children*, HarperCollins, 1995, pp. 125–56.

Wright, Richard. "The Man Who Was Almost a Man." *Eight Men: Short Stories*, Harper Perennial Modern Classics, 2008.

Wright, Richard. *Native Son*. Harper Perennial Modern Classics, 2008.

INDEX

Abrams, M. H., 19
"Adam Robinson Acquires Grandparents and a Sister" (E. P. Jones), 118, 120
"Advancing Luna and Ida B. Wells" (A. Walker), 30, 65, 82–83
African American Literature, 20
African American Vernacular English (AAVE), 11–12, 17, 23, 39, 41–43, 46–49, 52–54, 57, 61, 69, 106, 119–20
Afro-American Writing (Long and Collier), 34
Alabama, 4, 11, 66, 68–70, 120
Albert, Richard N., 87
Aldrich, Thomas Bailey, 42
All Aunt Hagar's Children (E. P. Jones), 4, 12, 14, 70, 107, 112, 116, 119, 121, 127, 128, 131, 135
"All Aunt Hagar's Children" (E. P. Jones), 110–11, 113, 115, 116, 119–20
Allen, Robert L., 37
"Almos' a Man" (Wright), 8, 25, 37, 61, 70
Anderson, Sherwood, 81
Anderton, May, 77
Andrews, William L., 33
Angelou, Maya, 11, 36
anthologies, 3–4, 6–9, 12, 19–39, 42, 45, 51, 55–56, 62, 78–79, 100–101, 103, 114, 133, 136; alphabetical approach, 32, 37; birthdate approach, 36–38; chronological approach, 16, 20, 27–28, 32–34, 36–38; genre approach, 37; thematic approach, 32, 37–38

Anthology of the American Short Story (Nagel), 24
Arkansas, 41, 60
Arrested Development, 70
Aswell, Ed, 24
"Asylum" (G. Jones), 28
Atlantic Monthly, 42, 45

"Back Room, The" (Hurston), 30
"Bad Neighbors" (E. P. Jones), 14, 110, 111–12, 117–18, 128
Baker, Barbara, 42
Baker, Houston A., Jr., 33, 41
Baldwin, James, 3–4, 7, 10, 12–15, 16–17, 21, 23–24, 26, 32, 34, 35, 64–65, 72–74, 76–78, 86–93, 96–97, 99, 105, 112, 131–34
Bambara, Toni Cade, 3–4, 10, 12–14, 16–17, 21, 27–28, 31–32, 34, 86–87, 99–105, 131, 133–34
Baraka, Amiri, 4, 12, 13, 16, 17, 37, 87, 93, 97–99
Barksdale, Richard, 33
"Battle Royal" (Ellison), 4, 5, 8, 15–16, 25, 65–68
Bennett, Gwendolyn B., 27
Benston, Kimberly, 33
Best American Short Stories of 1958 (Foley and Burnett), 24
Best Short Stories by Negro Writers, The (Hughes), 30
"Big Boy Leaves Home" (Wright), 25, 57–59, 61, 70

Big 7, 3–4, 7–8, 11, 16, 20, 21–27, 31–32, 34, 39, 41, 103, 131–33
"Big 7 Short Story Dataset," 131
"Bird Cage, The" (White), 28
Birmingham, Kevin, 74
Black Boy (Wright), 24, 60
"Black Brother" (Smith), 30
"Black Death" (Hurston), 49
Black-Eyed Susans (Washington), 28
Black-Eyed Susans/Midnight Birds (Washington), 20, 28
Black Noir (Penzler), 38
"Black Short Story Dataset, The," 6, 8, 16, 21, 23, 26–27, 32, 37
Black Voices (Chapman), 7
Black Woman, The (Bambara), 27–28, 100
Black Writers of America (Barksdale and Kinnamon), 33–34
"Blindsided" (E. P. Jones), 110, 111, 120, 128
"Bone of Contention, The" (Hurston), 29–30
Bonetti, Kay, 31
Boyd, Herb, 37
"Bright and Morning Star" (Wright), 8, 11, 24, 25, 59–61
Brotherman (Boyd and Allen), 37
Brown, Sterling, 93, 106
"Brownies" (Packer), 11
Burke, Patrick, 98
Burnett, David, 24
Burroway, Janet, 14
Butler, Octavia E., 20, 27, 38, 72
Butler, Robert, 12
"Butterfly on F Street, A" (E. P. Jones), 110, 116, 129

Callahan, John, 65
Callaloo, 19
Call & Response, 33, 36
Campbell, Hazel V., 28
Card, Orson, 14–15
Cataliotti, Robert H., 13
Cavalcade (David and Redding), 23, 32–34
Chaffee, Patricia, 71
"Changing Same (R&B and New Black Music), The" (Baraka), 97

characters, 4, 12–14, 41, 49, 53, 63–64, 66–67, 78, 85, 87–88, 91, 93, 98, 108–12, 118–19, 121–23, 125–27, 128, 130–36; Black, 3, 5, 10, 13, 17, 22, 25, 41, 45, 48–50, 65, 69, 78–79, 100, 114–16, 124–25, 127; homegrown, 14–15, 16–18, 43–44, 49–50, 54, 61, 65, 72–74, 78, 80, 84–85, 86–88, 91–92, 95–96, 98–105, 106–27, 129, 134–36; homegrown outsider, 14–16, 63–85, 129, 134–36; outsider, 14–15, 17, 72, 75, 77–78, 84, 87, 92–99, 129, 135–36; southern, 22, 41, 43, 45, 48, 53, 57, 62, 70, 93; white, 11, 17, 41, 47, 56, 64, 72–78, 83, 96–97, 104
Chaudhary, Hira, 131
Chesnutt, Charles, 3, 8, 11, 15, 16–17, 21, 22–24, 26, 32, 34, 37–39, 40–49, 57, 62, 63, 105, 120, 131, 133–34
Chicago Defender, 26
Childress, Alice, 28
Chinn, Nancy, 51
Christian, Barbara, 5
City in African-American Literature, The (Hakutani and Butler), 12
"City of Refuge" (Fisher), 12, 15, 16, 70, 93–95
civil rights, 11, 73–74, 82–83
Claborn, John, 88
Clair, Maxine, 28
Clifton, Lucille, 73
Coates, Ta-Nehisi, 106
Cobb, William Jelani, 115–16
Coleman, Anita Scott, 29
"Common Law" (E. P. Jones), 111, 115, 116
Complete Stories, The (Hurston), 30
Conjure Woman, The (Chesnutt), 22
Connolly, Cyril, 26
"Conscience of the Court, The" (Hurston), 30
Cooper, Tim, 111
Corbett, David, 14
Cornwell, Anita R., 28
Cortez, Jayne, 93
"Cross Crossings Cautiously" (Coleman), 29
Csicsila, Joseph, 7

cultural geo-tagging, 9–14, 18, 41–45, 47–49, 52–53, 55, 57, 64–65, 68, 78–79, 85, 86–88, 93, 105, 106–27, 130, 133, 135–36
culture, 3–5, 9–10, 12, 14, 43, 49, 53–54, 57, 63, 73, 78–79, 84–85, 86, 93, 96–97, 99, 106–7, 111, 129, 134–36; Black, 16–17, 42, 53, 55–56, 69, 92, 94–96, 98, 111; folk, 10, 41, 55–56; southern, 17, 80, 93

Danticat, Edwidge, 13, 36
Dark Matter: A Century of Speculative Fiction from the African Diaspora (Thomas), 38
Dark Matter: Reading the Bones (Thomas), 38
"Dark Night, A" (E. P. Jones), 112, 116
data and datasets, 6–8, 16, 20–23, 129–36. *See also specific datasets*
Davis, Arthur P., 23, 32–33
Davis, Thadious M., 10, 62, 63, 72, 79
Dean, Jeremy, 113
Delany, Samuel R., 38
Dennis, Michael, 130
Dickson-Carr, Darryl, 7
Dittmar, Linda, 97
Dixon, Melvin, 37
dream sequences, 63, 67–68, 71
"Drenched in Light" (Hurston), 30
Du Bois, W. E. B., 22, 38
Dumas, Henry, 4, 12, 13, 15, 17, 37, 38, 87, 93, 96–99
Dunbar, Paul Laurence, 23, 73, 106
Dunbar-Nelson, Alice, 26, 106
Duncan, Charles, 47
Dunn, Elizabeth E., 51

Eatonville, FL, 29, 50, 53, 55. *See also* Florida
editors, 3–4, 6–8, 16, 19–39, 42, 87, 100, 133
Edwards, Brent Hayes, 33
Eight Men (Wright), 37, 61
Ellison, Ralph, 3–5, 8, 11, 15, 16–17, 21, 25–26, 32, 34, 35, 63–78, 100, 105, 131, 133–35
"Eternal Quest, The" (Coleman), 29

"Ethics of Living Jim Crow, The" (Wright), 24
"Evening Thought, An" (Hammon), 32
"Everyday Use" (A. Walker), 27, 30–31, 36, 65, 79–81
Exum, Pat Crutchfield, 27

Falkenstein, Misty, 130
Farrell, Susan, 80
Faulkner, William, 21, 65
Fauset, Jessie, 26, 28, 29
"Fine Line: A Story of the Color Line, The" (Minus), 29–30
"First Day, The" (E. P. Jones), 109, 116, 118
Fisher, Rudolph, 4, 12, 13, 15, 16, 17, 21, 38, 70, 87, 93–97, 99
Fitzgerald, F. Scott, 21
flashbacks, 11, 63, 67–69, 71, 74, 81, 88–90, 102, 113, 134
Florida, 4, 10, 12, 14, 40–41, 49–51, 54–55. *See also* Eatonville, FL
"Flying Home" (Ellison), 8, 65–66, 68–71
Foley, Martha, 24
Fordham, Mary Weston, 22
For My People (M. Walker), 35
'48: The Magazine of the Year, 26
Foster, Frances Smith, 33
Fox, Robert Elliot, 8
Frost, Robert, 21

Gaines, Ernest, 12, 16, 21, 22, 36, 53
Gates, Henry Louis, Jr., 5, 7, 29, 30, 33, 40, 49
gender, 25, 79, 84, 131. *See also* women
geographies, 8–10, 14, 16, 18, 25, 40–41, 45–46, 48–49, 62, 63–64, 66–67, 70–72, 74, 85, 86, 89, 94–95, 100, 102–3, 105, 107, 109, 114, 119, 121, 130–31, 133–36; cultural, 10, 16, 70, 106
Georgia, 4, 10, 78, 82
geo-tagging, 9–14, 18, 41–45, 47–49, 52–53, 55, 57, 64–65, 68, 78–79, 85, 86–88, 93, 105, 106–27, 130, 133, 135–36
"Gilded Six-Bits, The" (Hurston), 3, 12, 24, 27, 30, 50–51, 55
Giovanni, Nikki, 28

168 INDEX

"Girl Who Raised Pigeons, The" (E. P. Jones), 14, 111, 112–13, 115, 116, 118
"Going to Meet the Man" (Baldwin), 14, 72–74, 76–77, 87
"Goophered Grapevine, The" (Chesnutt), 8, 15, 22, 24, 42–44
Gorilla, My Love (Bambara), 31, 100
"Gorilla, My Love" (Bambara), 31, 100–103
"Gospel, The" (E. P. Jones), 112, 116, 128
Graham, Maryemma, 8, 106, 121, 130
Graham, Ottie Beatrice, 29
Great Migration, 12, 70, 86
Gussow, Adam, 56
Gustafson, Sandra, 34

Hager, Christopher, 35, 36
Hahn, William, 113
Hakutani, Yoshinobu, 12
"Half-Bright" (Minus), 29
"Hammer Man, The" (Bambara), 99
Hammon, Jupiter, 32
Hansberry, Lorraine, 35, 70
Harlem, NY, 12, 14–16, 49, 70, 86–97, 100–101, 103–5, 134
"Harlem Ghetto, The" (Baldwin), 90
Harlem Renaissance, 3, 7, 19, 29, 33–35, 49
Harper, Frances E. W., 22, 28
Harper, Michael, 93
Harper American Literature, Vol. 2 (McQuade), 20
Harper and Brothers, 24
Harper and Row, 29
Harper's Bazaar, 37
Harris, Joel Chandler, 23
Harris, Trudier, 12, 51, 59, 72
Harrison, John, 107
Heath Anthology of American Literature, The (Lauter), 7–8, 22
Heath Anthology of American Literature, Vol. 2, The (Lauter), 21
Hemenway, Robert, 29
Heroism and the Black Intellectual (Watts), 65
Hersey, John, 26
Himes, Chester, 26, 35, 37–38

"His Mother's House" (E. P. Jones), 116, 117
Hollister, Michael, 81
Home to Harlem (McKay), 13
Horizon magazine, 26
"Hound Dog," 83
Hughes, Langston, 26, 30, 70, 73, 93, 106
Hurst, Fannie, 49
Hurston, Zora Neale, 3–5, 8, 10, 12, 14, 16–17, 21, 24, 27–32, 34–35, 39, 40–42, 49–57, 62, 63, 65, 72, 78–79, 81, 93, 100, 105, 106, 112, 120, 131–34

identity, 5, 72, 110; cultural, 12; gender, 79; racial, 24–25, 79, 98; regional, 79
If He Hollers Let Him Go (Himes), 35
Invisible Man (Ellison), 5, 8, 25

Jackson, Blyden, 60
Jarrett, Gene, 36, 43
"Jazz and the White Critic" (Baraka), 97
Jessop, Martyn, 130
Jim Crow laws, 11, 13, 56, 60–61, 63, 66, 69, 78, 94
"John Redding Goes to Sea" (Hurston), 30
Johnson, Charles R., 12, 49, 72
Johnson, Georgia Douglass, 106
Johnson, James Weldon, 93
Johnson, Maria V., 85
Jones, Edward P., 3–4, 10, 12, 14–15, 17–18, 37–38, 70, 106–27, 128–35
Jones, Gayl, 20, 28, 93
Jones, Harry L., 73
Jones, Sharon Lynette, 55
Joseph, Philip, 53–54

Keeping the Faith (Exum), 27
Keller, Frances, 42
Kelley, William Melvin, 11
Kentucky, 11, 42, 46–47
Kim, Kukhyoung, 130
Kincaid, Jamaica, 27
King, B. B., 70
"King of the Bingo Game" (Wright), 11, 65–66, 70–71
Kinnamon, Kenneth, 19, 33

Knopf-Newman, Marcy, 27, 29
Knowles, Caroline, 9

landmarks, 9–10, 12–13, 17–18, 43, 86, 89, 100, 107–9, 111–13, 119, 122, 129, 132, 135
language, 5–6, 12–13, 28, 41, 46, 48, 52–54, 89, 101, 117, 125; African American Vernacular English (AAVE), 11–12, 17, 23, 39, 41–43, 46–49, 52–54, 57, 61, 69, 106, 119–20; Standard English, 46–49, 57, 61, 69, 119–20
Larsen, Nella, 29
Lauter, Paul, 22
Lemke, Sieglinde, 30, 49
"Lesson, The" (Bambara), 12, 27, 31, 100, 103–5
Liberator magazine, 100
Lieberman, Jennifer, 75
"Like a Winding Sheet" (Petry), 13
literature: African American, 3, 5, 7–8, 12, 17–18, 19–20, 25, 27, 29, 32–36, 38–39, 73, 86, 103, 108, 112, 127, 133; American, 18, 19, 25, 27, 29, 34, 38, 61, 105, 112
Locke, Alain, 3
"Long Black Song" (Wright), 25, 36, 37, 58–59, 62
Lopate, Phillip, 86
Lorde, Audre, 28
Lost in the City (E. P. Jones), 4, 14, 107–8, 112, 116, 119, 121, 127, 128, 131, 135
"Lost in the City" (E. P. Jones), 111, 115, 116, 119, 128
Lucy, Robin, 25, 69
lynching, 11, 14, 17, 48, 56–58, 63–65, 72–78, 83, 94, 135
Lynching: Violence, Rhetoric, and American Identity (Ore), 73

Maass, Donald, 14, 15
"Ma'Dear" (McMillan), 16
"Man Who Lived Underground, The" (Wright), 13, 37
"Man Who Was Almost a Man, The" (Wright), 8, 25, 37, 61, 70
"Marie" (E. P. Jones), 112, 116, 128

Marrs, Cody, 35, 36
Marshall, Paule, 13, 22, 28, 31, 36
Martin, Matthew R., 23
Mason, Theodore, Jr., 33
Massachusetts Review, 99
Mathews, Donald G., 76
Mathis, Ayana, 40
Mazurek, Raymond A., 74–75
McDowell, Deborah E., 5, 33, 35
McKay, Claude, 73
McKay, Nellie Y., 27, 33
McMillan, Terry, 16, 20
"Meditations on History" (S. A. Williams), 28
memory, 11, 60, 64, 67, 73, 77, 78, 81–83, 85, 88, 92, 106, 110, 113, 124–27, 129, 134
Meyer, Annie Nathan, 49
Midnight Birds (Washington), 28
migration, 5, 11–12, 70, 86, 106, 120
Miller, E. Ethelbert, 117
Minus, Marian, 29
Mishra, Pankaj, 40
"Miss Cynthie" (Fisher), 93–94
Mississippi, 4, 10–11, 25, 41, 60–61, 78
"Mississippi Ham Rider" (Bambara), 99
Mitgang, Herbert, 25
Morrison, Toni, 5, 70, 72, 93
Mosley, Walter, 37
movement, 47, 70, 87, 92, 100–105, 106–14, 117–23, 125–26, 128–30, 134–36
Ms. magazine, 29
Mullen, Bill, 27, 28
Mullins, Matthew, 80
music, 13, 17, 87, 92–99, 105, 111; blues, 13, 93; jazz, 13, 15, 91–93, 96–98, 134
Music in African American Fiction, The (Cataliotti), 13
Musser, Judith, 27, 29

Nagel, James, 5, 24
Native Son (Wright), 8, 24, 35, 56
Neely, Brooke, 10
Negro Digest, 96, 99
Newark, NJ, 16, 93, 97
New Cavalcade, The (Davis et al.), 21

"New Man, A" (E. P. Jones), 37, 109–10, 128
New Negro, The (Locke), 3
New York City, NY, 3–4, 8, 10–13, 17, 31, 37, 47, 65, 70, 72, 74, 78, 81–83, 86–105, 106, 134; Harlem, 12, 14–16, 49, 70, 86–97, 100–101, 103–5, 134
New York Herald Tribune, 25
"Night Rhonda Ferguson Was Killed, The" (E. P. Jones), 108–9, 111, 116
"Nineteen Fifty-Five" (A. Walker), 11, 30, 65, 83–85
North Carolina, 12, 15, 41, 42–45, 48, 70, 94, 129
Norton Anthology of African American Literature, The (Gates and McKay), 7–8, 21, 33–36
Norton Anthology of African American Literature, Vol. 2, The (Gates and McKay), 21, 33–37
Norton Anthology of African American Literature, Vol. 3, The (Gates and Smith), 21, 33–36
Norton Anthology of American Literature, Vol. 2, The (Baym), 21
Norton Anthology of Literature by Women, The (Gilbert), 27
"Not in the Record" (Reeves), 30
novels, 3, 5–6, 8, 24–25, 38, 51, 134

O'Connor, Flannery, 21
Ohio, 11, 42, 46, 72, 75
Oklahoma, 65, 70, 78
"Old Boys, Old Girls" (E. P. Jones), 38, 107, 121, 123–27
O'Meally, Robert G., 33, 65
Opportunity magazine, 3, 29, 49
"Orange Line Train to Ballston, An" (E. P. Jones), 109, 115
Ore, Ersula, 73
Ossom-Williamson, Peace, 131
"Outing, The" (Baldwin), 23, 87

Packer, ZZ, 11
Paradise (Morrison), 5

Parrish, Timothy, 65
Partisan Review, 24
"Party Down at the Square, A" (Ellison), 8, 72, 74–78
"Passing of Grandison, The" (Chesnutt), 11, 22, 24, 45, 46–48
Patterson, Tiffany Ruby, 52
Penzler, Otto, 38
Petry, Ann, 13, 20, 21, 22, 35
Pierpont, Claudia Roth, 40
place, 4–6, 9–10, 12–15, 17–18, 33, 41–43, 52–54, 57, 64, 68, 72–73, 79, 86–93, 99, 105, 106–8, 111–13, 115–16, 121–22, 126, 129–30, 132, 134–36
Plant, Deborah, 49
plantations, 23, 40–49
Plath, Sylvia, 21
Poe, Edgar Allan, 132
poetry, 5, 26, 28, 35–36, 70, 93, 117
politics, 13, 43, 66, 69, 82, 103–5, 108, 113, 115, 122, 127
"Po' Sandy" (Chesnutt), 22, 42–44
poverty, 63, 88, 90
power, 55, 61–62, 66–67, 70, 75, 93, 96, 98, 104, 113, 124
Prentice Hall Anthology of African American Literature, The (Smith), 30, 36
Presley, Elvis, 83
prison, 4, 38, 48, 83, 89, 115, 121, 124–26, 135

race, 5, 10, 24–25, 40–45, 52, 56–58, 61, 63, 65–66, 68–69, 74–76, 79, 83–85, 96, 108, 130, 135; Black, 3–17, 19–39, 40–56, 58–70, 72–79, 81–84, 87–89, 92–105, 106–8, 111, 113–18, 121–27, 129–36; biracial, 45, 48; interracial relationships, 11, 83; interracial tension and conflicts, 4, 42, 51, 56–57, 59–60, 63, 82–84, 100, 134; intraracial tension, 51, 78, 100, 106, 115; white, 4, 10–11, 15, 16–17, 19, 23, 43, 47–49, 51, 57–61, 63–65, 67–69, 71–78, 82–84, 94–98, 104, 108, 120, 134–35
racism, 11, 13, 23, 43, 52, 57, 60–61, 66, 68–70, 72–77, 135

Raisin in the Sun, A (Hansberry), 35
Ralph Ellison and the Genius of America (Parrish), 65
Rampersad, Arnold, 33
Randolph, Ruth Elizabeth, 27
Random House, 25
rape, 59, 82–83, 120, 125. *See also* violence
"Raymond's Run" (Bambara), 14, 31, 100–101, 103
"Recitatif" (Morrison), 5
Redding, Saunders, 23, 32–33
"Reena" (Marshall), 13, 28
Reeves, Elizabeth Walker, 30
"Resurrecting Methuselah" (E. P. Jones), 116
Revolutionary Tales (Mullen), 20, 28, 29
Reynolds, Paul, Jr., 24
"Rich Man, A" (E. P. Jones), 112, 128
Rivas, Dan, 108, 114
Roberts, W. Adolphe, 38
Roosevelt, Eleanor, 56
Roses, Lorraine Elena, 27
Rustin-Paschal, Nichole, 110–11
Ryan, Melissa, 58

Salaam, Kalamu ya, 37
Samura, Michelle, 10
Sanchez, Sonia, 93
Scary Mason-Dixon Line, The (Harris), 72
"Screamers, The" (Baraka), 16, 37, 97–99
segregation, 11, 69, 72–73, 76, 82, 108
"Seven" (Danticat), 13
Shaffer, Donald M., Jr., 44
Shakur, Tupac, 70
Sherard, Tracey, 93
"Sheriff's Children, The" (Chesnutt), 22, 38, 42, 45, 48
"Sky Is Gray, The" (Gaines), 16
slavery, 11, 23, 41, 43–48, 63, 67
Sleeper Wakes, The (Knopf-Newman), 29
Smith, Cordelia T., 30
Smith, Rochelle, 30
Smith, Valerie, 33
social class, 16, 25, 43, 45–46, 48, 56, 69, 75, 88, 98, 103–5, 119

"Sonny's Blues" (Baldwin), 12–13, 15, 17, 23–24, 87–94, 105, 132, 134
South, the, 3–4, 8–13, 16–17, 22, 25, 31–32, 37, 39, 40–62, 63, 65–67, 69–80, 82–85, 87, 90, 93–95, 104–5, 106, 120, 132, 134
Southscapes (Davis), 10
spaces, 4, 9–10, 13–14, 49–50, 58, 67–68, 71, 74, 89–94, 96–99, 103–4, 106, 108, 117, 134–35
"Spanish in the Morning" (E. P. Jones), 113, 116, 118
Spillers, Hortense, 33, 35
"Spunk" (Hurston), 3, 12, 14, 30, 54–55, 132
Standard English, 46–49, 57, 61, 69, 119–20
"Steady Going Up" (Angelou), 11
Steinbeck, John, 21
Stepto, Robert, 5
stereotypes, 16, 76, 127, 134
"Store, The" (E. P. Jones), 111, 113, 116, 128
Storm, Anna, 55
Story magazine, 37
storytelling, 3–4, 108, 114, 134, 136; African American, 4, 6, 17, 44, 92
Street, The (Petry), 35
"Strike and Fade" (Dumas), 37
"Sunday Following Mother's Day, The" (E. P. Jones), 111
"Sweat" (Hurston), 3, 12, 24, 27, 30, 51–53, 55
symbolism, 12, 62, 75, 85, 107

Tackach, James, 87
Tales and Short Stories for Black Folks (Bambara), 30, 31, 100
Taylor, Frank, 25–26
Taylor, Sara, 77
"Tell It to Us Easy" and Other Stories (Musser), 29
Tennyson, Alfred Lord, 46
Tewarie, Bhoendradatt, 66
Their Eyes Were Watching God (Hurston), 3, 5, 29, 35, 40, 53
Thier, Aaron, 119
"This Morning, This Evening, So Soon" (Baldwin), 23, 87

Thomas, Lorenzo, 97
Thomas, Sheree, 38
Thompson, Eloise Bibb, 29
Thornton, Big Mama, 83
Till, Emmett, 83
Timelines of American Literature (Marrs and Hager), 36
"To Hell with Dying" (A. Walker), 16, 30–31, 65, 81–82
Tompkins, Grace W., 28
Toomer, Jean, 65
Trouble the Water (Ward), 35–36
Tunc, Tanfer, 45
Twain, Mark, 81
"Two Offers" (Harper), 28

Uncle Tom's Children (Wright), 24, 40, 56, 62
University of Texas at Arlington, 128, 129

Van Vechten, Carl, 49
violence, 10–11, 40–41, 52, 56–62, 65, 72–78, 82–84, 100, 106, 120, 121, 124–25, 127, 132, 135

Walker, Alice, 3–4, 10–12, 16–17, 21, 27–32, 34, 36, 53, 63–65, 78–85, 105, 131–34, 136
Walker, Margaret, 35, 65
Wall, Cheryl A., 33
Ward, Jerry W., Jr., 8, 36
Warmth of Other Suns, The (Wilkerson), 70
War of the Walls (Bambara), 100
Washington, Booker T., 22
Washington, DC, 4, 10, 12, 14–15, 17–18, 70, 105, 106–27, 128–30, 134–36
Washington, Mary Helen, 27–28
Watts, Jerry Gafio, 65
Wells, Ida B., 83
West, Dorothy, 12, 29
Wheatley, Phillis, 40

White, Paulette Childress, 28
Whitehead, Colson, 36, 72
"Wife of His Youth, The" (Chesnutt), 8, 22, 24, 37, 42, 45–46
Wife of His Youth and Other Stories of the Color-Line, The (Chesnutt), 22, 45
Wiley Blackwell Anthology of African American Literature, The, 36
Wilkerson, Isabel, 70
Williams, Sherley Anne, 28, 61
Williams, Tennessee, 65
"Will the Circle Be Unbroken" (Dumas), 15, 96–97
Wilson, August, 70
women, 16–17, 20, 27–28, 32, 78–79, 85, 101, 116–17, 119, 126–27, 131; Black, 13, 17, 20, 27, 31–32, 50, 55, 59–61, 79, 81–84, 87, 99–105, 117; white, 16, 74, 82–83
Women Working (Hedges et al.), 27
Wright, Richard, 3–5, 7–8, 10–11, 13, 16–17, 21, 24–26, 32, 34–37, 39, 40–42, 56–62, 63, 66, 70, 72–73, 84, 100, 105, 112, 120, 131–35
writers: Big 7, 3–4, 7–8, 11, 16, 20, 21–27, 31–32, 34, 39, 41, 103, 131–33; Black, 3–10, 13, 19–22, 25–35, 37–38, 40–41, 51, 63, 65, 69–70, 72–78, 83, 100, 105, 106, 112, 117, 125, 132–35; short stories, 3–5, 11–12, 25–26, 34, 36–39, 41, 63, 78, 99, 104–5, 107, 114, 124; southern, 31, 65; women, 16, 27–32, 100, 117
Writing New York (Lopate), 86
W. W. Norton & Company, 33

"Young Lions" (E. P. Jones), 107, 111, 121, 122–23, 126–27, 128

Zitting, Angela, 131
Zora Neale Hurston: A Literary Biography (Hemenway), 29

ABOUT THE AUTHOR

Kenton Rambsy is assistant professor of English and digital humanities at the University of Texas at Arlington. His ongoing digital humanities projects use quantitative and qualitative datasets to illuminate the significance of recurring trends and thematic shifts as they relate to African American literature and history.

www.ingramcontent.com/pod-product-compliance
Lightning Source LLC
Chambersburg PA
CBHW022023220426
43663CB00007B/1186